The Musée Picasso,
Paris

'What is sculpture?
What is painting?
Everyone clings to old-fashioned ideas
and outworn definitions,
as if it were not precisely
the role of the artist to provide new ones.'

Picasso, quoted by Brassaï in **Picasso & Co.**, New York, 1966, London 1967
(*Conversations avec Picasso*, Paris, 1964)

The Musée Picasso, Paris

Paintings
Papiers collés
Picture reliefs
Sculptures
Ceramics

Introduction	Dominique Bozo
Catalogue	Marie-Laure Besnard-Bernadac
	Michèle Richet
	Hélène Seckel
Chronology	Laurence Marceillac

With 871 illustrations, 58 in colour

Thames and Hudson
Editions de la Réunion des musées nationaux

ISBN :-

0500   234 612 ✓

Translated from the French
Musée Picasso: Catalogue sommaire des collections
by Alexander Lieven

This edition © 1986 Thames and Hudson Ltd, London
© 1985 Editions de la Réunion des musées nationaux
    10, rue de l'Abbaye, 75006 Paris
© 2- 7118- 0264- 7/SPADEM, Paris 1985

Photos (except where otherwise stated):
Réunion des musées nationaux, Paris

Printed and bound in Italy by Amilcare Pizzi, Milan, Italy

Contents

Picasso and Romuald Dor de la Souchère in the great hall of the Antibes Museum, 1952
(Musée Picasso Document, photo Denise Colomb)

Introduction: Picasso at Home

What was it that led the French State to pursue a purchasing policy whereby all the non-academic art of the late nineteenth and early twentieth centuries was deliberately ignored for the greater benefit of second-rate artists? Neither recent publications connected with exhibitions devoted to the contents of official collections at the turn of the century nor Jeanne Laurent's highly relevant and critical study of the relationship between the world of art and the State[1] provide fully satisfactory answers to this fundamentally important question. A solidly researched and thoroughgoing analysis of the underlying reasons for this situation is needed. It must include an honest account of the contribution made to it by bureaucracy and by clashes between individuals and schools of thought if the indifferent quality of French collections of twentieth-century art – even though, paradoxically, consisting mainly of works conceived on French soil – is ever to be properly understood. Dare one mention, now that one of the museums most representative of this century has opened, that Picasso, along with Matisse, Léger and Brancusi among others, was wholly neglected by the Beaux-Arts administration in his own lifetime? In fact, the State was only able to purchase a few of his works, and that somewhat belatedly. Even these were mostly of secondary importance, with a few exceptions: the *Nu assis* (*Seated Nude*) of 1905, the *Tête* (*Head*) for *Les Demoiselles d'Avignon* of 1907 and the *Tête de femme rouge* (*Woman's Head in Red*), 1906. Both of the latter were bought by right of preemption at the Lefèvre sale in 1965.

Thus, in 1945, when Jean Cassou set out to open a national museum of modern art, a project delayed by events since 1937, the national collection assembled in the Musée du Jeu de Paume des Tuileries, though regarded as more up to date than the Luxembourg, owned only one work by Picasso. This was the *Portrait of Gustave Coquiot*, dating from 1901 and bequeathed to the museum by Coquiot's widow in 1933. Picasso's contemporaries fared no better. The contrast with Swiss, American and Soviet museums, the latter with their Morozov and Shchukin collections, was startling. Apart from the Jeu de Paume, only one museum in France – the Musée des Beaux-Arts at Grenoble – owned two paintings by Picasso, the *Femme lisant* (*Woman Reading*), 1920, and *L'enfant à la poupée* (*Child with a Doll*), 1900–1, the former presented by the artist, the latter purchased in 1935. All in all, there were thus only three of his paintings in French public collections in 1945. On the strength of his friendship with Jean Cassou and Georges Salles, then Director of the Musées de France, Picasso gave the new museum ten paintings from his personal collection, chosen with special care. These included *L'atelier de la modiste* (*The Milliner's Workshop*), 1925–26, *L'Aubade*, 1942, and *La casserole émaillée* (*The Enamel Saucepan*), 1945.

It is now idle to speculate what this gift might have amounted to if the best part of his collection, including *Guernica*, had not then still been housed at The Museum of Modern Art, New York, where the war had caught it after the 1939 Retrospective Exhibition. Even so, Picasso became the Musée National d'Art Moderne's main patron, an example soon followed, first by Paul Eluard and Paul Rosenberg, and later by D.-H. Kahnweiler, Baronne Gourgaud, André Lefèvre, Georges Salles, Marie Cuttoli and Henri Laugier. Thereafter, Picasso was unstintingly generous with his gifts to French museums – Antibes, as we all know, Lyons, Arles and Céret. It should also be remembered that he handed over his personal art collection to the State. This represented an exceptionally interesting set of works by fellow artists which Jean Leymarie has described as 'a painter's links with painters and painting'.

Georges Salles, Picasso and Julien Cain at the centenary exhibition of the Imprimerie Mourlot, Paris, 1952 (Musée Picasso Document, photo Hélène Adant)

(1) Jeanne Laurent, *Arts et pouvoirs en France de 1793 à 1981: histoire d'une démission artistique*, Saint-Etienne, CIEREC, 1982.

This collection, housed for a time at the Louvre, is now displayed in its proper place alongside Picasso's own works, where it forms a kind of continuous dialogue with a lifework that never ceases to confront, define and celebrate the universal nature of painting. The artist who had originally created this collection thus put us even more deeply in his debt. It is not generally enough known that Picasso, motivated by loyalty to Spain, displayed the same degree of generosity on two separate occasions to the museum in Barcelona; as he did also to the Basel Kunstmuseum, to enable it to retain two pictures on loan to it which it was in danger of losing: the Rose period masterpiece *Les deux frères* (*The Two Brothers*) of 1905 and the famous *Arlequin* (*Harlequin*), 1923. More recently, shortly before his death, Picasso handed over to William Rubin for The Museum of Modern Art, New York, the famous sheet-iron *Guitar*, 1912 – a fine act of gratitude directed to a museum which had always concerned itself with his output and followed its development.

Finally, some years after Picasso's death, a law of a new kind was enacted in France allowing the gift of works of art to the nation in settlement of death duties. This enabled the core of his output, which he had always jealously kept for himself – Picasso's Picassos, as they were sometimes called – to be transferred to the national collections. They provided the basis for a museum of unrivalled excellence devoted to works assembled with the passionate, patient and secret connivance of the artist himself. Although he never admitted it in public, Picasso would almost certainly have agreed to the setting up of such a museum in his lifetime, if any suitable location in Paris had been offered to him. The old Musée du Luxembourg seems to have been suggested at one stage. However, in so far as his own output was concerned, he would very probably have shrunk during his lifetime from any action that might have smacked of arrogance, whereas he had already decided that his personal collection of the works of other artists was to be handed over to the French national museums by his heirs.

One may therefore safely assume that Picasso secretly looked forward to the establishment of such a museum dedicated to his works and that he left it to time to make up, or even to overcompensate, for the mistakes of the past. After all, the State can only be expected to turn its attention to those who make specific demands on it for help.

Picasso's Picassos – The Artist's Own Choice

Early-flowering genius, an exceptionally long life span, relentless work extending over the best part of a century – the 'unwearying creative activity' that never flagged – all no doubt helped Picasso to produce a large body of work and to keep the nucleus of it in his own possession without being forced to yield to the demands of the market-place. That much is certain, but other factors must also be taken into account if one is to understand how it came about that an astonishing number of major works – of masterpieces, indeed – were included in this collection.

The historic character of certain works that are genuinely unique provides a sufficient explanation in some cases, such as the *Nature morte à la chaise cannée* (*Still-life with Chair-caning*, cat. 35) with which Picasso had already refused to part in 1912, the monumental *Homme à la mandoline* (*Man with a Mandolin*, cat. 33) of 1911 and *La flûte de Pan* (*The Pipes of Pan*, cat. 76), 1923, which Jean Leymarie attempted to purchase in 1969. Similarly, Picasso was well aware that the unique series of Cubist constructions should not be broken up, that it illustrated the coherent evolution of his output and that it must therefore be retained intact for posterity.

In other cases, Picasso's retention of the works was more a matter of emotional, personal or family context, such as the portraits of Olga, Marie-Thérèse, Dora Maar, Françoise and Jacqueline, or those of Paulo, Maya, Claude and Paloma. There are other examples, too, whose presence is not explained simply by their hermetic or enigmatic nature, by what we would now call their 'museum work' character. It can be said, with hindsight, that their inclusion indicates Picasso's own special liking for them.

Such works were barely marketable, if at all, when they were first produced, however enlightened the collectors may have been. Now they are more familiar to us, and time enables us to look at them in a more informed and detached way when we assess their importance and meaning. After all, it was more than fifteen years before *Les Demoiselles d'Avignon* entered Jacques Doucet's collection, and thirty before it reached a museum.

Lastly, one must bear in mind the works produced at the very end of his life by an artist who remained entirely uninhibited and as inventive as ever. He refused to 'repeat himself' and was indeed incapable of doing so. The startled and irritated reactions which greeted these works when they were shown at Avignon in 1970, provoked by the almost insolent brushwork and gamut of colours, come to mind when one considers how many contemporary artists now find themselves on home ground among them. The energy packed by these works disturbs us. Yet their reassessment at the 1979 Grand Palais exhibition revealed the range of their impact on work now being done.

Picasso, like Matisse and Léger, belonged to a generation at work before the upheavals of the 1950s set in, a generation whose roots reached back into the nineteenth century and which had launched the twentieth. But its work kept to the Old Masters' way, steadily resorting to every technique available, every mode of expression, every way of studying and developing a work. Over and above this, Picasso was probably the first artist for whom the concept of 'analysis' and the need to practise it involved the retention of successive stages in the production of a single work. For him, moreover, as for Matisse, the theme and its variations were for all intents and purposes equally important, so that he set the same value on a finished work, on an experiment and on a project, either contemplated or in course of production. Hence a 'production process' that – perhaps for the first time – favoured an analytical approach, as opposed to that of classical painting. Instead of erasing, it imparted significance to each creative moment – or, at any rate, recorded it – as though the artist meant to enrich the creative process with works left lying fallow and to fix every stage in the recognition of the subject.

As we have seen, the gap separating Picasso's most advanced works from the taste, even at its most daring, of his dealers was too wide to ensure acceptance of all these exploratory works. The lucidity and candid vision of poets such as Aragon and Breton were needed to understand in their day *Les Demoiselles d'Avignon*, the fearsome guitars of 1926 or *La Crucifixion* (*The Crucifixion*, cat. 108). Not all collectors lagged behind, though some of them did so. It was only in the 1930s, and even more after the Second World War, that they fully caught up with Picasso's work. He had the better of them because his key works were still in his possession (not necessarily because that was what he wanted) and he therefore found no difficulty in holding on to his early output. He had always, for instance, refused to let the Tate Gallery have *The Dance* and only his friendship with Roland Penrose persuaded him to let it go in 1965.

It is said that Picasso hoarded everything. This applied to whatever he acquired or found or made, as well as to anything that caught his eye and could be manipulated or transformed. One need only glance at the many photographs of his various, sometimes very temporary, studios where he invariably created such an atmosphere of activity that, as Penrose remarked, an alchemist's laboratory would have seemed dull by comparison. His output was an integral part of this everyday world of life and labour.

Anyone fortunate enough to have seen all that Picasso preserved or simply kept will have been struck, regardless of its material nature or significance, by the virtual absence of those unfinished or rejected things commonly found in studios. In addition to the main works with which we are familiar and to what may be regarded as material for possible future use, there were works of uncertain quality, but nevertheless always finished. Contrary to what is sometimes said, it seems that Picasso did not return to his canvases or go over them again. X-ray examination practically always reveals the absence of *pentimenti*: changes do sometimes occur in the drawing, but seldom in the application of colour. Whenever changes do appear, they tend to be the outcome either of exuberance or of study but never in any sense integral elements of the work concerned, of its intention or of its spontaneous quality. Hence such a wealth of drawings, linked experiments and inspired sketches.

Picasso turned all these canvases and sculptures into a living backdrop for his day-to-day existence. In so far as he was concerned, these were stray objects, at once stimulating and necessary, waiting, as it might be, to catch the artist's eye or to find some object to complement them. The photographs of the studios in his various dwellings bear witness to this, and one can spot some specially favoured works which followed him from place to place and were awarded a conspicuous position on each occasion. 'Found' objects, other painters' pictures, tokens of friendship or admiration stand cheek by jowl with his own works. The bicycle saddle which, together with the handlebars picked up at the funeral of Gonzalez, would eventually go to make up the *Tête de taureau* (*Head of a Bull*, cat. 370) already hangs on the wall of the studio at Royan, next to Matisse's Fauve still-life acquired just before the 1940 exodus from Paris. Picasso of course put this ludicrous yet portentous object into his luggage when he came back. Was this perhaps already the quintessence of a work in the making?

Picasso only rarely lent works from his personal collection. A study of his main one-man exhibition catalogues reveals that he personally chose the works concerned (either on his own or with the help of his friends Alfred Barr, Roland Penrose, Franco Russoli, Maurice Jardot, Douglas Cooper and Jean Leymarie) not only for the very first such exhibition, organized at the Galerie Georges Petit in 1932, but for that at The Museum of Modern Art, New York, in 1939, and for that in Paris in 1966. In every case, the basic component came from his own collection. Between 1932 and 1966 few works left his studio. That is why we can still see them together today, and why the great retrospective exhibition at The Museum of Modern Art, New York, in 1980 could only be arranged after the estate had been settled and a sizable contribution borrowed from the Musée Picasso – no fewer than three hundred works. This in itself proves the present importance of this new museum which leaves virtually no gaps in the output. Recent accessions and others yet to come will contribute to making it the focus of an infinitely varied universe. It will display the artistic creation itself, together with its sources, its variations and its achievements.

This is not the place to describe in great historical detail the sequence of events that gradually brought this collection into being. That is dealt with later, in the individual introductions to the various categories of works housed in the museum. The principles applied in creating the museum must, however, be outlined, in view of the complex situation prevailing in France with regard to the national holding of modern art when a settlement in lieu of death duties became possible. The works by Picasso then in French museums were not only generally somewhat second-rate, but – more important – they lacked cohesion. They were scattered between the Musée National d'Art Moderne, the Musée d'Art Moderne de la Ville de Paris, a number of provincial museums – that of Antibes, in particular – and the collection destined for the museum at Villeneuve-d'Ascq, well provided with Picassos from the Masurel donation (Dutilleul-Masurel collection).

Should these various holdings be augmented and Picasso's Picassos dispersed? Should the settlement from the estate have the works held by the Musée National d'Art Moderne added to it, thereby segregating Picasso from his contemporaries? Various possibilities of this sort were considered, and each had its supporters, but nobody had the slightest idea of what the settlement was likely to contain. When, however, we became aware of the untold wealth of what was described at that time as an Aladdin's Cave, it was immediately obvious that this provided incomparable material for a museum of a very special and novel kind, and that these works must under no circumstances be dispersed. These considerations were embodied in the initial agreement concluded with Picasso's heirs. Their wishes and their generous response were in complete accord with the position adopted by the State, and the agreement was consequently closely adhered to. The heirs accepted that the normal procedure laid down for such cases should be reversed: they did not offer, as they would have been legally entitled to do, a selection of works on which they would probably have found it difficult to agree. Subsequent intricate negotiations would, in any case, most probably have thrown such a selection into disarray, have introduced an element of uncertainty into the choice that had been made, and perhaps even have spoiled it by the introduction of compromise solutions. Moreover, the

State would have had the right to reject it in the last resort. Instead, it was agreed that the State would be given first choice before any division of the estate was undertaken, precisely so as to ensure a completely coherent settlement. The heirs deserve great credit for the breadth of vision they displayed in subscribing to this arrangement. I was fortunate enough to be charged with the selection in consultation with Jean Leymarie, to whom I submitted my choice as I went along. It was carried out in total accord with all the heirs of Pablo Picasso.

Each of the latter drew up lists which were incorporated into our own selection. This produced a set of some six hundred and forty paintings on which the museum based its final choice of those destined to become the backbone of the collection. We retained more than two hundred. The choice of works in other techniques was more easily made.

The responsibility we faced was tremendous, and doubts arose in connection with a few works. We therefore thought it right to inform a small working party, consisting of Jean Leymarie, Roland Penrose, Pierre Daix and Maurice Besset, of our choice and to seek its advice even before we submitted our selection to the Commission Interministérielle d'Agrément, the ultimate State authority involved. The role of the working party was to review all the pictures and sculptures included in the settlement and to resolve any doubts, such as which of two versions of the same work should be chosen, as in the case of *La cuisine* (*The Kitchen*, cat. 174); which out of a number of thematically and formally closely related sculptures was to be retained; and whether the estimated values were mutually compatible and correct.

Existing French collections and possible future accessions were taken into account in the process of selection, as well as the fact that a museum entirely devoted to a genius of such protean character and magnitude must proffer a collection covering all aspects of his art, neither neglecting nor omitting any of its various phases, manifestations and techniques.

Our constant care clearly had to be to preserve this unique inheritance representing a many-faceted output, and to devise a museum that would not merely house an accumulation of masterpieces, but which would serve as an initiation into the studio of this creative genius; provide a collection that would reveal the bridges actually linking one phase in his output with another and one technique with the next; and offer a background on which leaps ahead and returns to the past could be highlighted, while the general unity of development was made plain. It would demonstrate how, to quote Christian Zervos, Picasso consulted his own existing works in terms of technique, in order to resolve present uncertainties, and attempted to establish an exchange from painting to sculpture and back again to painting in order to experiment with space and organize it.

If one were to attempt to classify in one's mind the various public collections of Picasso's works in France, one would find the extent to which they complement each other surprising. Thus the Rose period, rather poorly represented here, is sumptuously illustrated in the Walter-Guillaume collection, while the Cubism of 1908–9 is predominant in the Dutilleul-Masurel collection at Villeneuve d'Ascq. The museum at Antibes displays the output of the early post-war years. The only important gaps occur in the 1950s and 1960s, obviously because Picasso reached the peak of his success during that period and all his contemporary output was almost immediately bought up by collectors and museums. The entire *Femmes d'Alger* (*Women of Algiers*) series was snapped up by a passionate admirer, while *Les Ménines* (*Las Meninas*) were destined for Barcelona.

Since the Museo Picasso in Barcelona is mainly devoted to the formative period of early works centring on *Science and Charity*, we thought it pointless to compete with it, particularly as it is not a great distance from Paris. Nevertheless, Picasso's early genius is represented in the Hôtel Salé by two well-known works painted when he was fourteen, *L'Homme à la casquette* (*Man with a Cap*, cat. 1) and *La fillette aux pieds nus* (*The Barefoot Girl*, cat. 2). Our collection however, properly begins with the *Self-portrait* of 1901 (cat. 4) painted during his first stay in Paris. The 1906 *Self-portrait* (cat. 8) formed part of Picasso's everyday existence. It not only shows the long way he had travelled since the Blue period, but, above all, heralds *Les Demoiselles d'Avignon*, the preparatory studies for which have virtually all been collected here (cat. 10–16), together with the corresponding sketchbooks. The phase of Cézanne Cubism, few samples of which survived in the estate apart from the highly classical *Paysage aux deux*

Nu au peigne
(*Nude with a Comb*),
1906, Paris,
Musée de l'Orangerie,
Walter-Guillaume Collection

figures (*Landscape with Two Figures*, cat. 26), is now represented by the *Nature morte au cuir à rasoir* (*Still-life with Razor Strop*, cat. 27), given by D.-H. Kahnweiler, the bronze *Tête de femme (Fernande)* (*Head of a Woman* [*Fernande*], cat. 286) and some tremendous monumental drawings. Two of the nine monumental Cubist compositions, *Homme à la mandoline* (*Man with a Mandolin*, cat. 33) and *Homme à la guitare* (*Man with a Guitar*, cat. 34), accompany the *Nature morte à la chaise cannée* (*Still-life with Chair-caning*, cat. 35), itself surrounded by an outstanding number of collages and by almost all the constructions on record. The *Man with a Guitar*, never previously shown, provided one of the revelations of the Grand Palais exhibition of 1979. It stands out as much by its architectural power as by the feeling of deliberately deceptive space it imparts, as though three-dimensional shapes were advancing towards the onlooker and had at long last become part of our own living environment, a work which strangely combines analysis with synthesis. We lack space to mention here other works no less important than *Homme à la pipe* (*Man with a Pipe*, cat. 39) on the 'way out' from Cubism. It marks a return to colour rediscovered through the practice of collage and brought back into painting. Here are the forerunners of the reinstatement of figurative art, of classicism or of antiquity – depending on which critic is speaking – embodied in *Le peintre et son modèle* (*The Painter and his Model*, cat. 48) and, more particularly, in the experimental and disturbing paraphrase of Le Nain's *Le retour du baptême* (*The Return from the Christening*, cat. 51).

Similarly, once the war was over and Cubism was being left behind, the quest began for a confrontation between the latter and a trend harking back to the classical approach, already perceptible in the sets and costumes for *Parade*. All the major canvases of this period are here, except for *Les trois musiciens* (*The Three Musicians*), from the Biarritz *Les baigneuses* (*The Bathers*, cat. 55) – a small masterpiece which represents a sort of tribute to Douanier Rousseau – to *La flûte de Pan* (*The Pipes of Pan*, cat. 76), another masterpiece. Between these two works of astonishing power and inherent energy, the subjects of which still remain enigmatic, come the sepia version of *Trois femmes à la fontaine* (*Three Women at the Fountain*, cat. 69), many hitherto unknown works, such as *La source* (*The Source*, cat. 70); the 'monumental' *Nature morte au pichet et aux pommes* (*Still-life with Pitcher and Apples*, cat. 59) and, above all, the strange *La lecture de la lettre* (*Reading the Letter*, cat. 67).

The Dance, a masterpiece in the Tate Gallery, finds its counterpart in *Le baiser* (*The Kiss*, cat. 81) which antedates *Le peintre et son modèle* (*The Painter and his Model*, cat. 82) and had not been seen since 1953. It proved possible to retain both *Guitars* (cat. 249, 250) dating from 1926, together with the extraordinary series of small collage constructions (cat. 251–258).

What other collection will ever be in a position in future to bring together a set comparable to that made up of *The Kiss*, *The Crucifixion* and the *Grand nu au fauteuil rouge* (*Large Nude in a Red Armchair*, cat. 99) or to *The Bathers*? The *Jeune fille au miroir* (*Young Girl before a Mirror*) of 1932 (New York, The Museum of Modern Art) would not be mentioned so often if there had been earlier access to the *Grande nature morte au guéridon* (*Large Still-life on a Pedestal Table*, cat. 112) of 1931, a work which is just as powerful and complex. Muses, women sleeping or reading, and women doing their hair are conjured up in an admirable set of works culminating in one of the collection's masterpieces, the huge collage of *Femmes à leur toilette* (*Women at their Toilette*, cat. 219). It was produced in 1938 and provides an essential counterpoint to *Guernica*. To round off the score, one should range over the entire collection and mention, for example, the three versions of *Corrida* (*Bullfight*, cat. 73, 122, 123) of 1922 and 1933, the major wartime works, *La cuisine* (*The Kitchen*, cat. 174), *Le Déjeuner sur l'herbe* (cat. 189–191) and the large canvases of the latter years shown at Avignon. One would also need to analyse the fifteen hundred drawings, studies and sketchbooks: these clearly reveal the artist's chosen path, the scope of his work and the incredible wealth of the projects he had in mind. All this was known and had been published to some extent, but was scattered through the different volumes and supplements of the Zervos catalogue.

As Jean Leymarie pointed out in his introduction to the catalogue of the 1955 retrospective exhibition, the bringing together there of Picasso's sculptures was an unprecedented event. It proved to be the exhibition's great revelation, since the first book entirely devoted to this aspect of his output, by Werner Spies, did not appear until 1971. This element of the exhibition was displayed on its own immediately afterwards in London and then New York. We have now become more clearly aware of the importance of these works, which had until then only been glimpsed in books by Kahnweiler and Brassaï and never exhibited, except for those produced after the war. Picasso retained all his sculptures. Thus there are Vollard's casts of *Le fou* (*The Jester*, cat. 272) and the *Tête de femme (Fernande)* (*Head of a woman* [*Fernande*], cat. 273), as well as the monumental statues produced after the Second World War, usually in limited editions of one or two copies or, more frequently still, as a unique cast.

The collection of sculptures brought together by the settlement can never again be matched elsewhere, because it contains everything that exists as one of a kind. This equally applies to the Cubist constructions and picture reliefs, as well as to the two main 1928 models for a monument to Guillaume Apollinaire (cat. 306, 307). As to the complete series of bronze heads from Boisgeloup, the casts are accompanied in almost every case by the plaster original, something almost unparalleled in collections of sculptures at any time. Apart from the larger figures such as *La femme au jardin* (*The Woman in the Garden*, cat. 310), *L'homme au mouton* (*Man with a Sheep*, cat. 375), *La femme à la poussette* (*Woman with a Push Chair*, cat. 382), *La chèvre* (*The Goat*, cat. 384), *La guenon et son petit* (*Baboon with Young*, cat. 390), *La femme à l'orange* (*The Woman with an Orange*, cat. 361), the Boisgeloup series mentioned above and the wood carvings of 1930, some previously unknown works must be mentioned, such as the wood carvings dating from the period of *Les Demoiselles d'Avignon*, including the outstanding wooden mirror of 1907 entitled *Trois nus* (*Three Nudes*, cat. 283). These provide conclusive evidence of what was already known about Gauguin's influence. But the most astonishing sequence belongs to the 1912–15 period and, as we have seen, is firmly linked with contemporary pictorial problems. It begins with the 1912 cardboard *Guitar* (cat. 287), no doubt antedating the sheet-metal version in New York, continues with musical instruments and constructions in wood not previously shown and culminates in the painted sheet-iron work dating from 1915. This sequence illustrates, better than any other, the way in which space, colour and volume are compellingly treated – or rather resolved in succession – both on the flat picture surface and in the three dimensions of sculpture. The entire question of Cubism – the dissection, elimination and reinstatement of space – is confronted here. This matchless sequence, when juxtaposed with paintings, collages and *papiers collés*, addressed problems that are at once perennial and more topical than ever, concerning the illusion and reality of space, transparency and thickness, depth and limitation, to enumerate very briefly only a few of these. It is hard to imagine a more telling and coherent set of works aimed at conveying the basic complex of problems stated by Cubism.

The eighty-eight pieces of ceramics housed in the museum are mostly one-off works. This part of the output was already so well represented in French collections, particularly at Antibes, that no more was required than a selection indicating the range and variety involved.

The collection of drawings is similarly unrivalled. The principles we followed, when Michèle Richet joined us to organize the museum, were to keep the large compositions and not to break up sets, such as sketchbooks, subsidiary sheets, details, models and studies for the ballet. This was done deliberately and at the cost of abandoning some outstanding examples.

Picasso's engravings are known to the interested public through a few famous plates or proofs. In this case also, Picasso retained all the unique proofs, as well as the successive states, of which he – or occasionally Fort or Delâtre – usually pulled a very restricted number of copies. Geiser and Bloch provide a full account of all this. Later, he first gave the plates which he wished to publish to Roger Lacourière, then to Aldo and Piero Crommelynck, while the lithographs were done by Fernand Mourlot. What those who were given access to Picasso's estate experienced in this case was akin to entering an art lover's Garden of Eden. Everything had been preserved and looked after – unique works, successive stages of printing, copper plates and wood blocks, and a variety of proofs. It is safe to say that from the first beginnings up to the 1940s only the published sets were distributed. Here again, we thought it incumbent upon us not to disperse whatever belonged together and not to disregard single copies, even those that were of no more than subsidiary importance. With this purpose in mind, it was also decided not necessarily to retain all the plates already available in the Bibliothèque Nationale. On the other hand, all the previous stages relevant to the *Vollard Suite* have been systematically preserved in the present collection. This approach was supplemented by Madame Lacourière's uniquely generous gift in 1982, comprising a hundred plates marked 'approved for printing', an outstanding donation to commemorate Roger Lacourière's contribution to Picasso's engraved output. Our collection is undoubtedly the largest and most complete in existence and it contains, moreover, almost all Picasso's illustrated books, as well as the lay-out for Reverdy's *Le chant des morts*.

Picasso and Daniel-Henry Kahnweiler in the garden of La Californie (Musée Picasso Document, photo Edward Quinn)

A Growing Collection

Although Picasso's Picassos provide the backbone of this museum, they are supplemented by some works from the Musée National d'Art Moderne as a result of exchanges carried out in the interests of coherence and balance in both collections. Thus the monumental *Portrait of Gustave Coquiot* has been brought to the Musée Picasso to highlight the legacy of Lautrec and Gauguin, the interest in Van Gogh and, in a sense, what was to turn into Fauvism. Picasso avoided this trend, but *Les Demoiselles d'Avignon* and its antecedents went a long way towards 'Art Sauvage'. In the Musée National d'Art Moderne collection, this portrait of Coquiot did not provide an essential link or fill an unbridgeable gap, while at the Hôtel Salé it reveals the whole mastery with which Picasso, aged nineteen when he painted it in 1901, already used well-marked contrasts to assert the character of his art.

The museum was strengthened by major donations even before it opened its doors. In 1980, Daniel-Henry Kahnweiler bequeathed to it the very handsome *Nature morte au cuir à rasoir* (*Still-life with Razor Strop*, cat. 27) of 1909. It marks the end of the Cézanne Cubist phase and the introduction of a type of modelling that already split forms and analysed them; it was a work that the museum very much needed. Madame Lacourière presented the outstanding set of the *Vollard Suite* to the museum in 1982.

While we were assembling the collection, Louise and Michel Leiris informed me that they proposed to contribute to the establishment and endowment of the future museum by giving it several works from their own collection, some of which had previously belonged to Kahnweiler. This offer made it possible for us to do without some works from the estate, *Le verre d'absinthe* (*The Glass of Absinthe*) in particular, and to consider other possibilities elsewhere. This also made it possible to fill certain other gaps in some aspects of the output not represented by canvases. I will only mention, among so many others, the *Nu étoilé* (*Starry Nude*) of 1936 and the monumentally nacreous *Pisseuse* (*Pisser*), with its milky quality and tonalities rare in Picasso's output. This donation (reserving the right of usufruct) also includes the most important and perfect piece of monumental concrete statuary ever produced by Picasso, the *Femme aux bras écartés* (*Woman with Outstretched Arms*), the sheet-iron model for which the museum already owns (cat. 407). As in the case of the Apollinaire monument (an enlargement of one of the models for which was authorized by the artist's heirs), visitors to the museum will be able to see from the rooms in which the models are housed its full-scale version in the garden.

Maurice Jardot, Michel Leiris, Picasso, M. Guttierez and Claude Laurens at Vauvenargues, about 1958–59 (Picasso Archives)

Recently this museum, which is under an obligation to complement various aspects of its collection, was able to acquire the very exceptional *Composition au papillon* (*Composition with a Butterfly*, cat. 267) of 1932. This was thought to have been lost, but thanks to the understanding attitude of Madame Dora Maar it has now been allowed to rejoin a unique set of the collages and picture reliefs which regularly punctuate the artist's output by a stark contrast between painting and reality. This butterfly, fixed for all time in white paint, caused André Breton to ask himself what it was that 'made its absolute incorporation in the painting suddenly call forth that unique emotion which, when it overcomes us, indicates without any possible shadow of doubt that we have just been vouchsafed a revelation'.

The museum has also benefited from generous donations which now accompany the items mentioned above. Picasso's holograph writings are very few and far between – he received much correspondence, but wrote little himself. His letter to André Salmon in 1915 is therefore all the more valuable, quite apart from its decoration. Monsieur and Madame Alain Mazo were moved to hand it over to the museum soon after they had acquired it. There can be few contemporary documents capable of providing a counterpoint of this kind to the artist's output.

Picasso at the Hôtel Salé

'Picasso versus Louis XIV', a journalist wrote quite recently concerning the establishment of the museum in the Hôtel Salé (officially the Hôtel Aubert de Fontenay), as though the twentieth century were the only period of history unable to cohabit with its past. This choice of location, made in 1975 by M. Michel Guy, Secretary of State for Culture, was based on a number of considerations, not least that of restoring to a building of this sort a lasting public function for the permanent benefit of people at large. The proposal to house the Picasso collection in it required sound scrutiny. The architect Roland Simounet was appointed to carry out a study of the building and its potential, its ability to house such a large collection and to stand up to the traffic of so many visitors. No location could have been more appropriate for this artist's output. The proportions of the rooms match those of the various apartments and houses in which Picasso had worked throughout his life. Here are genuine echoes of studios at the rue des Grands-Augustins in Paris, at Boisgeloup and Mougins, even at La Californie and Fournas. The past is recalled and a dialogue is set up with it. This becomes obvious when paintings from Fontainebleau or sculptures from Boisgeloup are seen in the seventeenth-century setting provided by Martin Desjardins and the Marsy brothers. But undoubtedly the most astonishing feature of the Hôtel Salé is the way in which the sequence of the permanent collection not only chimes with the building, but, one may safely claim, redeems the values of the spatial organization within it and shows off the restrained use of its rooms and levels. This even involves the stable yard, roofed over in the nineteenth century, which now provides a home for the sculptures arranged in a contrast of different periods. Moreover, there could hardly be any building better attuned to this *œuvre* than a historic dwelling with a past as varied as that of the Hôtel Salé. Nor, indeed, any architecture as grandly on the scale of what Gaëtan Picon described as 'the Picasso civilization, that Louvre from another planet'. The very encounter between his own output, his personal collection and this unusual location has a place in the Picasso universe. It is appropriate that his collection of works by other artists, which sums up the twentieth century and the classical art of the West, should also be housed here. It is accompanied by objects of primitive art that had belonged to Picasso, such as the two figures from New Caledonia (cat. T.88, T.89), the Punu mask (cat. T.84), the great Nimba mask from Guinea (cat. T.82) and the New Hebrides idol (cat. T.80) that Matisse gave Picasso when he visited his older colleague at the Hôtel Régina in Nice. Finally, mention must be made of the wealth of – sometimes unpretentious – works which recall the admiration or affection of the artist's companions, such as the collage (cat. T.53) dating from 1947 and inscribed 'Affectionately to Picasso, Henri Matisse' – that fellow-voyager and interlocutor who was so different from him, but to whom his entire affection and admiration were all the more freely given. In this sense also the Musée Picasso is not a normal specialist museum; it is not, indeed, an ordinary museum at all. As we see it, it is perhaps an ideal museum as an introduction to the art of the twentieth century or, at least, an essential way of approach to an understanding of twentieth-century man.

D.B.

Notes

If ever an artist's output inexorably defied all attempts at classification by techniques and made them appear completely idiosyncratic, it is that of Picasso. What possible chance is there of drawing a line between painting and sculpture when his entire creative energy was, in fact, directed at breaking up these traditional categories and alternating between two and three dimensions at will? Where is one to place *papiers collés*, picture reliefs and assemblages which stand at the junction of different modes of expression and by this very fact bring into being an entirely new plastic idiom?

In order to meet the requirements of a concise catalogue, the purpose of which is to list in a conveniently identifiable sequence all the items on show in a museum, we have chosen for reasons of convenience to adopt a system of classification by types of technique: Paintings, *Papiers collés*, Picture reliefs, Sculptures, Ceramics.

Drawings and sketchbooks will be dealt with in another volume. Prints will form the subject of a further publication listing all the engravings held by official collections in France.

A new system of numbering has been devised for this catalogue and used in its texts. The M.P. inventory numbers have been retained only for the drawings, the catalogue of which is in the course of preparation.

Dating

The works have been classified in chronological order within each of the catalogue's five sections, although the order adopted here does not invariably take exact account of the date on which any work was produced within a given year. Broad dates usually take precedence over more precise statements, except when a particular work can be reliably dated and therefore allow a whole series to be dated by analogy. A date and place of origin shown in square brackets indicate that they rest on an assumption, usually made on stylistic grounds, but are not sufficiently well documented to eliminate all doubt. The date quoted for bronze casts is invariably that of the original. Certain dates have been altered since the inventory was drawn up and the catalogue of the settlement published in 1979.

Abbreviations

M.P. refers to the museum's inventory numbering.
Dimensions are given in centimetres: height × width × depth.
Only inscriptions in the artist's own hand are given. They are printed in italics in the catalogue.
S.   signed
D.   dated
a.   above
b.   below
l.   left
r.   right
c.   centre
Inscr.   inscribed

References to Other Publications

These are quoted in the catalogue captions in chronological order:

D.B.   Pierre Daix and Georges Boudaille, *Picasso 1900–1906, catalogue raisonné de l'œuvre peint*, Neuchâtel, 1966.

D.R.   Pierre Daix and Joan Rosselet, *Picasso: The Cubist Years 1907–1916*, London, 1979.

Duncan   David Douglas Duncan, *Picasso's Picassos*, London, New York, 1961.

G.   Bernhard Geiser, *Picasso peintre-graveur*, Vol.1, illustrated catalogue of the engraved and lithographed output, 1899–1931, Berne, published by the author, 1933–1955; Vol. 2, *catalogue raisonné* of the engraved output and monotypes, 1932–1934, Berne, 1968.

P.i.F.   Josep Palau i Fabre, *Picasso, 1881–1907: Life and Work of the Early Years*, Oxford, 1981.

T.l.o.p. (¹) *Tout l'œuvre peint de Picasso, périodes bleue et rose*, Paris, 1980.

T.l.o.p. (²) *Tout l'œuvre peint de Picasso, 1907–1916*, Paris, 1977.

R.   Georges Ramié, *Céramique de Picasso*, Paris, 1974.

S.   Werner Spies, *Picasso, Das plastische Werk* (sculpture catalogue in collaboration with Christine Piot), Stuttgart, 1983.

Z.   Christian Zervos, *Pablo Picasso*, Paris, Vol. I, 1932, to Vol. XXXIII, 1978.

Acknowledgments

This catalogue is based on the initial work carried out by Dominique Bozo, Michèle Richet and Philippe Thiébaut in producing the catalogue for the exhibition of the settlement of the estate at the Grand Palais in 1979.

We would like to express our deep gratitude for the frequently crucial assistance afforded to us in the preparation of the various sections of this catalogue:

for sculpture to

Christine Piot and Werner Spies;

for ceramics to

Elisabeth Fontan, Antoinette Hallé, Yvan Oreggia, Alain Ramié and Jean Ramié;

for primitive and Iberian art to

Françoise Beck, Annie Caubet, Jacques Kerchache, François Lupu, Jean-Louis Paudrat and Pierre Rouillard;

for the De Chirico sketchbook to

Maurizio Fagiolo dell'Arco.

We are also grateful to Paule Mazouet for her invaluable assistance in the technical supervision of the catalogue's production.

Picasso in his rue Schoelcher studio in
1915 with the unfinished *L'homme accoudé
sur une table* (*Man Leaning on a Table*)
(Picasso Archives)

Paintings

The full wealth and diversity of this collection of paintings cannot be conveyed – nor a detailed analysis of the main works undertaken – in the limited space available here. The highlights of the museum are dealt with in a separate illustrated volume, while a scientific analysis of each work, together with its preliminary studies, will provide the material for a further publication – the *catalogue raisonné* of Picasso's works held in France. Dominique Bozo has outlined in his introduction, 'Picasso at Home', the principles that guided him in picking the collection, and described its strong points. We shall therefore confine ourselves here to citing the main historical factors which enable one to understand the formation and evolution of Picasso's output from 1895 to 1973, and to providing summary descriptions of what seem to us to be the main works of each period.

La fillette aux pieds nus (*The Barefoot Girl*, cat. 2) in Picasso's studio in 1914 (Picasso Archives)

(1) G. Apollinaire, 'Les jeunes: Picasso peintre', *La Plume*, 15 May 1905.

Youth, the Blue Period, Gosol 1895–1906

Although the Musée Picasso's holding of youthful works is comparatively limited, it is nevertheless indicative of the various stages through which the artist's output passed between the first canvases of 1895 and the achievement of an individual style in 1906. The museum has two paintings dating from a time of apprenticeship so richly illustrated in the Museo Picasso, Barcelona – *L'homme à la casquette* (*Man with a Cap*, cat. 1) and *La fillette aux pieds nus* (*The Barefoot Girl*, cat. 2), both of which date from the stay in Corunna, where the Ruiz family went to live in 1891. Picasso was then fourteen and one cannot help being struck, despite the conventional handling, by the early maturity of a young painter already reacting to his model's inner life, in this instance, the human face of sadness and poverty.

In the likeness of his departed friend, represented in *La mort de Casagemas* (*The Death of Casagemas*, cat. 3), the museum preserves an essential piece of evidence about the dramatic event which threw the artist's life into confusion and launched the Blue period. Despite its sharp colours and areas of heavy *impasto*, characteristic of the bright and colourful Parisian period and well exemplified in the *Portrait of Gustave Coquiot* (on loan from the Musée National d'Art Moderne) with its Pointillist touches, this small canvas with a tragic theme heralds the transition to an art that is both Expressionist and emotional. The Blue period is sparsely represented, but one particular work – the *Self-portrait* of 1901 (cat. 4) – sums up both its spirit and its style. This picture of the artist, his face emaciated and scored by the rigours of winter and illness, was painted during his stay in Paris in 1901. It is somewhat reminiscent of certain self-portraits by Van Gogh in which one recognizes the same psychological intensity and the half-haunted look of the eyes. The blue tonality expresses the moral and physical wretchedness of a human race doomed to be victims: 'For the space of a year', wrote Apollinaire, 'Picasso's existence was immersed in this wetness of paint, blue as the damp bottom of the abyss, and pitiful.'[1]

During the summer of 1906, Picasso and his mistress Fernande Olivier went to stay in Gosol, a small village tucked away in the Catalan hills. This trip marked the beginning of a new phase in his output and promoted that far-reaching change which had already started to take shape in the *Saltimbanques* series of 1905. He now abandoned the sentimental and literary aesthetics of the Blue period, with its emaciated faces and images of woe and solitude, and turned to a world full of beauty, balance and serenity. This period is characterized by a sculptural treatment of the human figure, stylized gestures and a colour range based on ochre, rose and grey, the tonalities of Gosol's own soil. It represents a crucial stage in the painter's development – the assertion of his maturity as an artist, a seeding of his Cubist approach and his first return to Mediterranean sources and an archaizing approach.

Les deux frères (*The Two Brothers*, cat. 6), despite their nudity and their sculptural treatment, still faintly hark back to the world of the circus (witness the drum and the theme of youngsters with neatly drawn features), but the *Jeune garçon nu* (*Nude Boy*, cat. 7) and the *Self-portrait* (cat. 8) display an archaic simplicity and a determination to schematize and simplify which lead to a purely plastic and pictorial expression. Picasso treats his face as a mask in the *Self-portrait*, in other words as a set of clear, near-geometrical shapes devoid of all individual character. He was to do the same in the *Portrait of Gertrude Stein* (New York, The Metropolitan Museum of Art). The influence of Iberian statuary which Picasso had seen in the Louvre at the exhibition of recent excavations in Osuna is apparent in the treatment of the eyes with their empty look, the eyebrows and the nose. This degree of stylization marked the last stage before work began on *Les Demoiselles d'Avignon* (New York, The Museum of Modern Art). The distance travelled between the Blue and the Rose period *Self-portraits* is obvious enough.

Les Demoiselles d'Avignon 1907

Even though the museum does not own this key monument of twentieth-century painting, it can nevertheless provide pointers to it, thanks to the series of sketches and preliminary studies which accompanied the work. These studies in fact provide an understanding of how the various stages in the production of the finished painting are related to each other. Picasso worked out each figure in the composition separately. The various nude figures, the sailor's (or woman's) head and shoulders, the girl with raised arms, all represent characters which testify to the various stages through which this subject had passed before reaching its final version. The differences in treatment from one canvas to the next are revealing in terms of the complexity of the finished work, the combination of influences involved and the pictorial problems tackled at one stroke by the artist, such as the statement of volume and movement, the integration into the background and the part played by outline and colour. The transition from the primitive archaism of Gosol to 'barbaric dissymmetry' (Daix) can be seen in the development of the face which has occurred between the *Buste d'homme* (*Head and Shoulders of a Man*, cat. 12) and the *Buste* (*Head and Shoulders*, cat. 15), or between *Nu assis* (*Seated Nude*, cat. 10) and *Femme aux mains jointes* (*Woman with Clasped Hands*, cat. 14). The Iberian influence, expressed by an exaggerated disregard of proportions in the enlargement of the chin and lower part of the face, the heavily outlined eyes, outsize ears and empty look, becomes more marked. Picasso carried out his research on the rendering of volume in two different directions. The girls at the centre of the picture represent flat figures in which plasticity is suggested by a deviation of outlines and changes in scale, while on the right-hand side of the canvas the figures carried out with hatched or striped bands of colour are modelled by means of contrasts in the colouring. He thus abruptly switched from rounded bodies to geometrical angularity. The first series is derived from canvases that somewhat resemble colour sketches, with broad brown strokes on backgrounds of broken grey and muted pinks. Infra-red photographs of the *Woman with Clasped Hands* (cat. 14) and *Head and Shoulders* (cat. 15) have revealed, beneath the final layer of paint and on the back of the canvas, a preliminary

Les Demoiselles d'Avignon, 1907, New York, The Museum of Modern Art

Infra-red photograph of *Femme aux mains jointes* (*Woman with Clasped Hands*, cat. 14) (Research Laboratory of the Musées de France)

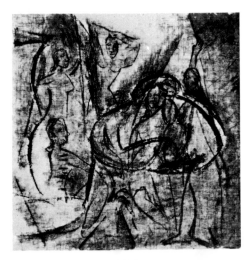

Infra-red photograph of the back of *Buste* (*Head and Shoulders*, cat. 15) (Research Laboratory of the Musées de France)

sketch of the whole composition and a number of figure studies, including one identical with the *Petit nu de dos aux bras levés* (*Small Nude from the Back with Raised Arms*, cat. 11) and the profile of a figure holding up the drapery. A form of hatching that is not to be mistaken for African scarification recurs in the *Buste de femme ou de marin* (*Head and Shoulders of a Woman or Sailor*, cat. 13) and in *L'arbre* (*The Tree*, cat. 19), the first abstract landscape in the history of painting. The ruthless revival of colour which coincided with the late Fauvist canvases of Matisse and Derain is exemplified in *Mère et enfant* (*Mother and Child*, cat. 17), a painting of extraordinarily violent expression, both in its vivid colours and in the marked schematization of the faces. Finally, the *Demoiselles* series would not be complete without the primitive-looking, rough-hewn wooden sculptures, the treatment of which Picasso subjected to the same stylistic principles as his paintings.

Cubism 1908–1916

Although the large Cubist compositions are not here, the museum nevertheless again contains a series of smaller-scale works and drawings that enable one to follow the main stages in the evolution of Cubism from 1908 to 1914. The Cézanne phase, with its concentration on the study of volume, space and light, is illustrated by the three variations on *Tête d'homme* (*Head of a Man*, cat. 24, 25, 28), the *Nu couché avec personnages* (*Reclining Nude with Figures*, cat. 22) and the *Paysage aux deux figures* (*Landscape with Two Figures*, cat. 26), which may be compared with Braque's L'Estaque works dating from the same period. The 'passage' technique, in other words the dissection of volumes along their leading edges to ease the passage between object and spatial shell, appears in the *Nature morte au cuir à rasoir* (*Still-life with Razor Strop*, cat. 27, D.-H. Kahnweiler bequest). The crucial stage arising from the visit to Horta de Ebro in 1908, in the course of which the fragmentation of solid surfaces into facets was perfected, appears in the *Landscapes* in the collection of The Museum of Modern Art, New York. The 'analytical' phase is represented by two major works, *Homme à la mandoline* (*Man with a Mandolin*, cat. 33) and *Homme à la guitare* (*Man with a Guitar*, cat. 34). The identification of the figure in the first, more abstract, of these is virtually impossible and one recognizes no more than the armchair and the musical instrument. The picture is painted on two pieces of canvas roughly joined together, and appears to be unfinished in the lower part, thus making it possible to show the artist's method of work. The second, also painted on two pieces of canvas, incorporates some points of reference that enable one to identify the man with his moustache, the guitar and the armchair. This picture was painted in successive stages, as the inscriptions – '1911, 12, 13' – on the back indicate.

In so far as the Cubist period is concerned, however, the wealth of the collection essentially resides in the unique set of collages, picture reliefs and constructions dating from 1912–15, among which the *Nature morte à la chaise cannée* (*Still-life with Chair-caning*, cat. 35) of 1912 deserves pride of place. Picasso incorporated in it an actual piece of oilcloth printed with a chair-caning pattern. This first collage was to revolutionize twentieth-century art as a whole, both because of the new form of space thus generated by the material employed and its autonomous relation to the background, and because it undermined the conventional concept of pictorial illusion. Why 'represent' that which can be 'presented'? In this particular instance, the treatment was all the more ambiguous because the oilcloth was in fact itself only an illusion of canework. In other words, this was at one and the same time a case both of highlighting and of questioning a method of representation. This was also the first occasion on which Picasso used scrap materials in a way that was to become very familiar in his 1912–15 constructions and in his picture reliefs.

Starting out from the invention of collage, Cubism was to develop in three closely connected directions – painting, *papier collé* and sculpture – so that the reliefs represent three-dimensional extensions of the *papiers collés*, the paintings are imitations of the *papiers collés*, and so on. Picasso thoroughly explored all the techniques and opportunities provided by his new plastic idiom and used the greatest possible variety of supports and materials – tins, turned pieces of wood, bits of string and nails, cigar boxes, etc. At the same time, he set out to establish a veritable inventory of actual, everyday reality by drawing for his subjects on the most ordinary objects, such as a glass, a bottle, a café table, a pipe, playing cards, popular song sheets, all kinds of things redolent of humanity. Armed with the freedom won by creating a new pictorial space and a means of representation now based on symbols, Picasso indulged after 1914 in a colourful and decorative form of Cubism characterized by a Pointillist technique which enabled him to convey translucence and the play of light on objects. In *Homme à la cheminée* (*Man at the Fireplace*, cat. 49) he combined a formulation of superimposed planes derived from *papiers collés* with a naturalistic formulation of the fireplace's framework, thereby contrasting Cubist and perspective space. The introduction of figurative details marked a step in the return to figuration which Picasso undertook as early as 1914 in his portrait drawing of Vollard,[2] and which in painting is first exemplified by a picture that the settlement from the estate brought to light, *Le peintre et son modèle* (*The Painter and his Model*, cat. 48). This unfinished work, in which Picasso combined Cézanne's influence with Ingres's graphic style, deals with a subject he often studied in drawings – such as that of a man leaning on a table – and brings into play one of the artist's basic themes, that of the confrontation with his model. This may be the only existing representation of Picasso's new mistress, Eva Gouel, to whom he had already indirectly alluded in some canvases by the description *Ma Jolie* (*My Pretty One*).

The Neo-classical Period 1917–1925

This period, described as the neo-classical or Ingres phase, and often regarded – somewhat recklessly – as part of the general 'recall to order' of the 1920s, is in fact one of the richest and most complex phases in the general evolution of Picasso's art. It witnessed the parallel development of several very sharply differing and seemingly conflicting styles. It embraced a summing-up of Cubism which both culminated and branched out in *The Three Musicians* (New York, The Museum of Modern Art, and Philadelphia Museum of Art); the apogee of a classicism drawn from Ingres and antiquity, as in *Trois femmes à la fontaine* (*Three Women at the Fountain*, New York, The Museum of Modern Art, and cat. 69), *La flûte de Pan* (*The Pipes of Pan*, cat. 76) and *La source* (*The Source*, cat. 70); and, lastly, a bout of intense work for the theatre, such as the sets and costumes for the *Parade*, *Mercure*, *Pulcinella* and *Cuadro Flamenco* ballets. All this bears witness in various ways to the figurative and stylistic opportunities generated by the Cubist revolution. Much controversy was caused by Picasso's reversion to a classical style and traditional figurative work which began in 1914, but came to full expression between 1920 and 1923. Some observers at first treated this as a betrayal, others as a return to good order by the Cubist 'revolutionary'. All these superficial opinions can be explained by the post-war ideological climate. It was intensely nationalist, pilloried Cubism as 'Boche' and advocated a return to Mediterranean sculpture, with its traditional values of order and balance. Some simplistic interpretations of Picasso's classicist style during this period also rely to some extent on his new way of life. After his marriage to Olga in 1917, the move to the rue La Boétie and the switch to the Rosenberg gallery, Picasso began to associate with a more worldly, bourgeois set whose conformist tastes revelled in such a smooth and reassuring revival of antiquity, seen as a new start after the troubles of war. But it is also entirely beyond doubt that, though this return to antiquity chimed with the cultural mood of the period – that of Cocteau's *Antigone*, Stravinsky's *Oedipus Rex* and Valéry's *Jeune Parque* – Picasso's classicism can in no sense be equated with academicism. In fact, as Pierre Daix has pointed out, this was a 'booby-trapped classicism'; armed with the spatial freedoms won by

(2) Zervos II², 922.

Photograph of Olga Kokhlova taken by Picasso, Montrouge, 1917 (Picasso Archives)

Cubism, it used antiquity as Negro masks had earlier been used to put it to new purposes and reinterpreted conventional figurative models in the light of Cubist experience.

In 1917 Picasso was swept off to Italy by Jean Cocteau to join up with Diaghilev's ballet company and prepare sets and costumes for *Parade*. It was in Rome that he met Olga Kokhlova, a dancer in the Ballets Russes who was to become his wife. He has left us a very close likeness of her, judging by a photograph which he used as a model, in *Portrait d'Olga dans un fauteuil* (*Portrait of Olga in an Armchair*, cat. 50). The realistic detail, the purity and economy of line and the pose are reminiscent of some of Ingres's great portraits. This virtuoso, though rather mawkish, classicist manner was succeeded by a far more radical interpretation of Ingres, involving the expressive distortion of forms and elongation of figures, exemplified in the strange little canvas of *Les baigneuses* (*The Bathers*, cat. 55), a paraphrase of Ingres's *The Turkish Bath*. This harking back to the past necessarily involved a resort to the masters, such as the Pointillist *Le retour du baptême, d'apres Le Nain* (*The Return from the Christening, after Le Nain*, cat. 51) of 1917 and a 1919 Cubist interpretation – *Les amoureux* (*The Lovers*, cat. 57) – of Manet's *Nana*. The dual nature of Picasso's pictorial idiom at this time is very apparent in *Etudes* (*Studies*, cat. 60), which brings together and sums up several pictures in a single work: small, virtually abstract Cubist geometrical compositions on the one hand and, on the other, studies of hands and figures borrowed from antiquity.[3] The Musée Picasso collection includes life-size examples of both these styles – the glass, playing card and pipe compositions (cat. 53, 54), *Tête de femme* (*Head of a Woman*, cat. 65) and *La danse villageoise* (*The Village Dance*, cat. 71).

Visits to the seaside, first at Biarritz and later on the Côte d'Azur, provided Picasso with new themes in which sunbathing, water sports and the nude bodies of women bathers found a place among everyday scenes of life on the beach. These themes supplemented recent studies of dancers – the outcome of time spent with the Ballets Russes – and prompted Picasso to undertake an accurate and systematic study of the female form, its movements, its attitudes and the opportunities it offered for transformation. The outsize proportions of these monumental giantesses derive in equal measure from models provided by Roman statuary and from a symbolic conception of womanhood as the 'Alma Mater'. They also have a strictly pictorial function, however, as another way of increasing the area of vision and encompassing the material, physical reality of these bodies. Picasso tends to spread out their limbs over the entire picture surface, to blow them out so as to impart equal significance and value to every one of them and thus completely fill the picture plane.

The latter-day Cubism of the early 1920s may be comparatively poorly represented in the collection, but the neo-classical phase provides a wealth of remarkable works. *La flûte de Pan* (*The Pipes of Pan*, cat. 76), the universally acknowledged masterpiece of this period, takes pride of place. This is followed by the second, sanguine version of *Trois femmes à la fontaine* (*Three Women at the Fountain*, cat. 69), a supremely 'Greek' work, which embodies all the canons of classical beauty; and another, second charcoal version of a canvas entitled *La source* (*The Source*, cat. 70),[4] a composition derived from a picture of the Fontainebleau School. The settlement from the estate revealed a hitherto unknown work – *La lecture de la lettre* (*Reading the Letter*, cat. 67) – an enigmatic and stylistically unique picture which may represent a tribute to Apollinaire, the friend who had recently died. One might also mention two still-life pictures, the first – *Nature morte sur la commode* (*Still-life on the Chest of Drawers*, cat. 58) – treated with advanced realism, and the second – *Nature morte au pichet et aux pommes* (*Still-life with Pitcher and Apples*, cat. 59) – endowed with great formal purity. There is also a small gouache, *Deux femmes courant sur la plage (La course)* (*Two Women Running on the Beach* [*The Race*], cat. 74), 'a real monument in action, two forceful and gigantic beauties who could hardly be more integrally part of their environment, yet are timeless, free and powerful, about to take off'.[5] This gouache served as a model for the curtain of *Le Train bleu*, a ballet by Cocteau on a score by Darius Milhaud.

In 1921, Olga gave birth to a son, Paulo. A mysterious and poetic picture, *Famille au bord de la mer* (*Family on the Sea-shore*, cat. 75), reflected this recent introduction to fatherhood. Picasso would later produce famous and delightful portraits of his son, *Paul en arlequin* (*Paulo as Harlequin*, cat. 79) and *Paul en pierrot* (*Paulo as Pierrot*, cat. 80).

(3) An X-ray photograph by the Research Laboratory of the Musées de France has revealed the copy of an engraving by Rembrandt, *The Raising of Lazarus*, under Picasso's picture.

(4) Painted version, Zervos, IV, 304.

(5) D. Bozo, *Picasso, œuvres reçues en paiement des droits de succession*, Paris, Grand Palais, 1979–80, p. 119.

This set of works also enables one to appreciate the variety of combined techniques used by the artist – oil paint, charcoal, sanguine or gouache, on paper, canvas or panel – and throws light on his method of working, as well as on the changes he made from one version to the next of the same picture when he altered his medium.

Transformations – Surrealism 1925–1931

The whole of Picasso's output is punctuated from start to finish by unexpected departures which suggest a radical switch from what had gone before. In fact, looked at more closely, it will be seen that such formal innovations had often long since been incorporated in forward-looking works which Picasso put aside until he thought the time ripe to revive them and develop them more thoroughly. Such trend-setting works in the development of his output carry the seeds of a new pictorial idiom and display in emblematic form the style and spirit of the fresh phase which they are launching. This applies to *Le baiser* (*The Kiss*, cat. 81), dating from a stay in Juan-les-Pins in 1925 with Olga and Paulo – an outstanding picture in a number of ways and comparable in importance to *The Dance* (London, Tate Gallery). Both carry to a different degree the same kind of aggressive mood and visual impact. Both are marked by the bursting asunder of forms, first dismembered, then freely associated as in a jigsaw puzzle; by exaggerations in the modelling and by the overlapping of planes and patterns involving both illusionist and Cubist space; and by an explosion of shrill and variegated colours. This outbreak of violence and eroticism in Picasso's output coincided with the emergence of Surrealism, together with the advocacy of 'convulsive beauty' and of the liberation of instincts. On a personal plane, it also coincided with the beginning of strains and conjugal clashes between him and Olga which were to prompt in Picasso feelings of violence and aggression towards the female sex.

Picasso's links with the Surrealists have caused a good deal of argument: an attempt by the group to take him over, according to some, and a matter of pure coincidence, according to others. Should one agree with Breton's statement that[6] 'he is one of us, and if Surrealism wishes to set a course of action for itself, it need only tread where Picasso has trodden, and will tread again'? Or should one follow Leiris,[7] who pillories this attempt 'more or less to identify him with the Surrealists' as a 'crude and pernicious mistake'?

Be that as it may, some facts point to a definite connection. In 1925, *La Révolution Surréaliste* published *Les Demoiselles d'Avignon*, the famous dot-and-line abstract sketch-book of Juan-les-Pins and the *Femme en chemise* (*Woman in a Chemise*). Picasso also took part in 1925 in the Galerie Pierre exhibition and, ten years later, in those of Pierre Colle and Charles Ratton.

In fact, however, except for certain drawings clearly inspired by Surrealism and dating from 1933–34, Picasso's work never touched upon the realm of dreams and the subconscious. His transformations may take him far afield, but he always stayed close to reality. His Surrealist leanings owed much more to currents running deep in his private life than to any involvement in an intellectual system.

The 1925–33 period, so brutally begun, proved the richest of his entire output in terms of both formal and thematic inventions. An entirely novel sculptural and pictorial idiom was then created, as well as a personal and subjective iconography which runs right through his work from this time on. This was the mature Picasso, violent and erotic, subjective and lyrical after his Cubist asceticism and the return to classicism – two aspects of the same harmonious and orderly universe in which the treatment of form took precedence over content – who now came back to his initial Expressionist leanings, intent on describing what Breton defined as 'the model within'. It seems as though, from 1925 on, Picasso could say and dare whatever he pleased, since he now commanded the entire range of his pictorial resources and the whole gamut of formal registers.

(6) A. Breton, *Le Surréalisme et la peinture*, Paris, 1965, p. 7.

(7) M. Leiris, 'Toiles récentes de Picasso', *Documents*, No. 2, 1930, pp. 55–71.

Picasso produced two monochrome works in 1926, *Le peintre et son modèle* (*The Painter and his Model*, cat. 82) and *L'atelier de la modiste* (*The Milliner's Workshop*, Paris, Musée National d'Art Moderne). They are almost like negatives of each other: a combination of grey and black curved shapes contrasts with a similar black contour. This network is inscribed into a background of grey monochrome areas which serve to stress the picture surface and suggest an element of depth. Such independence of drawing, colour and form is a corollary of the Cubist idiom. The curvilinear Cubism of the still-life pictures dating from 1925 was here taken to its uttermost limits, bordering on automatic writing. Indeed, it is the meanderings of the line which create a huge foot here, a hand elsewhere and a head in yet another place, while the painter with his palette stands on the right. The artist and his model are thus linked by a single network of lines, an apt description of the relationship between them. This tight skein of form-creating lines recurs, significantly enough, in the first drawings for *Le Chef-d'œuvre inconnu* by Balzac, dating from 1926.

Just as *The Dance* (London, Tate Gallery) and *Le baiser* (*The Kiss*, cat. 81) opened the way for all the formal dislocations and exaggerations produced by this period, *Le peintre et son modèle* (*The Painter and his Model*, cat. 82) was at the source of a whole series of works generated by the same graphic and linear treatment. *Figure* (cat. 86) and *Nu sur fond blanc* (*Nude on a White Background*, cat. 87) provide a schematic summary for these works by the contrast between their monochrome geometrical areas (which, as earlier in the *papiers collés*, indicate the background) and a line drawing which traces out a dislocated anatomy characterized by tiny heads and gigantic limbs. These figures are reflected three-dimensionally in *Métamorphose I* and *II* (*Metamorphosis I* and *II*, cat. 302, 303), in which Picasso renewed the dialogue between painting and sculpture initiated during the Cubist years. Side by side with such work featuring organic, soft, fluid and random shapes, a new language of severe, angular and rational forms came into being in connection with the theme of *The Studio* (New York, The Museum of Modern Art). This wide-meshed network of lines gradually stiffened and was reflected in the wire constructions (cat. 305–307), two of which were put forward as designs for a monument to Apollinaire and which are, in a sense, drawings in space.

In 1928 and 1929 Picasso spent the summer in Dinard and turned out the famous series of small canvases on the theme of women bathing: 'This cycle of images offering symbols, such as the key, the lock, the empty or transparent booth that is shut or about to be closed again, every one of them supplying potent poetic themes to make the Surrealists happy.'[8] These monumental forms, unfolding in the clear light of Normandy, also suggest anthropomorphic townscapes or models for gigantic statues. They were to grow immense, both in canvases dating from 1931 – *Femme lançant une pierre* (*Woman Throwing a Stone*, cat. 111) – and in the sculptures from Boisgeloup which they foreshadowed. Picasso subjected the female body to an interplay of organic transformations and permutations by setting up associations, such as that of genitalia and mouth, the *vagina dentata* – a perennial obsession. This treatment of the female body is not only an ultimate statement in terms of modelling and monumentality, but is also essentially Expressionist, as witness the *Grand nu au fauteuil rouge* (*Large Nude in a Red Armchair*, 1929, cat. 99), one of the most powerful representations of personal anguish ever painted. The woman's flaccid limbs, the head thrown back in a silent cry of distress, the crude and violent colours express the inner collapse of a being racked by pain and rejection. *The Crucifixion*, 1930 (cat. 108), is a major work of this period, both in its historical theme with personal overtones and in the complexity of its formal idiom, which brings together the various motifs employed by Picasso during this period: vagina-head, bony and biomorphic forms, and flat shapes, like those of *L'acrobate* (*The Acrobat*, cat. 106). The Crucifixion theme, to which Picasso was to return in 1932 in a series of studies after the Isenheim altarpiece, is indissolubly linked with that of the bullfight and the Minotauromachy. In 1928, Picasso produced a large collage (Paris, Musée National d'Art Moderne) and a painting of the *Minotaure courant* (*Running Monotaur*, cat. 91) in which this theme appears for the first time. During a visit to Spain in 1933, he painted two versions of the bullfight theme on the death of the torero (cat. 122, 123) – a bare-breasted young woman in one version. These two major works, together with the *Minotaure au javelot* (*Minotaur with Javelin*, cat. 124), belong to the famous cycle which properly began with the *Vollard Suite*, as well as the cover that Breton

(8) D. Bozo, op. cit., p. 121.

commissioned and Picasso designed for the Surrealist periodical *Minotaure*, published at that time by Tériade under a title suggested by Bataille. The Minotaur represented the central theme of Picasso's world, with the spatial arrangement of the labyrinth forming the link between two cultures joining the cult of Mithras to the bullfight and the offspring of Pasiphaë to the Spanish fighting bull. The Minotaur, with whom Picasso totally identified, is the quintessential symbol of duality – the duality of artistic output, of the human being, of creation as a whole. Part human, part beast and part divine, he embodies in a single being the monster, primitive animality, the dark forces of the subconscious, the executioner and the victim, Eros and Thanatos – love and death.

Boisgeloup 1931–1934

As an escape from the troubles of married life, Picasso set up a vast studio in the castle of Boisgeloup, near Gisors, in 1931, and launched into sculpture, especially free-standing work. This was prompted as much by his new surroundings as by the constant presence at his side of the ideal sculptural model – Marie-Thérèse Walter – whom he had met by chance in 1927. Her image was to dominate the entire 1931–36 period in his painting and sculpture. *Girl before a Mirror*, 1932 (New York, The Museum of Modern Art), regarded as the major work of this period, must be set against the powerful and vibrant *Grande nature morte au guéridon* (*Large Still-life with a Pedestal Table*, cat. 112), a complex, tense and perhaps even more radical work. Alfred Barr liked to recall Picasso's comment on it: 'Some still-life!' In fact, as Picasso later told Pierre Daix, it was a disguised portrait of Marie-Thérèse. From 1931, he employed a distinct pictorial idiom specifically derived from her, consisting of curves, rounded forms and arabesques, and it was ultimately she who provided the inspiration for the theme of women displayed in the innocence of sleep – *Nu couché* (*Reclining Nude*, cat. 120) – or seen with a book – *La lecture* (*Reading*, cat. 115).

All these 'Boisgeloup' works convey the model's unquestionably sculptural and monumental quality. Picasso analysed the robust fullness of the forms she offered, the elegance of her face and her characteristic attributes – the slit eyes, a nose that carried on the line of the forehead and the well-rounded breasts.

The canvases produced during this period, whether they refer to the appropriately topical theme of *Le sculpteur* (*The Sculptor*, cat. 113), to the *Femme au fauteuil rouge* (*Woman in a Red Armchair*, cat. 116) or to the *Femme assise dans un fauteuil rouge* (*Woman Sitting in a Red Armchair*, cat. 117), have a close connection with sculpture and represent the pictorial counterparts of three-dimensional experiments. But this formal idiom was equally derived from work on *The Crucifixion* and the Dinard *Metamorphoses*, as an aggressive and violent painting – *La femme au stylet* (*The Woman with a Stylet*, cat. 114) – shows, with its return to the distorted limbs and small, sharp-toothed head of earlier figures.

1934–1939

The years between 1934 and 1939 were troubled times for Picasso, personally and politically. He was to tell David Douglas Duncan: 'It's the worst period of my life.' The violent conjugal clashes with Olga, culminating in separation and a divorce petition in 1935, were closely accompanied by the birth of Maya, his daughter by Marie-Thérèse Walter, and a meeting with another woman, Dora Maar, a young photographer of Yugoslav origin who had been introduced to him by Paul Eluard.

The drama of the Spanish Civil War, which very deeply affected Picasso, followed by the rise of Fascism and the threat of global war, provide the background for the – admittedly very diverse – set of works produced during this period.

Caught in the cross-fire of his emotional upsets, Picasso seemed haunted during these years by the representation of the female form. The Marie-Thérèse cycle came to an end with the naked, rose-hued body of the *Nu dans un jardin* (*Nude in a Garden*, cat. 126), coiled like a seed about to burst into flowers and fruit. The arabesque brush routine gave way to a geometrical treatment and angularity, as in the *Nu au bouquet d'iris et au miroir* (*Nude with Bunch of Irises and Mirror*, cat. 125). This change of style went with a thematic evolution in which the sleeping woman was replaced by the woman reading, another form of dreaming. The large-nosed profile and the bird-shaped hands of the woman leaning over a table in *Femme lisant* (*Woman Reading*, cat. 127) may be compared with the figures of the *Muse* (Paris, Musée National d'Art Moderne).

Picasso stopped painting and set about writing poetry in Spanish and French between May 1935 and February 1936. This was published in May 1936 by André Breton in a special edition of *Cahiers d'Art*, 1930–35. In May 1936 he went to ground at Juan-les-Pins with Marie-Thérèse and Maya, who had just been born, and picked up his paintbrushes again. The women's heads which then emerged were among the most extravagant in his entire output: bobbin-heads (cat. 132), wire-heads (cat. 128) and women in hats with topsy-turvy anatomies (cat. 133), displaying the full range of transformations to which Picasso subjected the female face and the conflicting emotions which it inspired in him. Interiors with women in cramped surroundings, hopelessly scanning their mirrors (cat. 131, 134), culminate in the most monumental work of 1938 – the great collage of *Femmes à leur toilette* (*Women at their Toilette*, cat. 219), a tapestry cartoon produced on the same spot as *Guernica* in the Grands-Augustins studio from pieces of flowered wallpaper which had originally been used to fasten the earlier work in position.

Portraits of the two muses – Marie-Thérèse, the blonde, and Dora, the brunette – follow one another. The first is rendered in coldly lunar tones, with dominant blues and yellows in a constant evocation of sweetness and innocence, while the second asserts her elegance and vitality – long nails painted red, a determined chin and a radiant beauty.

Well-loved women's faces, however, did not wipe away expressions of violence and anger. The issue of Republican Spain runs through this period as a whole, but is explicitly stated only in *Guernica* (Madrid, Museo del Prado), a synthesis of the painter's personal iconography, derived from bullfights and the Minotauromachy, which achieved a universally symbolic value under the impact of a historical event. *Guernica* was by no means an isolated work of its kind and the Civil War continued to haunt Picasso's output. He was particularly obsessed by *La femme qui pleure* (*The Weeping Woman*, cat. 143), at once a symbol of the affliction of Spanish women and a portrait of Dora Maar. The theme of women bathing at the seaside recurs in two canvases of 1937, *Grande baigneuse au livre* (*Large Bather with a Book*, cat. 138) and *Deux femmes nues sur la plage* (*Two Nude Women on the Beach*, cat. 141), which hark back to the sculptural extravaganzas of the Dinard and Boisgeloup periods.

The brutish and voracious *Homme au chapeau de paille et au cornet de glace* (*Man with a Straw Hat and an Ice Cream Cone*, cat. 152) shows how Picasso gave artistic expression, with violence, humour and ferocity, to the psychological pressures weighing on him during this period.

The War and After 1939–1954

After the horrors of Guernica, political events continued on their savage course. Terror came to the whole of Europe in 1939. Picasso's painting was affected by the circumstances of the times and although he never actually represented the war, it is present in his canvases. This was essentially a period devoted to portraits of women and to still-life work. The faces of these women in hats are subjected to every possible permutation, not merely full-face and in profile, but with features displaced, volumes and proportions inverted, enlarged and distorted. Despite such handling, something of the model's own shape survives. As Breton points out, 'woman is treated not as a subject, but as an object, like a guitar or a lollipop'.[9] Picasso was trying to convey at one and the same time the sentiments the model inspired in him and her own personality.

This ruthless treatment of the human face has often been regarded as an expression or paraphrase in artistic terms of 'the horrors of war'. Similarly, the difficulties of life under the German occupation are conveyed in a series of still-life pictures, with a skeleton, a candle, a skull and food (cat. 168, 169, 172), reminiscent of Spanish *Vanitas* paintings by their iconography and by a handling that is as austere and bare as in a work by Zurbarán.

Much comment was caused by Picasso's decision to join the Communist Party in October 1944. Like many other intellectuals, he soon found himself facing the problems posed by committed art, and his refusal to submit to the dogmas of Socialist Realism was to unleash violent polemics in the press and within the Party. In addition to the *Portrait of Stalin* (published in *Les Lettres françaises*) and *Le charnier* (*The Charnel House*), another important work – *Massacre en Corée* (*Massacre in Korea*, cat. 177) – also deserves a mention. This allegory of war, inspired by Goya's *The Third of May* and Manet's *Execution of the Emperor Maximilian*, provides an excellent illustration of the constraints and limitations inherent in commissioned art.

In November 1948, Picasso painted two versions of *La cuisine* (*The Kitchen*, New York, The Museum of Modern Art, and cat. 174) at the Grands-Augustins. As Françoise Gilot reported, 'essentially, the kitchen was an empty white cube, with only the birds and the three Spanish plates to stand out from the whiteness. One night Pablo said, "I'm going to make a canvas out of that – that is, out of nothing."'[10] The graphic character of this work, closely related to the illustrations for Reverdy's *Le Chant des Morts* in 1948, structured the picture surface and defined its tensions by means of lines and dots. The first version, in The Museum of Modern Art, New York, is the more abstract of the two and remained at the purely graphic stage with its network of black lines on a grey background, while the second version is more practical and decorative. The structure, outlined by Françoise Gilot and Javier Vilato, served as a starting point for Picasso when he filled in and completed the picture, although altering its sense.

1950–1973

A series of important events in the 1950s was to influence Picasso's style and mood during this period: the death in 1954 of Matisse, with whom he had kept up a constant dialogue; the departure of Françoise Gilot, the mother of Claude and Paloma; the entry into his life of Jacqueline Roque, whom he was to marry in 1961; and finally, in 1955, the move to La Californie, an early twentieth-century (Belle Epoque) villa in Cannes, surrounded by a luxuriant garden.

The reaction to Matisse's death took the form of an oblique tribute to him in the Studio series, with *L'atelier de La Californie* (*The Studio of La Californie*, cat. 185), and in the variations on *Les femmes d'Alger d'après Delacroix* (*The Women of Algiers after Delacroix*)

(9) A. Breton, 'Pablo Picasso, réponse à une enquête', *Le Surréalisme et la peinture*, Paris, 1965, p. 115.

(10) F. Gilot, C. Lake, *Life with Picasso*, New York, 1964, London, 1965, p. 210.

which all pay homage to colour and odalisques. Jacqueline was closely involved in this series through her striking resemblance to the woman with a hookah in Delacroix's painting. Picasso painted a number of portraits of her in Turkish costume and her presence permeated the whole of his *œuvre* from now on.[11]

The output of the 1950–63 period was internally linked by the variations on Old Masters – Delacroix, Velázquez and Manet – and was punctuated by Picasso's successive residences – La Californie, Vauvenargues and Mougins – each of which has left the stamp of its environment and atmosphere on the canvases produced there.

The monumental and sculptural *Femmes à leur toilette* (*Women at their Toilette*, cat. 219), closely related to *Femmes sur la plage* (*Women on the Beach*, Paris, Musée National d'Art Moderne), was derived from studies of nudes for *The Women of Algiers*. The largest and most Matisse-like painting in the collection, *The Studio of La Californie* (cat. 185), came shortly before the work on *Las Meninas* (Barcelona, Museo Picasso), the quintessence of the great 'Studio' work. *La baie de Cannes* (*The Bay of Cannes*, cat. 186) and the *Nature morte à la tête de taureau* (*Still-life with Bull's Head*, cat. 187), however, followed *Las Meninas*. In fact, after painting 'interior landscapes', Picasso set up his studio on the second floor of the villa and opened its window on to the sea. The *memento mori* theme, first broached in 1908 in connection with the death of Wiegels, now acquired a special significance. Pierre Daix kept the artist in touch with the political crisis that resulted from events in Algeria. The version of *Le Déjeuner sur l'Herbe* (cat. 189), together with two studies for it, forms part of the last and most important set of paraphrases. This cycle, started in August 1959 and completed in July 1962, comprises twenty-seven paintings, 140 drawings and three lino-cuts, as well as ten cardboard maquettes for sculptures. By measuring up to Manet, Picasso 'encompassed the painting of the nineteenth century and his great triumph is to have reached out beyond this tradition in order to assert his independence and his supremacy'.[12]

Rewarding as these achievements may have been, one cannot help wondering whether such a resort to the Old Masters and the appropriation of art from the past did not also represent an admission that he could discover no proper subjects during this era of spiritual crisis and prevailing abstraction.

Be that as it may, the test to which these conflicts subjected Picasso enabled him to break with the burden of the past and to make a fresh, entirely novel, departure – the so-called Avignon period.[13] This ultimate phase, the importance of which has been consistently underrated, made an essential contribution to the history of art in the West. It not only represented the culmination of a personal creative universe and the artistic testament of a painter endowed with genius, but also revealed a source of new pictorial opportunities, a way to the renewal of figurative language and a plea for lyrical potency in painting. This phase was decried for many years because it was at first imperfectly understood by a whole generation conditioned to obeying a formalist and post-Matisse point of view. It was seen as no more than the obsessional vagaries of a painter, well past his prime, who belonged to another era. But it has recently achieved recognition and will provide art in the 1980s with a point of reference and a guiding light, much as Matisse's paper cut-outs did for the decade following 1965. This rediscovery was most probably prompted by the present climate in art, which favours a return to painterliness, figuration, expressionism and subjectivity, thus making these canvases more accessible and revealing what is at stake in them. It would seem that today's avant-garde is indeed taking over where Picasso left off a decade or so ago. A new pictorial idiom, based on absolute freedom and the supremacy of spontaneity, is in the making, aimed at expressing an obsessive and hallucinatory universe. This requires a resort to mythologies, both collective and personal; to a deliberately primitive and brutish aesthetic approach, resulting in 'badly' painted, sketchy work; to pictorial quotations, which in Picasso's case were drawn from his own output; and to an explicit emphasis on paint as a material.

Towards the end of his life, Picasso increasingly seemed to regain his Spanish quality. His themes, manner and atmosphere all carried a strong Hispanic flavour. Matadors, swordsmen, guitarists and water-melon eaters are the key figures in this 'world of tarot cards' to which Malraux referred. Grey and black harmonies predominate, occasionally enlivened by displays of garish, brilliant tones, rose-red, golden yellow and orange. Finally, the baroque

(11) It is a matter of great regret that the Musée Picasso collection includes no portrait of Jacqueline.

(12) D. Cooper, *Les Déjeuners*, Paris, 1962, p. 35.

(13) This designation was derived from the great exhibitions of 1970 and 1973 in the Palace of the Popes at Avignon.

mood and the exaggeration, the humour, ridicule and tragic sense of death lodged in these canvases made them worthy successors of others by Velázquez and Goya.

'One should dwell on each of these canvases: the Mougins *Paysage* [*Landscape*, cat. 201], nocturnal as a Golgotha; the *Jeune fille assise* [*Seated Girl*, cat. 199], probably a portrait of Jacqueline, reminiscent of portraits from Fayyum, or those – equally monumental – of the Empress Theodora. Beside *Le jeune peintre* [*The Young Painter*, cat. 202] which provides continuity, one should note the impressive and lifelike self-portrait in the *Vieil homme assis* [*Seated Old Man*, cat. 196]. This ultimate dramatic image of the painter at the second threshold of his life echoes the *Arlequin pensif* [*Pensive Harlequin*, New York, private collection] from as long ago as 1909, with the same weary attitude, or the likeness of Renoir with paralysed hands, as a photographer caught it at the end of his life, Vincent's straw hat, the last picture of Cézanne's gardener'[14] and Matisse's Romanian blouse.

In the majority of these pictures, the paint has been thickly applied in places, hastily spread elsewhere, and shows the trail of the brush. This 'smudged' effect results from the interplay of transparencies, the overlapping of layers and subtle scales of tonal values. 'The painting remains to be done', Picasso would say towards the end of his life, as though it all needed to be done again from the start, as though his painting was as yet only in its early days, in a primeval phase, at its first, stuttering beginnings. In what passed for old age, he provided a perfect model for the return to art in its infancy.

In fact, after jeopardizing the heritage of the Renaissance in his Cubist period by attacking one of its foundations – perspective illusion – Picasso created a fresh pictorial space and was able to endow painting with new fields for investigation. Then, at the end of 'this agonizing journey', after saying all that could be said in every conceivable way, and even shouldering the burdensome heritage of the past in his closing years, he faced the ultimate question, the doubt cast on all knowledge: what is painting and how is it to be done?

M.-L. B.-B.[15]

(14) D. Bozo, op. cit., p. 224.

(15) We are grateful to Philippe Thiébaut and Dominique Bozo for allowing us to use material from their introductions to the catalogue of the exhibition 'Picasso, œuvres reçues en paiement des droits de succession', Paris, Grand Palais, 1979–80.

Fig. 1
Sketchbook sheet, Dinard, 1922
(Artist's Estate)

Technical Note

All works on canvas or wood supports, whatever the medium used – oil, gouache, charcoal, pastel, ink or pencil – have been grouped as paintings. Works on paper pasted on canvas for protection, such as the two nude studies for *Les Demoiselles d'Avignon* (M.P. 12, M.P. 13), have been reclassified as drawings. We have, however, made two exceptions to this rule for gouache works on cardboard: *Les deux frères* (*The Two Brothers*, cat. 6) and *Buste de femme ou de marin* (*Head and Shoulders of a Woman or Sailor*, cat. 13) have remained among the paintings in view of their specifically pictorial treatment.

Verre sur un guéridon (*Glass on a Pedestal Table*, cat. 38), at one time listed as a *papier collé*, has now been included among the paintings, since it is for all intents and purposes an oil painting on canvas, despite the pieces of paper pinned on to it. *Femmes à leur toilette* (*Women at their Toilette*, cat. 219), on the other hand, has now been included among the *papiers collés*.

Changes in Dating

In most cases, the paintings have been dated by Picasso, either on the back (on the stretcher or canvas) or on the front. When there is no date, we have adopted Zervos's dating, or that of Pierre Daix for the Cubist period. Certain changes have been made with respect to the dating quoted in the catalogue of the Grand Palais settlement exhibition, 1979.

Cat. 1 and 2 (M.P. 1 and 2)
These two pictures were painted at Corunna and must therefore date from the first quarter of 1895, since the Ruiz family left for Barcelona in April. The date inscribed on cat. 2 is difficult to read and is more likely to be 1.3 than 1.9.

Cat. 17 (M.P. 19)
Mère et enfant (*Mother and Child*). This canvas is later than *Les Demoiselles d'Avignon* and earlier than the *Nu à la draperie* (*Nude with Drapery*, Leningrad, The Hermitage Museum); it must therefore date from the summer of 1907.

Cat. 24–26 (M.P. 25, 26, 28)
These have been dated to the autumn of 1908. See W. Rubin, *Pablo Picasso: A Retrospective*, New York, The Museum of Modern Art, 1980.

Cat. 75 (M.P. 80)
A peparatory drawing in a sketchbook used in Dinard in 1922 (Z.XXX, 322) makes it possible to date this picture to the summer of that year (Fig. 1).

Cat. 84 (M.P. 98)
Dated 1927 on the strength of a drawing in a 1927 sketchbook (M.P. 1873, Fig. 2).

Cat. 87 (M.P. 102)
Dated 1927 on the strength of a drawing in a 1927 sketchbook (M.P. 1874, Fig. 3).

Only those drawings are mentioned above which provide a precise date for an otherwise undated picture, but none of those that merely represent preparatory work for pictures dated by Picasso himself.

Fig. 2
Sketchbook sheet, Paris, 1926/27
(M.P. 1873)

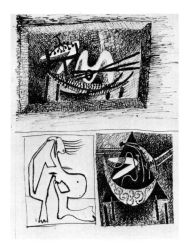

Fig. 3
Sketchbook sheet, Cannes, 1927
(M.P. 1874)

4   Self-portrait

1
L'homme à la casquette
Man with a Cap
Early 1895
Corunna
Oil on canvas
72.5 × 50
Z.I, 4; P.i.F., 64
M.P. 1

2
La fillette aux pieds nus
The Barefoot Girl
Early 1895
Corunna
Oil on canvas
75 × 50
S.D.a.r.: *P. Ruiz/ 1.9* (or *3* [?]).
Z.I, 3; Duncan, p. 203; P.i.F., 69
M.P. 2

3
La mort de Casagemas
The Death of Casagemas
Summer 1901
Paris
Oil on wood panel
27 × 35
Z.XXI, 178; D.B. VI-5; P.i.F., 676
M.P. 3

4
Autoportrait
Self-portrait
Late 1901
Paris
Oil on canvas
81 × 60
Z.I, 91; Duncan, p. 204; D.B. VI-35;
T.l.o.p.[1], 21; P.i.F., 715
M.P. 4

5
Portrait d'homme
Portrait of a Man
Winter 1902–1903
Paris–Barcelona
Oil on canvas
93 × 78
S.a.r.: *Picasso*
Z.I, 142; D.B. VIII-1; T.l.o.p.[1], 46; P.i.F., 782
M.P. 5

6
Les deux frères
The Two Brothers
Summer 1906
Gosol
Gouache on cardboard
80 × 59
Z.VI, 720; D.B. XV-8; T.l.o.p.[1], 257;
P.i.F., 1299
M.P. 7

6   The Two Brothers

7
Jeune garçon nu
Nude Boy
Autumn 1906
Paris
Oil on canvas
67 × 43
T.l.o.p.(1), 346; P.i.F., 1384
M.P. 6

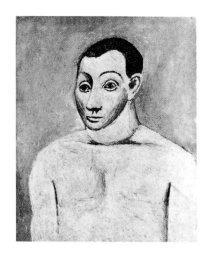

8
Autoportrait
Self-portrait
Autumn 1906
Paris
Oil on canvas
65 × 54
S. on back, a.l.: *Picasso*
Z.II[1], 1; D.B. XVI-26; T.l.o.p.(2), 1;
T.l.o.p.(1), 347; P.i.F., 1376
M.P. 8

9
Marins en bordée
Sailors on a Spree
Winter 1906–1907
Paris
Oil on wood panel
17.6 × 13.5
D.R. 2
M.P. 9

10
Nu assis
Seated Nude
(Study for *Les Demoiselles d'Avignon*)
[Winter 1906–1907]
Paris
Oil on canvas
121 × 93.5
Z.II[2], 651; D.R. 15; T.l.o.p.(2), 76; P.i.F., 147
M.P. 10

11
Petit nu de dos aux bras levés
Small Nude from the Back with Raised Arms
(Study for *Les Demoiselles d'Avignon*)
May 1907
Paris
Oil on wood panel
19.1 × 11.5
D.a.l.: *mai 07*; Inscr.: *L. de garance foncée/*
L. de garance rose/ Garance d'alumine/
L. de Smyrne claire/ L. de Smyrne moyenne/
J. cadmium citron/ Vert de cadmium/
Sulfure de cadmium/ Oxyde de chrome
D.R. 18
M.P. 11

12
Buste d'homme
Head and Shoulders of a Man
(Study for *Les Demoiselles d'Avignon*)
Spring 1907
Paris
Oil on canvas
56 × 46.5
Z.XXVI, 12; T.l.o.p.(2), 39; D.R. 22
M.P. 14

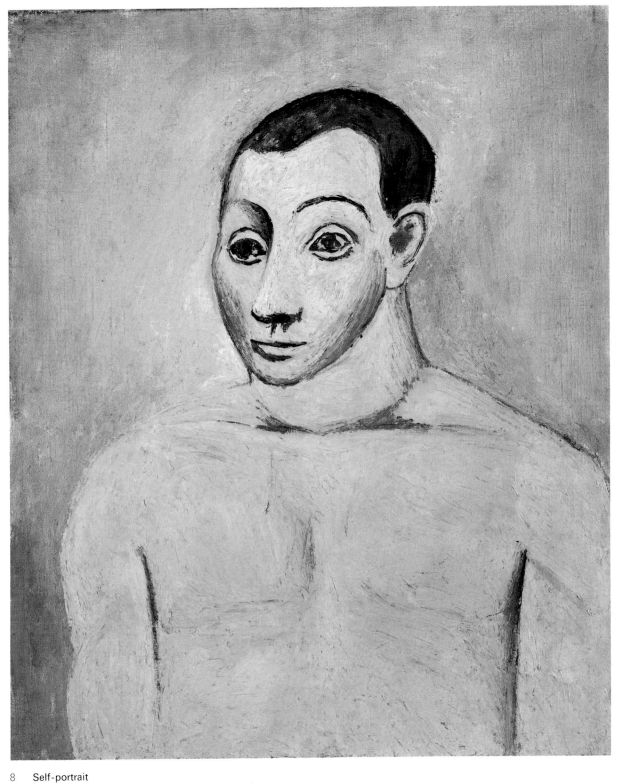

8   Self-portrait

1907

13   Head and Shoulders of a Woman or Sailor

17   Mother and Child

13
Buste de femme ou de marin
Head and Shoulders of a Woman or Sailor
(Study for *Les Demoiselles d'Avignon*)
Spring 1907
Paris
Oil on cardboard
53.5 × 36.2
D.R. 28
M.P. 15

14
Femme aux mains jointes
Woman with Clasped Hands
(Study for *Les Demoiselles d'Avignon*)
Spring 1907
Paris
Oil on canvas
90.5 × 71.5
Z.II², 662; T.l.o.p.(²), 40; D.R. 26; P.i.F., 1439
M.P. 16

15
Buste
Head and Shoulders
(Study for *Les Demoiselles d'Avignon*)
Spring 1907
Paris
Oil on canvas
60.5 × 59.2
Z.XXVI, 18; D.R. 23; P.i.F., 1440
M.P. 17

16
Buste de femme
Head and Shoulders of a Woman
(Study for *Les Demoiselles d'Avignon*)
Spring 1907
Paris
Oil on canvas
58.5 × 46.5
Z.II², 617; D.R. 24; P.i.F., 1434
M.P. 18

17
Mère et enfant
Mother and Child
Summer 1907
Paris
Oil on canvas
81 × 60
Z.II¹, 38; T.l.o.p.(²), 50; D.R. 52
M.P. 19

18
Petit nu assis
Small Seated Nude
Summer 1907
Paris
Oil on wood panel
17.6 × 15
Z.XXVI, 262; Duncan, p. 204; D.R. 71
M.P. 20

19
L'arbre
The Tree
Summer 1907
Paris
Oil on canvas
94 × 93.7
Z.II², 681; T.l.o.p.(2), 62; D.R. 62
M.P. 21

20
Nu couché
Reclining Nude
Spring 1908
Paris
Oil on wood panel
27 × 21
Z.XXVI, 364; Duncan, p. 56; D.R. 156
M.P. 22

21
Nu debout
Standing Nude
Spring 1908
Paris
Oil on wood panel
27 × 21.2
Z.XXVI, 365; Duncan, p. 55; D.R. 157
M.P. 23

22
Nu couché avec personnages
Reclining Nude with Figures
Spring 1908
Paris
Oil on wood panel
36 × 62
S. on back, a.l.: *Picasso*
Z.II², 688; T.l.o.p.(2), 134; D.R. 164
M.P. 24

23
Nature morte au vase et à l'étoffe verte
Still-life with Vase and Green Drape
Spring–summer 1908
[Paris]
Oil on canvas
27.1 × 21.3
Z.XXVI, 361; Duncan, p. 205; D.R. 178
M.P. 27

24
Tête d'homme
Head of a Man
Autumn 1908
Paris
Gouache on wood panel
27 × 21.3
Z.XXVI, 394; Duncan, p. 65; D.R. 152
M.P. 25

25
Tête d'homme
Head of a Man
Autumn 1908
Paris
Gouache on wood panel
27 × 21.3
Z.XXVI, 392; Duncan, p. 67; D.R. 153
M.P. 26

26
Paysage aux deux figures
Landscape with Two Figures
Autumn 1908
[Paris]
Oil on canvas
60 × 73
Z.II¹, 79; Duncan, p. 205; T.l.o.p.(2), 144;
D.R. 187
M.P. 28

27
Nature morte au cuir à rasoir
Still-life with Razor Strop
1909
Oil on canvas
55 × 40.5
S. on back: *Picasso*
Z.II¹, 135; D.R. 227
Verbal bequest by D.-H. Kahnweiler, 1980
M.P. 1980–1

28
Tête d'homme
Head of a Man
Spring 1909
Paris
Gouache on wood panel
27.1 × 21.3
Z.XXVI, 412; Duncan, p. 69; D.R. 251
M.P. 29

29
Le Sacré-Cœur
The Sacré-Coeur
Winter 1909–1910
Paris
Oil on canvas
92.5 × 65
S. on back: *Picasso*
Z.II¹, 196; D.R. 339
M.P. 30

30
Verre, pomme, livres
Glass, Apple, Books
Spring 1911
Paris
Oil on canvas
22.5 × 45.5
Z.II², 720; T.l.o.p.(2), 399; D.R. 379
M.P. 31

26   Landscape with Two Figures

31
Journal, porte-allumettes, pipe et verre
Newspaper, Match-holder, Pipe and Glass
[Autumn] 1911
Paris
Oil on canvas
26.8 × 21.8
Z.II², 729; T.l.o.p.⁽²⁾, 409; D.R. 433
M.P. 32

32
Grenade, verre et pipe
Pomegranate, Glass and Pipe
[Autumn] 1911
Paris
Oil on canvas pasted on cardboard
24 × 29
Z.II², 721; T.l.o.p.⁽²⁾, 408; D.R. 431
M.P. 33

33
Homme à la mandoline
Man with a Mandolin
Autumn 1911
Paris
Oil on canvas
162 × 71
Z.II¹, 290; T.l.o.p.⁽²⁾, 439; D.R. 428
M.P. 35

34
Homme à la guitare
Man with a Guitar
Autumn 1911 [–1913]
Paris
Oil on canvas
154 × 77.5
S.D. on back: *Picasso/ K 11 & 12/ ET 13*
Z.XXVIII, 57; D.R. 427
M.P. 34

35
Nature morte à la chaise cannée
Still-life with Chair-caning
Spring 1912
Paris
Oil and oilcloth on canvas edged with rope
29 × 37
Z.II¹, 294; Duncan, p. 207; T.l.o.p.⁽²⁾, 461;
D.R. 466
M.P. 36

36
Guitare 'J'aime Eva'
'I Love Eva' Guitar
Summer 1912
Sorgues
Oil on canvas
35 × 27
Z.II¹, 352; T.l.o.p.⁽²⁾, 492; D.R. 485
M.P. 37

37
Guitare
Guitar
[Spring 1913]
[Céret]
Oil on canvas pasted to wood panel
87 × 47.5
D.R. 597
M.P. 38

38
Verre sur un guéridon
Glass on a Pedestal Table
1913
Céret
Oil on canvas, pasted and pinned paper
20.5 × 20.5
Z.II^2, 758; T.l.o.p.$^{(2)}$, 487; D.R. 606
M.P. 378

39
Homme à la pipe
Man with a Pipe
[Spring 1914]
[Paris]
Oil on printed textile pasted on canvas
138 × 66.5
Z.II^2, 470; T.l.o.p.$^{(2)}$, 732; D.R. 760
M.P. 39

40
Homme à la moustache
Man with a Moustache
[Spring 1914]
[Paris]
Oil and printed textile pasted on canvas
65.5 × 46.6
Z.II^2, 468; T.l.o.p.$^{(2)}$, 719; D.R. 759
M.P. 40

41
Verre et pipe, chiffres et lettres
Glass and Pipe, Numbers and Letters
[Spring 1914]
[Paris]
Oil and charcoal on canvas
14 × 29
D.R. 721
M.P. 41

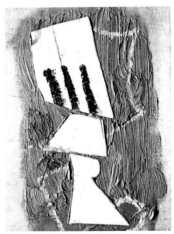

42
Verre
Glass
Spring 1914
Paris
Oil on wood panel with pieces of canvas
16 × 11.7
Z.XXIX, 35; Duncan, p. 207; D.R. 731
M.P. 42

33   Man with a Mandolin

35   Still-life with Chair-caning

1914

39   Man with a Pipe

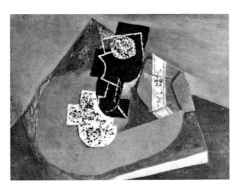

43
Verre et paquet de tabac
Glass and Packet of Tobacco
Spring 1914
Paris
Oil and beads stuck on wood panel
26.5 × 35
D.R. 736
M.P. 44

44
Verre et paquet de tabac
Glass and Packet of Tobacco
Summer 1914
Avignon
Oil and sand on wood panel
15.5 × 17.7 × 0.3
D. on back: *AVIGNON/1914*
Z.II², 851; T.l.o.p.(2), 701; D.R. 791
M.P. 49

45
Verre, paquet de tabac et as de trèfle
Glass, Packet of Tobacco and Ace of Clubs
Summer 1914
Avignon
Oil, crayon and sand on wood panel
15 × 17.7
Z.XXIX, 42; Duncan, p. 208; D.R. 792
M.P. 50

46
Verre
Glass
Summer 1914
Avignon
Oil and sand on wood panel
17.6 × 13.4 × 0.3
D. on back: *1914/Avignon*
Z.II², 828; T.l.o.p.(2), 697; D.R. 775
M.P. 51

47
Nature morte: Guitare, journal, verre et as de trèfle
Still-life: Guitar, Newspaper, Glass and Ace of Clubs
[1914]
[Paris]
Oil on canvas
41 × 27
Z.II², 510; T.l.o.p.(2), 760; D.R. 807
M.P. 52

48
Le peintre et son modèle
The Painter and his Model
Summer 1914
Avignon
Oil and crayon on canvas
58 × 55.9
D.R. 763
M.P. 53

49
Homme à la cheminée
Man at the Fireplace
1916
Paris
Oil on canvas
130 × 81
D.R. 891
M.P. 54

50
Portrait d'Olga dans un fauteuil
Portrait of Olga in an Armchair
Autumn 1917
Montrouge
Oil on canvas
130 × 88.8
Z.III, 83
M.P. 55

51
Le retour du baptême, d'après Le Nain
The Return from the Christening, after Le Nain
Autumn 1917
[Paris]
Oil on canvas
162 × 118
Z.III, 96
M.P. 56

52
Femme dans un fauteuil rouge
Woman in a Red Armchair
[1918]
[Paris]
Oil on wood panel
15 × 8.7
M.P. 57

53
Pipe, verre et carte à jouer
Pipe, Glass and Playing Card
1918
Paris
Oil on canvas
38 × 46
Z.III, 139
M.P. 58

54
Verre et pipe
Glass and Pipe
1918
[Paris]
Oil and sand on canvas
45.7 × 55
Z.III, 146
M.P. 59

50   Portrait of Olga in an Armchair

55
Les baigneuses
The Bathers
Summer 1918
Biarritz
Oil on canvas
27 × 22
Z.III, 237
M.P. 61

56
Paysage
Landscape
(Study for *The Three-Cornered Hat*)
1919
London
Oil on wood panel
10 × 15
Z.XXIX, 384
M.P. 60

57
Les amoureux
The Lovers
1919
Paris
Oil on canvas
185 × 140
Z.III, 438
M.P. 62

58
Nature morte sur la commode
Still-life on the Chest of Drawers
1919
[Paris]
Oil on canvas
81 × 100
Z.III, 443; Duncan, p. 208
M.P. 63

59
Nature morte au pichet et aux pommes
Still-life with Pitcher and Apples
1919
Oil on canvas
65 × 43
M.P. 64

60
Etudes
Studies
1920
Oil on canvas
100 × 81
Z.IV, 226
M.P. 65

1918

55   The Bathers

59   Still-life with Pitcher and Apples

1
Femme assise
Seated Woman
1920
Paris
Oil on canvas
92 × 65
Z.IV, 179
M.P. 67

62
Paysage de Juan-les-Pins
Landscape at Juan-les-Pins
Summer 1920
Juan-les-Pins
Oil on canvas
52 × 70
Z.IV, 107; Duncan, p. 208; T.l.o.p.[2], 949
M.P. 68

63
Baigneuses regardant un avion
Bathers Watching an Aeroplane
Summer 1920
Juan-les-Pins
Oil on plywood
73.5 × 92.5
Z.IV, 163
M.P. 69

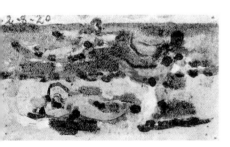

64
Trois personnages au bord de la mer
Three Figures on the Sea-shore
August 1920
Juan-les-Pins
Oil on canvas
37 × 16.9
D.a.l.: *2.8.20*
M.P. 70

65
Tête de femme
Head of a Woman
1921
[Paris]
Oil on canvas
55 × 46
Z.XXX, 236
M.P. 66

66
Femme au chapeau
Woman with a Hat
1921
Charcoal and pastel on canvas
130 × 97
Z.IV, 365
M.P. 71

67   Reading the Letter

71   The Village Dance

1921–1922

67
La lecture de la lettre
Reading the Letter
1921
[Paris]
Oil on canvas
184 × 105
M.P. 72

68
Etude pour 'Trois femmes à la fontaine'
Study for 'Three Women at the Fountain'
1921
Fontainebleau
Crayon and body on wood panel
21.5 × 27
M.P. 965

69
Trois femmes à la fontaine
Three Women at the Fountain
Summer 1921
Fontainebleau
Sanguine on canvas
200 × 161
M.P. 74

70
La source
The Source
Summer 1921
Fontainebleau
Soft crayon on canvas
100 × 200
M.P. 75

71
La danse villageoise
The Village Dance
[1922]
[Paris]
Fixed pastel and oil on canvas
139.5 × 85.5
Z.XXX, 270
M.P. 73

72
Instruments de musique sur une table
Musical Instruments on a Table
[1922]
Paris
Oil on wood panel
15 × 9.9
M.P. 76

74   Two Women Running on the Beach (The Race)

75   Family on the Sea-shore

76   The Pipes of Pan

73
Corrida
Bullfight
[1922]
Oil and crayon on wood panel
13.6 × 19
M.P. 77

74
**Deux femmes courant sur la plage
(La course)**
*Two Women Running on the Beach
(The Race)*
Summer 1922
Dinard
Gouache on plywood
32.5 × 41.1
Z.IV, 380; Duncan, p. 208
M.P. 78

75
Famille au bord de la mer
Family on the Sea-shore
Summer 1922
Dinard
Oil on wood panel
17.6 × 20.2
M.P. 80

76
La flûte de Pan
The Pipes of Pan
Summer 1923
Antibes
Oil on canvas
205 × 174
Z.V, 141; Duncan, p. 209
M.P. 79

77
Paul dessinant
Paulo Drawing
1923
Paris
Oil on canvas
130 × 97
Z.V, 177
M.P. 81

78
Mandoline sur une table
Mandolin on a Table
[Spring] 1924
[Paris]
Oil and sand on canvas
97 × 130
Z.V, 188
M.P. 82

79
Paul en arlequin
Paulo as Harlequin
1924
Paris
Oil on canvas
130 × 97.5
Z.V, 178; Duncan, p. 209
M.P. 83

80
Paul en pierrot
Paulo as Pierrot
28 February 1925
Paris
Oil on canvas
130 × 97
D. on back on the stretcher: *28.II.XXV.*
Z.V, 374; Duncan, p. 210
M.P. 84

81
Le baiser
The Kiss
Summer 1925
Juan-les-Pins
Oil on canvas
130.5 × 97.7
D. on back on the stretcher:
Juan-les-Pins/1925
Z.V, 460
M.P. 85

82
Le peintre et son modèle
The Painter and his Model
1926
[Paris]
Oil on canvas
172 × 256
Z.VII, 30; Duncan, p. 211
M.P. 96

83
Femme à la collerette
Woman with a Collar
Summer 1926
Juan-les-Pins
Oil on canvas
35 × 27
D. on back on the stretcher:
Juan-les-Pins 1926
Duncan, p. 210
M.P. 97

84
Dormeuse
Sleeping Woman
1927
[Paris]
Oil on canvas
46 × 38
M.P. 98

79   Paulo as Harlequin

80 Paulo as Pierrot

81   The Kiss

82   The Painter and his Model

85
Femme dans un fauteuil
Woman in an Armchair
Summer 1927
Cannes
Oil on canvas
130 × 97
D.a. on fold-over of canvas: *Cannes 27*
Z.VII, 68
M.P. 99

86
Figure
Figure
1927
Oil on plywood
129 × 96
Z.VII, 137; Duncan, p. 211
M.P. 101

87
Nu sur fond blanc
Nude on a White Background
1927
Oil on canvas
130 × 97
M.P. 102

88
Tête de femme
Head of a Woman
[1927–1928]
Oil and sand on canvas
55 × 55
Z.VII, 124; Duncan, p. 212
M.P. 100

89
Figure et profil
Figure and Profile
1928
Oil on canvas
72 × 60
Z.VII, 129
M.P. 103

90
Peintre à la palette et au chevalet
Painter with Palette and Easel
1928
Oil on canvas
130 × 97
M.P. 104

91
Minotaure courant
Running Minotaur
April 1928
[Paris]
Oil on canvas
162.5 × 130
D. on back on the stretcher: *avril/1928*
Z.VII, 423; Duncan, p. 212
M.P. 105

92
Baigneuse
Bather
6 August 1928
Dinard
Oil on canvas
22 × 14
D. on back: *Dinard 6 août 1928/ (nº 3)*
M.P. 106

93
Baigneuse ouvrant une cabine
Bather Opening a Beach Hut
9 August 1928
Dinard
Oil on canvas
32.8 × 22
D. on back on the stretcher:
Dinard 9 août 1928 (nº 2)
Z.VII, 210; Duncan, p. 212
M.P. 107

94
Baigneuses sur la plage
Bathers on the Beach
12 August 1928
Dinard
Oil on canvas
21.5 × 40.4
D. on back: *Dinard 12 Août/1928*
Z.VII, 216; Duncan, p. 212
M.P. 108

95
Joueurs de ballon sur la plage
Ball Players on the Beach
15 August 1928
Dinard
Oil on canvas
24 × 34.9
D. on back on the stretcher:
Dinard 15 Août 1928
Z.VII, 223; Duncan, p. 121
M.P. 109

96
Baigneuses jouant au ballon
Bathers Playing with a Beach Ball
20 August 1928
Dinard
Oil on canvas
21.7 × 41.2
D. on back on the stretcher:
Dinard 20 Août 1928 (nº 1)
Z.VII, 234; Duncan, p. 212
M.P. 110

93   Bather Opening a Beach Hut

99   Large Nude in a Red Armchair

97
L'atelier
The Studio
1928–1929
Paris
Oil on canvas
162 × 130
Duncan, p. 243
M.P. 111

98
Femme au fauteuil rouge
Woman in a Red Armchair
1929
Paris
Oil on canvas
64.5 × 54
S.D.b.r.: *Picasso/29*
Z.VII, 291
M.P. 112

99
Grand nu au fauteuil rouge
Large Nude in a Red Armchair
5 May 1929
Paris
Oil on canvas
195 × 129
D. on back on the stretcher: *5 mai XXIX*
Z.VII, 263; Duncan, p. 213
M.P. 113

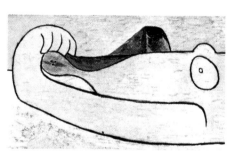

100
Baigneuses à la cabine
Bathers at the Beach Hut
19 May 1929
Paris
Oil on canvas
33 × 41.5
D. on back on the stretcher: *19 mai XXIX*
Z.VII, 276
M.P. 114

101
Grande baigneuse
Large Bather
26 May 1929
Paris
Oil on canvas
195 × 130
D. on back: *Dimanche XXVI mai XXIX*
Z.VII, 262; Duncan, p. 213
M.P. 115

102
Femme étendue sur la plage
Woman Stretched out on the Beach
24 August 1929
Dinard
Oil on canvas
14.1 × 23.7
D. on back on the stretcher:
Dinard 24 Août XXIX
Duncan, p. 123
M.P. 116

105   The Swimmer

108   The Crucifixion

103
Le baiser
The Kiss
25 August 1929
Dinard
Oil on canvas
22 × 14
D. on back on the stretcher:
Dinard–Dimanche 25 Août XXIX/n° IV
M.P. 117

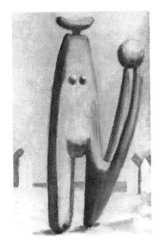

104
Baigneuse au ballon
Bather with a Beach Ball
1 September 1929
Dinard
Oil on canvas
21.9 × 14
D. on back on the stretcher:
Dinard/Dimanche/1er septembre XXIX
Duncan, p. 214
M.P. 118

105
La nageuse
The Swimmer
November 1929
Paris
Oil on canvas
130 × 162
D. on back on the stretcher: *Novembre 1929*
Z.VII, 419; Duncan, p. 214
M.P. 119

106
L'acrobate
The Acrobat
18 January 1930
Paris
Oil on canvas
162 × 130
D. on back on the stretcher: *18.I.XXX*
Z.VII, 310; Duncan, p. 214
M.P. 120

107
Tête sur fond rouge
Head on a Red Background
2 February 1930
Paris
Oil on wood, panel
26 × 21
D. on back: *2.II.XXX*
Z.VII, 301
M.P. 121

108
La Crucifixion
The Crucifixion
7 February 1930
Paris
Oil on plywood
51.5 × 66.5
D. on back: *7-II-XXX-*
Z.VII, 287; Duncan, p. 214
M.P. 122

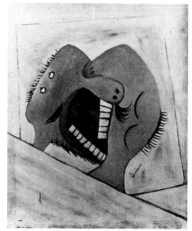

109
Figures au bord de la mer
Figures on the Sea-shore
12 January 1931
Paris
Oil on canvas
130 × 195
D. on back on the stretcher: *-12-I-XXXI-*
Z.VII, 328
M.P. 131

110
Le baiser
The Kiss
12 January 1931
Paris
Oil on canvas
61 × 50.5
D. on back on the stretcher: *12-I-XXXI*
Z.VII, 325
M.P. 132

111
Femme lançant une pierre
Woman Throwing a Stone
8 March 1931
Paris
Oil on canvas
130.5 × 195.5
D. on back: *8-III-XXXI*
Z.VII, 329; Duncan, p. 215
M.P. 133

112
Grande nature morte au guéridon
Large Still-life with a Pedestal Table
11 March 1931
Paris
Oil on canvas
195 × 130.5
D. on back on the stretcher: *-11-III-XXXI-*
Z.VII, 317; Duncan, p. 214
M.P. 134

113
Le sculpteur
The Sculptor
7 December 1931
Paris
Oil on plywood
128.5 × 96
D. on back: *7-Décembre/M.CM.XXXI*
Z.VII, 346
M.P. 135

114
La femme au stylet
The Woman with a Stylet
19–25 December 1931
[Paris]
Oil on canvas
46.5 × 61.5
D. on back on the stretcher:
25 Décembre XXXI 19–20 Décembre XXXI
M.P. 136

109   Figures on the Sea-shore

112   Large Still-life with a Pedestal Table

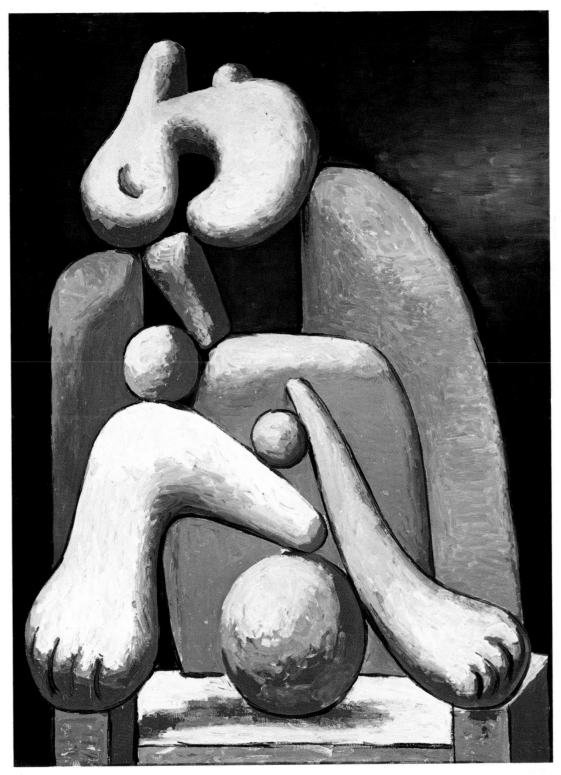

116   Woman in a Red Armchair

115
La lecture
Reading
2 January 1932
Boisgeloup
Oil on canvas
130 × 97.5
D. on back on the stretcher:
2 janvier M.CM.XXXII
Z.VII, 358
M.P. 137

116
Femme au fauteuil rouge
Woman in a Red Armchair
27 January 1932
Boisgeloup
Oil on canvas
130.2 × 97
D. on back on the stretcher: *27 janvier XXXII.*
Z.VII, 330
M.P. 138

117
Femme assise dans un fauteuil rouge
Woman Sitting in a Red Armchair
1932
Boisgeloup
Oil on canvas
130 × 97.5
Duncan, p. 215
M.P. 139

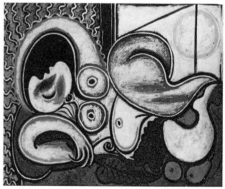

118
Nature morte: Buste, coupe et palette
Still-life: Bust, Bowl and Palette
3 March 1932
Boisgeloup
Oil on canvas
130.5 × 97.5
D. on back on the stretcher: *3 Mars XXXII*
Duncan, p. 215
M.P. 140

119
Boisgeloup sous la pluie
Boisgeloup in the Rain
30 March 1932
Boisgeloup
Oil on cloth
47.5 × 83
D. on back: *30 mars XXXII.*
Z.VII, 339
M.P. 141

120
Nu couché
Reclining Nude
4 April 1932
Boisgeloup
Oil on canvas
130 × 161.7
D. on back on the stretcher:
Boisgeloup 4 avril M.C.M.XXXII
Z.VII, 332
M.P. 142

120   Reclining Nude

123   Bullfight: Death of the Torero

121
Baigneuses au ballon
Bathers with a Beach Ball
4 December 1932
Paris
Oil on canvas
81 × 100
D. on back on the stretcher:
PARIS. 4 Décembre XXXII
M.P. 143

122
Corrida: la mort de la femme torero
Bullfight: Death of the Woman Torero
6 September 1933
Boisgeloup
Oil and crayon on wood panel
21.7 × 27
D.b.l.: *Boisgeloup/ 6 septembre/ M.CM.XXXIII*
Z.VIII, 138
M.P. 144

123
Corrida: la mort du torero
Bullfight: Death of the Torero
19 September 1933
Boisgeloup
Oil on wood panel
31 × 40
D. on back: *Boisgeloup- 19 septembre/ XXXIII*
Z.VIII, 214
M.P. 145

124
Minotaure au javelot
Minotaur with Javelin
25 January 1934
Paris
Indian ink on plywood
97 × 130
D.a.r.: *Paris 25 janvier XXXIV-*
Z.VIII, 167; Duncan, p. 215
M.P. 146

125
Nu au bouquet d'iris et au miroir
Nude with Bunch of Irises and Mirror
22 May 1934
Boisgeloup
Oil on canvas
162 × 130
D. on back on the stretcher:
Boisgeloup 22 mai XXXIV-
Z.VIII, 210
M.P. 147

125a
Femme à la bougie, combat entre le taureau et le cheval
Woman with a Candle, Fight between Bull and Horse
24 July 1934
Boisgeloup
Pen and Indian ink; brown crayon on cloth pasted on plywood
31.5 × 40.5
D. on back above, in pencil:
Boisgeloup 24 juillet/ XXXIV
Z.VIII, 215
M.P. 1136

126
Nu dans un jardin
Nude in a Garden
4 August 1934
Boisgeloup
Oil on canvas
162 × 130
D. on back on the stretcher:
Boisgeloup 4 Août XXXIV-
M.P. 148

127
Femme lisant
Woman Reading
9 January 1935
Paris
Oil on canvas
162 × 113
D. on back on the stretcher:
Paris-mercredi 9 janvier XXXV.
Z.VIII, 260
M.P. 149

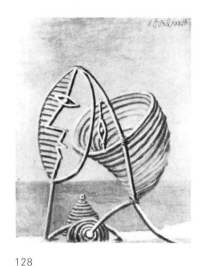

128
Portrait de jeune fille
Portrait of a Girl
3 April 1936
Juan-les-Pins
Oil on canvas
55.5 × 46
D.a.r.: *3 Avril XXXVI;* on back on the stretcher:
Juan les Pins/ 3 AVRIL XXXVI.
Duncan, p. 82
M.P. 150

129
Femme au buffet
Woman at the Sideboard
9 April 1936
Juan-les-Pins
Oil on canvas
55 × 46
D.b.r.: *9 avril XXXVI;* on back on the stretcher:
9 avril XXXVI.
Duncan, p. 88
M.P. 151

130
Dormeuse aux persiennes
Sleeping Woman with Shutters
25 April 1936
Juan-les-Pins
Oil and charcoal on canvas
54.5 × 65.2
D. on back on the stretcher: *25 avril XXXVI.*
Duncan, p. 105
M.P. 152

131
Femme à la montre
Woman with a Watch
30 April 1936
Juan-les-Pins
Oil on canvas
65 × 54.2
D.a.l.: *30 avril/XXX.VI*
Duncan, p. 111
M.P. 153

126   Nude in a Garden

127   Woman Reading

133   The Straw Hat with Blue Leaves

132
Tête
Head
1 May 1936
Juan-les-Pins
Oil on canvas
61 × 50
D.b.r.: *1er mai XXXVI*.; on back on the
stretcher: *1er mai XXXVI*
Duncan, p. 112
M.P. 154

133
Le chapeau de paille au feuillage bleu
The Straw Hat with Blue Leaves
1 May 1936
Juan-les-Pins
Oil on canvas
61 × 50
D.a.l.: *1 mai XXXVI*.; on back on the stretcher:
1 mai XXXVI
Duncan, p. 113
M.P. 155

134
Femmes dans un intérieur
Women in an Interior
2 May 1936
Juan-les-Pins
Oil on canvas
61 × 50.5
S.b.r.: *Picasso*; D.a.l.: *2 mai XXXVI*; on back
on the stretcher: *2 mai XXXVI*.
Duncan, p. 115
M.P. 156

135
Nature morte à la lampe
Still-life with Lamp
29 December 1936
[Tremblay-sur-Mauldre]
Oil on canvas
97 × 130
D.c.l.: *29/DÉCEMBRE*; on back on the stretcher:
29 D.XXXVI.
Duncan, p. 219
M.P. 157

136
Portrait de Dora Maar
Portrait of Dora Maar
1937
[Paris]
Oil on canvas
92 × 65
D. on back on the stretcher: *1937*.
Z.VIII, 331; Duncan, p. 219
M.P. 158

137
Portrait de Marie-Thérèse
Portrait of Marie-Thérèse
6 January 1937
[Paris]
Oil on canvas
100 × 81
D. on back on the stretcher: *6.1.37*.
Z.VIII, 324; Duncan, p. 220
M.P. 159

136   Portrait of Dora Maar

137   Portrait of Marie-Thérèse

139   Seated Woman in front of a Window

1937

143   The Weeping Woman

138
Grande baigneuse au livre
Large Bather with a Book
18 February 1937
Paris
Oil, pastel and charcoal on canvas
130 × 97.5
D. on back on the stretcher: *18-2-37.*
Z.VIII, 351; Duncan, p. 221
M.P. 160

139
Femme assise devant la fenêtre
Seated Woman in front of a Window
11 March 1937
[Tremblay-sur-Mauldre]
Oil and pastel on canvas
130 × 97.3
D. on back on the stretcher: *11.3.37.*
Duncan, p. 123
M.P. 161

140
Femme assise aux bras croisés
Seated Woman with Arms Crossed
1937
[Tremblay-sur-Mauldre]
Oil on canvas
81 × 60
Duncan, p. 222
M.P. 162

141
Deux femmes nues sur la plage
Two Nude Women on the Beach
1 May 1937
Paris
Indian ink and gouache on wood panel
22 × 27
D.b.r.: *1 Mai XXXVII*
Z.IX, 217
M.P. 163

142
Portrait de Dora Maar
Portrait of Dora Maar
1 October 1937
Paris
Oil and pastel on canvas
55 × 45.5
D. on back on the stretcher: *1.10.37.*
Duncan, p. 225
M.P. 164

143
La femme qui pleure
The Weeping Woman
18 October 1937
Paris
Oil on canvas
55.3 × 46.3
D. on back on the stretcher: *18 Octobre 37.*
Duncan, p. 133
M.P. 165

144
Portrait de Dora Maar
Portrait of Dora Maar
23 November 1937
Paris
Oil on canvas
55.3 × 46.3
D. on back on the stretcher: *23 novembre 37.*
Z.IX, 136; Duncan, p. 226
M.P. 166

145
Portrait de Marie-Thérèse
Portrait of Marie-Thérèse
4 December 1937
Paris
Oil and crayon on canvas
46 × 38
D.b.l.: *4.D.37.*
Duncan, p. 135
M.P. 167

146
La suppliante
The Suppliant
18 December 1937
Paris
Gouache on wood panel
24 × 18.5
D.b.l.: *18 D 37.*
Duncan, p. 138
M.P. 168

147
Tête de femme à la palette
Head of a Woman with a Palette
18 December 1937
Paris
Oil on wood panel
22.3 × 16
D.a.r.: *18 D 37.*
Duncan, p. 227
M.P. 169

148
Maya à la poupée
Maya with a Doll
16 January 1938
Paris
Oil on canvas
73.5 × 60
D.b.l.: *16.1.38.*
Z.IX, 99; Duncan, p. 230
M.P. 170

149
La coiffure
Hairdressing
22 March 1938
Paris
Oil on canvas
57 × 43.5
D. on back on the stretcher: *22.3.38.*
Duncan, p. 232
M.P. 171

148   Maya with a Doll

150
L'artiste devant sa toile
The Artist in front of his Canvas
22 March 1938
Paris
Charcoal on canvas
130 × 94
D. on back on the stretcher: *22.3.38.*
M.P. 172

151
La fermière
The Farmer's Wife
23 March 1938
Paris
Charcoal and oil on canvas
120 × 235
D. on back on the stretcher: *23.3.38.*
Z.IX, 78; Duncan, p. 232
M.P. 173

152
Homme au chapeau de paille et au cornet de glace
Man with a Straw Hat and an Ice Cream Cone
30 August 1938
Mougins
Oil on canvas
61 × 46
D.c.b.: *30 A 38*
Z.IX, 205; Duncan, p. 236
M.P. 174

153
Tête d'homme barbu
Head of a Bearded Man
[1938]
Oil on canvas
55 × 46
Duncan, p. 228
M.P. 175

154
Femme couchée lisant
Reclining Woman Reading
21 January 1939
Tremblay-sur-Mauldre
Oil on canvas
96.5 × 130
D.c.r.: *21.1.39.*; on back on the stretcher: *21.1.39.*
Z.IX, 253
M.P. 177

155
Chat saisissant un oiseau
Cat Catching a Bird
22 April 1939
Paris
Oil on canvas
81 × 100
D.a.l.: *22-4.39.*; on back on the stretcher: *22.4.39.*
Z.IX, 296; Duncan, p. 241
M.P. 178

152   Man with a Straw Hat and an Ice Cream Cone

156
Femme assise au chapeau
Seated Woman with a Hat
27 May 1939
Paris
Oil on canvas
81 × 54
D.c.r.: *27.5.39*; on back on the stretcher:
27.5.39.
Z.IX, 301; Duncan, p. 241
M.P. 179

157
Buste de femme au chapeau rayé
*Head and Shoulders of a Woman with a
Striped Hat*
3 June 1939
Paris
Oil on canvas
81 × 54
D. on the hat: *3.6.39.*; on back on the
stretcher: *3.6.39.*
Duncan, p. 167
M.P. 180

158
Femme au chapeau bleu
Woman with a Blue Hat
3 October 1939
Royan
Oil on canvas
65.5 × 50
D.b.l.: *3.10.39*; on back: *Royan/3.10.39.*
Z.IX, 353
M.P. 181

159
Tête de femme
Head of a Woman
4 October 1939
Royan
Oil on canvas
65.5 × 54.5
D.b.l.: *4.10./39*; on back: *Royan/4.10.39.*
Z.IX, 357
M.P. 182

160
Tête de femme
Head of a Woman
30 November 1939
Royan
Oil on canvas
65 × 54
D.a.l.: *30.11.39.*; on back: *Royan/30.11.39.*
Z.IX, 375
M.P. 183

161
Café à Royan
Café at Royan
15 August 1940
Royan
Oil on canvas
97 × 130
D. on back: *Royan/15.8.40*; on the stretcher:
Royan 15.8.40.
Z.XI, 88; Duncan, p. 243
M.P. 187

157   Head and Shoulders of a Woman with a Striped Hat

162
Buste de femme au chapeau
Woman with a Hat
9 June 1941
Paris
Oil on canvas
92 × 60
D.a.l.: *9 juin/41.*; on back on the stretcher:
9 juin 41.
Z.XI, 155
M.P. 188

163
Jeune garçon à la langouste
Boy with a Crayfish
21 June 1941
Paris
Oil on canvas
130 × 97.3
D. on back on the stretcher: *21 juin 41.*
Z.XI, 200
M.P. 189

164 ·
Le Vert-Galant
Square du Vert-Galant
25 June 1943
Paris
Oil on canvas
64.5 × 92
D. on back: *25/juin/43.*
Z.XIII, 64; Duncan, p. 243
M.P. 190

165
Grand nu couché
Large Reclining Nude
28 June 1943
Paris
Oil on canvas
130 × 195.3
D. on back: *28/juin/43.*
Z.XIII, 65
M.P. 191

166
L'enfant aux colombes
The Child with Doves
24 August 1943
Paris
Oil on canvas
162 × 130
D. on back: *24 At 43.*
Z.XIII, 95
M.P. 192

167
Buste de femme au chapeau bleu
Woman with a Blue Hat
7 March 1944
Oil on canvas
92 × 60.2
D. on back: *7 mars/44.*
Z.XIII, 302; Duncan, p. 243
M.P. 193

168
Pichet et squelette
Pitcher and Skeleton
18 February 1945
Paris
Oil on canvas
73 × 92.2
D. on back: *18.2.45*; on the stretcher: *P.*
Z.XIV, 78
M.P. 194

169
Nature morte à la bougie
Still-life with Candle
21 February 1945
Paris
Oil on canvas
92.2 × 73
D. on back: *21.2./45.*
Z.XIV, 69
M.P. 195

170
Femme assise
Seated Woman
5 March 1945
Paris
Oil on canvas
131.5 × 81
D. on back: *5.3.45.*
Z.XIV, 77
M.P. 196

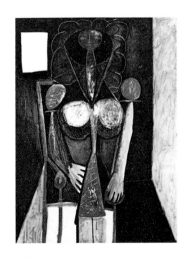

171
Femme dans un fauteuil
Woman in an Armchair
3 July 1946
Paris
Oil and gouache on canvas
130.2 × 97.1
D. on back: *3 juillet/46*
M.P. 197

172
Crâne, oursins et lampe sur une table
Skull, Sea Urchins and Lamp on a Table
27 November 1946
[Antibes–Paris]
Oil on plywood
81 × 100
D. on back: *27.11./46.*
Z.XIV, 290
M.P. 198

173
Chouette dans un intérieur
Owl in an Interior
7 December 1946
Paris
Oil on plywood
81 × 100
D. on back: *7.12.46*
M.P. 199

174
La cuisine
The Kitchen
November 1948
Paris
Oil on canvas
175 × 252
Z.XV, 107
M.P. 200

175
La chèvre
The Goat
1950
Vallauris
Oil and charcoal on plywood
93 × 231
Z.XV, 153
M.P. 201

176
Fumées à Vallauris
Smoke Clouds at Vallauris
12 January 1951
Vallauris
Oil on canvas
59.5 × 73.5
D. on back: *12/1/51*
Z.XV, 174; Duncan, p. 244
M.P. 202

177
Massacre en Corée
Massacre in Korea
18 January 1951
Vallauris
Oil on plywood
110 × 210
D. on back: *Vallauris/18 janvier/1951*
Z.XV, 173
M.P. 203

178
Jeux de pages
Pages at Play
24 February 1951
Vallauris
Oil on wood panel
54 × 65
D. on back: *24.2.51*
Z.XV, 184; Duncan, p. 244
M.P. 204

179
Nature morte au pichet
Still-life with Pitcher
7 November 1951
Vallauris
Oil, chalk and charcoal on plywood
105 × 136.5
D. on back: *Vallauris/7.11.51.*
M.P. 205

174   The Kitchen

183   Claude Drawing, Françoise and Paloma

180
Crâne de chèvre, bouteille et bougie
Goat's Skull, Bottle and Candle
25 March 1952
Paris
Oil on canvas
89 × 116
D. on back: *Paris/92. Gay-Lussac/25.3.52.*
Z.XV, 201
M.P. 206

181
La liseuse
Woman Reading
29 January 1953
Vallauris
Oil on plywood
114 × 146
D. on back: *Vallauris/29.1.53.*
Z.XV, 237
M.P. 207

182
L'ombre
The Shadow
29 December 1953
Vallauris
Oil and charcoal on canvas
129.5 × 96.5
D. on back: *29.12.53.*
Z.XVI, 100; Duncan, p. 182
M.P. 208

183
Claude dessinant, Françoise et Paloma
Claude Drawing, Françoise and Paloma
17 May 1954
Vallauris
Oil on canvas
116 × 89
D. on back: *17.5.54.*
Z.XVI, 323; Duncan, p. 246
M.P. 209

184
Femmes à la toilette
Women at their Toilette
4 January 1956
Cannes
Oil on canvas
195.5 × 130
D. on back: *4.1.56.*
Z.XVII, 54; Duncan, p. 247
M.P. 210

185
L'atelier de La Californie
The Studio of La Californie
30 March 1956
Cannes
Oil on canvas
114 × 146
D. on back: *30.3./56.*
Z.XVII, 56; Duncan, p. 247
M.P. 211

186
La baie de Cannes
The Baý of Cannes
19 April–9 June 1958
Cannes
Oil on canvas
130 × 195
D. on back: *19.4.58./20.4.58./21.4.58./*
22.4.58./23.4.58./24.4.58./25.4.58./26.4.58./
27.4.58./31.5.58./1.6.58./7.6.58./9.6.58.
Z.XVIII, 83; Duncan, p. 257
M.P. 212

187
Nature morte à la tête de taureau
Still-life with Bull's Head
25 May–9 June 1958
Cannes
Oil on canvas
162.5 × 130
D.b.l.: *28.5.58*; on back: *28.5./58/29.5.58./*
30.5.58./31.5.58./7.6.58./9.6.58.
Z.XVIII, 237; Duncan, p. 265
M.P. 213

188
Le buffet de Vauvenargues
The Dresser at Vauvenargues
23 March 1959–23 January 1960
Cannes–Vauvenargues
Oil on canvas
195 × 280
D. on back: *Cannes./fait cette après-midi/*
23.3.59./entre 3 Hs et 7 Hs-11 Hs./24.3.59./
25——/26-1.4.59./2.4.59. 3.4.5.6.25.26./
Vauvenargues/29.5.59/16.6.59. 17.18. 30.31/
19.20. 1.6 2.6./3.6. 4./23.1.60 5.6.7./
8.9.10.11
Z.XVIII, 395
M.P. 214

189
Le déjeuner sur l'herbe d'après Manet
Le Déjeuner sur l'Herbe after Manet
3 March–20 August 1960
Vauvenargues
Oil on canvas
130 × 195
D. on back: *3.3.60/1.8.60/12.8.60/13-/14/*
15/16/17/18/20
Z.XIX, 204
M.P. 215

190
Le déjeuner sur l'herbe d'après Manet
Le Déjeuner sur l'Herbe after Manet
12 July 1961
Mougins
Oil on canvas
81 × 99.8
D. on back: *12.7.61./n.D. de V.*
Z.XX, 89
M.P. 216

191
Le déjeuner sur l'herbe d'après Manet
Le Déjeuner sur l'Herbe after Manet
13 July 1961
Mougins
Oil on canvas
60 × 73
D. on back: *13.7.61/N. de Vie*
Z.XX, 90
M.P. 217

185   The Studio of La Californie

189   Le Déjeuner sur l'Herbe after Manet

195   The Family

192
Femme assise
Seated Woman
26 May 1963
Mougins
Oil on canvas
195 × 130
D. on back: *26.5.63*
M.P. 218

193
Nu couché
Reclining Nude
14 June 1967
Mougins
Oil on canvas
195 × 130
D. on back: *14.6.67.*
Z.XXVII, 35
M.P. 219

194
Le baiser
The Kiss
26 October 1969
Mougins
Oil on canvas
97 × 130
D. on back: *26.10.69.*
Z.XXXI, 484
M.P. 220

195
La famille
The Family
30 September 1970
Mougins
Oil on canvas
162 × 130
D. on back: *30.9.70.*
Z.XXXII, 271
M.P. 222

196
Vieil homme assis
Seated Old Man
26 September 1970–14 November 1971
Mougins
Oil on canvas
145.5 × 114
D. on back: *26.9./70 14.11.7/:/1/25./9./70.*
Z.XXXII, 265
M.P. 221

197
Le matador
The Matador
4 October 1970
Mougins
Oil on canvas
145.5 × 114
D. on back: *4.10.70.*
Z.XXXII, 273
M.P. 223

198
Nu couché et homme jouant de la guitare
Reclining Nude and Man Playing a Guitar
27 October 1970
Mougins
Oil on canvas
130 × 195
D. on back: *27.10.70*
Z.XXXII, 293
M.P. 224

199
Jeune fille assise
Seated Girl
21 November 1970
Mougins
Oil on plywood
130.3 × 80.3
D.a.r.: *21.11.70*; on back: *21.11.70*
Z.XXXII, 307
M.P. 225

200
Maternité
Mother and Child
30 August 1971
Mougins
Oil on canvas
162 × 130
D. on back: *DIMANCHE/LUNDI/30.8.71.*
Z.XXXIII, 168
M.P. 226

201
Paysage
Landscape
31 March 1972
Mougins
Oil on canvas
130 × 162
D. on back: *vendredi/31/mars/1972*
Z.XXXIII, 331
M.P. 227

202
Le jeune peintre
The Young Painter
14 April 1972
Mougins
Oil on canvas
91 × 72.5
D. on back: *VENDREDI./14.4.72./III*
Z.XXXIII, 350
M.P. 228

203
Musicien
Musician
26 May 1972
Mougins
Oil on canvas
194.5 × 129.5
D. on back: *26.5./72.*
Z.XXXIII, 397
M.P. 229

196   Seated Old Man

199   Seated Girl

The boulevard Raspail studio in 1912 (Picasso Archives)

Papiers collés

(1) See below the texts by H. Seckel on 'Picture Reliefs' and 'Sculptures'.

(2) See the catalogue of the 'Picasso' exhibition, Marseilles, Musée Cantini, 1959, No. 19.

(3) See above M.-L. Besnard-Bernadac's comments on *Nature morte à la chaise cannée* (*Still-life with Chair-caning*, cat. 35).

(4) *Guitare 'J'aime Eva'* ('*I Love Eva' Guitar*, cat. 36). The gingerbread has not survived.

(5) See the catalogue of the exhibition 'Georges Braque. Les papiers collés', Paris, Centre Georges Pompidou, Musée National d'Art Moderne, 1982, No. 1, and D. Cooper's article in it.

(6) There may have been two of these: see the article by I. Monod-Fontaine in 'Georges Braque. Les papiers collés' catalogue.

(7) No comprehensive comparative study of these two artists' output has so far been carried out. It might well be undertaken as part of a general work on Cubist *papiers collés*, including those by Gris and Laurens.

(8) Reproduced in P. Daix, J. Rosselet, *Picasso: The Cubist Years 1907–1916*, London, 1979, p. 358, and on the facing page.

(9) '*J'emploie tes derniers procédés papéristiques et pusiereux [sic].*' Letter published by I. Monod-Fontaine (see note 6) by courtesy of M. and Mme Claude Laurens.

(10) First noted, to the best of our knowledge, by I. Monod-Fontaine, op. cit., p. 42.

It has become customary to include *papiers collés* (literally 'stuck' or 'pasted papers') among the broader category of collages. Listed under the present heading, however, are *papiers collés* in the strict sense: paper elements – pieces of wallpaper and newsprint, various other scraps, cigarette packets, playing cards – cut out and 're-articulated', as Jean Paulhan put it. These usually fill out elements of drawing and are fastened to a paper or cardboard support by glue or pins.

In addition to *Nature morte à la chaise cannée* (*Still-life with Chair-caning*, cat. 35), *Verre sur un guéridon* (*Glass on a Pedestal Table*, cat. 38) has also been retained among the paintings. It was originally listed as a *papier collé* and does embody elements that have been pasted and pinned, but on to canvas rather than paper. Two Cubist pictures which incorporate pasted pieces of the same printed textile – *Homme à la pipe* (*Man with a Pipe*, cat. 39) and *Homme à la moustache* (*Man with a Moustache*, cat. 40) – also remain classified as paintings.

Constructions are included among the sculptures, while picture reliefs, 'a two-dimensional background on which some elements stand out in relief' with pronounced three-dimensional features, are grouped under a heading of their own.[1]

The chronology of Picasso's collages and *papiers collés* had long been in dispute, but now appears to have been settled. The *Still-life with Chair-caning* (cat. 35) was carried out in the spring of 1912, probably in May, rather than in 1911–12 (as a number of art historians who followed Zervos had suggested) or even at the beginning of 1912, as John Golding supposed. It was then, as Picasso confided to Douglas Cooper,[2] that he first used a real object – a piece of oilcloth pasted on to canvas – to represent chair-caning.[3]

Picasso produced a second, more topical, 'collage' for a different purpose – as a declaration of love – when he stuck a piece of gingerbread inscribed with 'I love Eva'[4] on to a canvas picturing a guitar. He had been spending the summer at Sorgues, where he and Braque had rented adjoining houses. The two artists undoubtedly used the time spent there to discuss changes in the conception of space arising from the *Still-life with Chair-caning* and the questions raised by the new freedom of form and colour in relation to each other.

As he strolled through the streets of Avignon towards the end of August, Braque spotted a roll of paper with a wood-grain pattern in the window of a wallpaper shop, and immediately saw the opportunities it offered. As soon as Picasso left for Paris, Braque went back to buy it, cut some pieces from it and stuck them on a charcoal drawing so as to complete it and stress some of its features. The first *papier collé* (a wholly novel term) – *Fruit Bowl and Glass*[5] – had been created. Picasso was confronted with it on his return.[6]

Once back in Paris for good, in his new boulevard Raspail studio, Picasso took over the new technique, arranged it to his liking,[7] developed it and indulged in what may be described as visual games. So much is obvious from photographs of his studio with *papiers collés* pinned to the wall[8] and from a letter of 7 October 1912 to Braque, who had stayed behind in Sorgues: 'I am making use of your latest paperistic and pulverous processes.'[9]

Did Picasso immediately foresee all the new opportunities thus created? He set no separate tariff for 'embellished' drawings in the contract letter of 18 December 1912, which formalized his commercial transactions with Kahnweiler, unlike Braque, who had itemized 'drawings with paper, wood, marble or any other adjunct' in his contract signed a fortnight earlier.[10]

It is clear, on the other hand, that Picasso had a high opinion of his *papiers collés* and handed some over to Kahnweiler. He picked about ten of them for his first retrospective exhibition at the Galeries Georges Petit in 1932, and gladly made others available when Pierre Loeb arranged an exhibition of Picasso's *papiers collés* in 1935.

Guillaume Apollinaire was referring to collages and *papiers collés* by March 1913: 'And he [Picasso] would sometimes not think it beneath him to bring actual objects to light – a twopenny broadsheet, a real postage stamp, a scrap of daily paper or a piece of oilcloth printed with a chair-caning pattern. The painter's art would have added no vivid touch to the verity of these things.'[11]

Louis Aragon[12] and Tristan Tzara[13] also both sensed the poetical quality of *papiers collés* and analysed their specific features. Jean Paulhan was later to draw attention to the character of the space generated by such works.[14]

D.-H. Kahnweiler was immediately captivated by this art form. He recounted[15] that Vlaminck had told him in 1920: 'To think that at the rue Vignon you showed me a sheet with a few charcoal strokes and a scrap of newsprint stuck on to it, and told me that it was beautiful! . . . and the worst of it, Kahnweiler, is that I believed you.' This had been a *papier collé* by Picasso. Collectors of *papiers collés*, such as Marie Cuttoli and Henri Laugier,[16] Roger Dutilleul, André Lefèvre and Herman Rumpf to name only a few, were prompted by aesthetic considerations. These were 'objects of sheer pleasure'[17] in so far as they were concerned: they hardly felt that they were witnessing a 'revolution'.[18] There has recently been a proliferation of scholarly work on this subject in academic conferences, seminars and publications which, together with exhibitions, has provided some opportunities for reassessment.

Art historians have certainly not overlooked *papiers collés*, especially in works devoted to Cubism, but no detailed studies had appeared on this subject, to the best of our knowledge, until those by Greenberg in 1958[19] and Rosenblum in 1971.[20] In France, in 1973, Pierre Daix wrote an article on 'Some Chronological Discrepancies in the *Papiers collés* Revolution (1912–1914)',[21] as a tribute to Picasso immediately after his death. Daix followed Rosenblum's conclusions and suggested precise dates for the *papiers collés* as a whole. Given the present state of research in this field, the Musée Picasso has adopted, for the purposes of this catalogue, the dates suggested by Pierre Daix.

His classification involved three 'generations': the first covered works produced in Paris in November–December 1912, in the boulevard Raspail studio; the second, those from Céret in March–May 1913; while the third extended from March 1914 in Paris to early summer of that year in Avignon.

All three generations are respresented in the Musée Picasso's collections, which also include three post-Cubist *papiers collés*: *Oiseau en cage* (*Bird in a Cage*, cat. 217) of 1918–19, *Nature morte devant une fenêtre* (*Still-life in front of a Window*, cat. 218) of 1919 and, above all, *Femmes à leur toilette* (*Women at their Toilette*, cat. 219) of 1938, measuring some three by four and a half metres and made with pasted papers alone. There are four works in the first generation: *Violon* (*Violin*, cat. 204) includes part of a newspaper dated 17 November 1912; in *Bouteille sur une table* (*Bottle on a Table*, cat. 206) a newspaper dated 8 December 1912 replaces the paper background and acts as the support, a somewhat unusual technique. The coloured paper and newsprint cuttings stuck down in *Violon* (cat. 204) are treated as areas of colour; the same part is played in *Violon et feuille de musique* (*Violin and Sheet of Music*, cat. 205) by a musical score, while cut-outs provide the main component elements of the instrument in the other *Violon* (cat. 207). It is worth noting that a violin figures in three of these four works.

The second generation is brilliantly illustrated by seven works, including two Céret landscapes, a subject also tackled by Juan Gris. Picasso was then experimenting in search of a key to a pictorial sign language. The human face was often reduced to a simple ideogram, as in the *Tête* (*Head*, cat. 208). Spaces were marked out by the intersection and reduplication of abstract planes, as in *Bouteille de vieux marc et journal* (*Bottle of Old Marc and Newspaper*, cat. 210) and *Paysage de Céret* (*Céret Landscape*, cat. 211). Wallpaper usually replaced newsprint.[22] The latter does not appear in any of the works from this period in the museum's collection, although a newspaper is represented by the three letters drawn in *Bottle of Old*

(11) G. Apollinaire, 'Pablo Picasso', *Montjoie!*, 14 March 1913.

(12) L. Aragon, *La peinture au défi*, an introduction to the exhibition of *papiers collés* at the Galerie Goemans, Paris, 1930.

(13) T. Tzara, 'Le papier collé ou le proverbe en peinture', *Cahiers d'Art*, 1931, No. 2, and the preface to the catalogue of the exhibition of *papiers collés* (1912–1914) by Picasso at the Galerie Pierre, February–March 1935.

(14) J. Paulhan, 'L'espace cubiste ou le papier collé', *L'Arc*, 1960/2, reprinted in *La peinture cubiste*, Paris, 1971.

(15) D.-H. Kahnweiler, *Ma galerie et mes peintres, entretiens avec Francis Crémieux*, Paris, 1961, p. 104.

(16) His collection in this field has been offered to the Musée National d'Art Moderne.

(17) D. Bozo in his preface to the catalogue of the 'Georges Braque. Les papiers collés' exhibition.

(18) This has now become a standard description. One might therefore refer to the immediately preceding period as 'pre-revolutionary'. It was then that Picasso, just like Braque, introduced real-life items such as imitation wallpapers, numerals and letters into his pictures as well as gritting them with sand to alter their texture, in order to avoid producing an esoteric effect.

(19) C. Greenberg, 'The pasted-paper revolution', *Art News*, September, 1958.

(20) R. Rosenblum, 'Picasso and the coronation of Alexander III, a note on the dating of some Papiers collés', *Burlington Magazine*, October 1971.

(21) P. Daix, 'Des bouleversements chronologiques dans la révolution des papiers collés', *Gazette des Beaux-Arts*, Paris, October 1973. He returned to these dates in *Picasso: The Cubist Years 1907–1916*.

(22) The identical wallpaper recurs in cat. 210 and cat. 211.

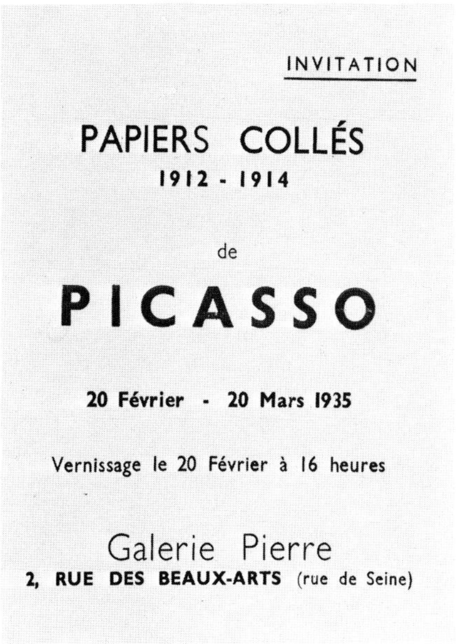

INVITATION

PAPIERS COLLÉS
1912 - 1914

de

PICASSO

20 Février - 20 Mars 1935

Vernissage le 20 Février à 16 heures

Galerie Pierre
2, RUE DES BEAUX-ARTS (rue de Seine)

Invitation card to the *papiers collés* exhibition at the Galerie Pierre in 1935 (Musée Picasso Document)

Marc and Newspaper. The *Guitare* (*Guitar*, cat. 209) is marked by the use of strips of wallpaper border. Components are often pinned into position rather than pasted.

The third generation is represented by two works: *Verre, as de trèfle, paquet de cigarettes* (*Glass, Ace of Clubs, Packet of Cigarettes*, cat. 215) and *Bouteille de vin et dé* (*Bottle of Wine and Die*, cat. 216). These fully meet Pierre Daix's criteria because 'the materials employed make a major contribution to the general effect'. Space is treated differently in these two works. *Bottle of Wine and Die*, powerfully effective through its restraint, has a piece of paper representing the die pinned to the stippled shadow of the bottle. In *Glass, Ace of Clubs, Packet of Cigarettes*, the drawn and pasted elements do not take up the whole of the supporting surface. These *papiers collés* must have been produced in Paris during the spring of 1914; the Musée Picasso would have no examples of that summer's work in Avignon if it were not for the glasses (cat. 227, 228) among its 'study items'.[23]

M.R.

(23) See Technical Note below.

Technical Note

Papers that had been cut out and in some cases painted, originating from the studio and incorporated in the museum's collection, either as part of the settlement or later donated by one or other of the heirs, have been collected under the heading of 'Study Items for *Papiers collés* and Paintings'. We know nothing about Picasso's working methods in 1912–14, when these items were probably produced, and one can therefore only speculate as to their state of completion and purpose. Included among them are attempted imitations of materials (cat. 223–226), scraps of paper prepared for pasting and paper cut-outs used as studies for paintings. Thus the patterns cut out in cat. 236–238 recur in painted form in the Musée National d'Art Moderne's *Portrait de jeune fille* (*Portrait of a Girl*).[1]

Many of these items contain pin-holes, indicating that they have at one time been pinned.

(1) Zervos XXX, 528; D.R. 784.

204
Violon
Violin
Autumn 1912
Paris
Pasted coloured papers, wallpaper and a piece
of newspaper on cardboard, charcoal
65 × 50
Z.II^2, 774; T.l.o.p.$^{(2)}$, 535; D.R. 517
M.P. 367

205
Violon et feuille de musique
Violin and Sheet of Music
Autumn 1912
Paris
Pasted coloured papers and musical score on
cardboard, gouache
78 × 63.5
Z.II^2, 771; T.l.o.p.$^{(2)}$, 533; D.R. 518
M.P. 368

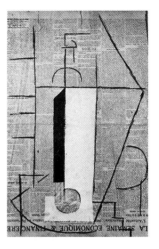

206
Bouteille sur une table
Bottle on a Table
Autumn/winter 1912
Paris
Pasted papers, ink and charcoal on newsprint
62.5 × 44
Z.II^2, 782; T.l.o.p.$^{(2)}$, 559; D.R. 551
M.P. 369

207
Violon
Violin
Autumn/winter 1912
Paris
Pasted paper and charcoal on paper
31.5 × 24
Z.XXVIII, 243; D.R. 531
M.P. 370

208
Tête
Head
Early 1913
[Paris–Céret]
Pinned coloured papers, charcoal and chalk
on drawing paper (papier Ingres)
61.7 × 46.8
Z.XXVIII, 284; D.R. 594
M.P. 371

209
Guitare
Guitar
[Spring 1913]
[Céret]
Coloured papers, wallpapers, piece of
newspaper, charcoal and pencil on cardboard
44 × 32.7
Z.XXVIII, 301; D.R. 598
M.P. 372

210
Bouteille de vieux marc et journal
Bottle of Old Marc and Newspaper
Spring 1913
Céret
Pinned pieces of wallpaper, charcoal and
chalk on drawing paper (papier Ingres)
47.8 × 62
Z.II², 332; T.l.o.p.⁽²⁾, 481; D.R. 611
M.P. 373

211
Paysage de Céret
Céret Landscape
Spring 1913
Céret
Pinned coloured papers and wallpapers, with
charcoal and chalk, on mauve drawing paper
(papier Ingres)
38 × 38.5
Z.II¹, 343; Z.VI, 1187; T.l.o.p.⁽²⁾, 484, 643;
D.R. 612; Duncan, p. 206
M.P. 374

212
Paysage de Céret
Céret Landscape
Spring 1913
Céret
Pasted and pinned coloured papers, with
pastel and charcoal on blue drawing paper
(papier Ingres)
47.8 × 62.5
Z.XXVIII, 60; D.R. 613
M.P. 375

213
Guitare, verre, bouteille de vieux marc
Guitar, Glass, Bottle of Old Marc
Spring 1913
Céret
Pinned coloured paper and wallpaper, with
charcoal and chalk, on blue drawing paper
(papier Ingres)
47.2 × 61.8
Z.II², 757; T.l.o.p.⁽²⁾, 590; D.R. 603
M.P. 376

214
Tête d'arlequin
Head of Harlequin
1913
Céret
Pinned paper, with charcoal, on drawing
paper (papier Ingres)
62.7 × 47
Z.II², 425; T.l.o.p.⁽²⁾, 601; D.R. 617
M.P. 377

215
Verre, as de trèfle, paquet de cigarettes
Glass, Ace of Clubs, Packet of Cigarettes
Spring 1914
Paris
Oil on paper and empty cigarette packet
pasted on drawing paper (papier d'Arches),
pastel and pencil
64 × 49
D.R. 673
M.P. 379

1912

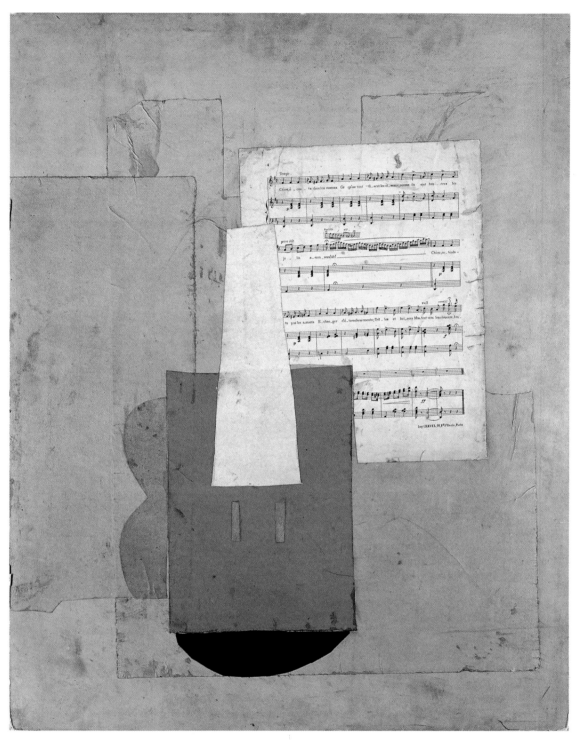

205   Violin and Sheet of Music

209   Guitar

216
Bouteille de vin et dé
Bottle of Wine and Die
Spring 1914
Paris
Charcoal on drawing paper (papier Ingres),
oil and gouache on pinned drawing paper
(papier Ingres)
49 × 43
Z.II², 459; D.R. 693; Duncan, p. 208
M.P. 380

217
Oiseau en cage
Bird in a Cage
Winter 1918–1919
Paris
Pinned pieces of tarred paper and charcoal on
cardboard
41 × 59
Z.III, 258; T.l.o.p.⁽²⁾, 916
M.P. 381

218
Nature morte devant une fenêtre
Still-life in front of a Window
1919
Paris
Coloured papers and piece of printed
illustration pasted on to paper
26.5 × 23.5
Z.XXIX, 457
M.P. 382

219
Femmes à leur toilette
Women at their Toilette
1938
Paris
Pasted wallpapers and gouache on backed
paper
299 × 448
Z.IX, 103
M.P. 176

219   Women at their Toilette

Study Items for *Papiers collés* and Paintings

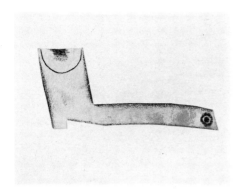

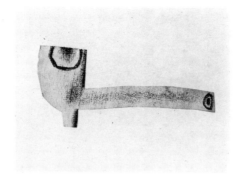

220
Pipe
Pipe
[1912]
Pencil, gouache on paper cut out in the shape of a pipe
5.3 × 11.8
Gift of Marina Ruiz-Picasso
M.P. 1982–162

221
Pipe
Pipe
[1912]
Pencil, gouache on paper cut out in the shape of a pipe
5 × 11.8
Gift of Marina Ruiz-Picasso
M.P. 1982–163

222
Pipe
Pipe
[1912]
Pencil, gouache on paper cut out in the shape of a pipe
4.3 × 10.5
Gift of Marina Ruiz-Picasso
M.P. 1982–164

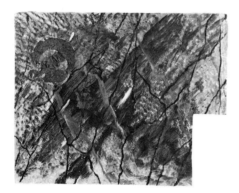

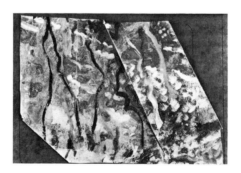

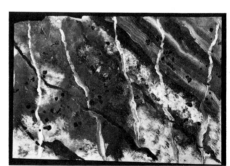

223
Essai d'imitation de matériau
Trial Imitation of Building Material
[1913–1914]
Oil and composition on packing paper
50 × 65
M.P. 383

224
Essai d'imitation de matériau
Trial Imitation of Building Material
[1913–1914]
Oil on paper
22.5 × 34
M.P. 384

225
Essai d'imitation de matériau
Trial Imitation of Building Material
[1913–1914]
Oil on paper
21 × 30.8
M.P. 385

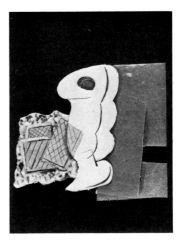

226
Essai d'imitation de matériau
Trial Imitation of Building Material
[1913–1914]
Oil on paper
29.5 × 49
M.P. 386

227
Trois verres
Three Glasses
1914
Avignon
Oil on packing paper
30 × 15.5
Z.II², 822; T.l.o.p.⁽²⁾, 811–814
M.P. 387

228
Verre et biscuits
Glass and Biscuits
1914
Avignon
Oil and crayon on blue felted paper cut-outs
19 × 21.8
Z.II², 825; T.l.o.p.⁽²⁾, 811–814
M.P. 388

229
Eléments de guitare
Parts of a Guitar
[1914]
a) Oil on paper
     47 × 7.2
b) Oil on paper
     21.5 × 18.7
c) Oil on paper
     23.5 × 7
d) Pencil on paper
     27.5 × 5.5
e) Charcoal on pastel paper
     13.5 × 5
f) Charcoal and oil on paper
     21.5 × 5.8
M.P. 389

230
Sèche
Squid
[1914]
Pencil on paper cut-out
29.1 × 17.5
Z.II², 815; T.l.o.p.⁽²⁾, 803–810
M.P. 390

231
Verre
Glass
[1914]
Pastel and oil on paper cut-out
13 × 7.5
Z.II², 820; T.l.o.p.⁽²⁾, 803–810
M.P. 391

232
Carte à jouer: as de trèfle
Playing Card: Ace of Clubs
[1914]
Varnished oil and pencil on paper
9.5 × 7
Z.II², 819; T.l.o.p.⁽²⁾, 803–810
M.P. 392

233
As de trèfle
Ace of Clubs
[1914]
Oil on cut-out packing paper
8 × 5.3
Z.II², 817; T.l.o.p.⁽²⁾, 803–810
M.P. 393

234
Poire et sa feuille
Pear with Leaf Attached
[1914]
Oil and pencil on paper cut-out
15 × 5.3
Z.II², 816; T.l.o.p.⁽²⁾, 803–810
M.P. 394

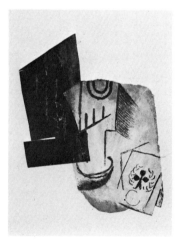

235
As de trèfle, verre, élément de guitare
Ace of Clubs, Glass, Part of a Guitar
[1914]
Varnished oil and pencil on cut-out and
pinned papers
27.5 × 22
Z.II², 806; T.l.o.p.⁽²⁾, 689–695
M.P. 395

236
**Eléments d'étude pour le tableau
'Portrait de jeune fille': Plume**
Study Items for 'Portrait of a Girl': Feather
1914
Avignon
Gouache on paper cut-out
24 × 13
Z.II², 791; T.l.o.p.⁽²⁾, 677–688
M.P. 396

237
**Eléments d'étude pour le tableau
'Portrait de jeune fille': Ampoules**
Study Items for 'Portrait of a Girl': Light Bulbs
1914
Avignon
a) Oil on tracing paper
    15 × 8.5
    Z.II², 798
b) Oil on paper
    12 × 7.2
    Z.II², 795
c) Pencil on both sides of paper
    10 × 5.8
    Z.II², 797; T.l.o.p.⁽²⁾, 677–688
M.P. 397

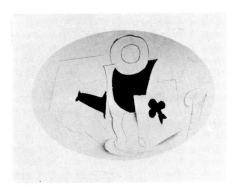

238
Eléments d'étude pour le tableau 'Portrait de jeune fille': Mains
Study Items for 'Portrait of a Girl': Hands
1914
Avignon
a) Gouache and pencil on packing paper
    10.5 × 7
    Z.II², 802
b) Pencil on paper
    11.5 × 7
    Z.II², 796
c) Pencil on packing paper
    12 × 6.5
    Z.II², 801
d) Pencil on packing paper
    14 × 5.2
    Z.II², 793; T.l.o.p.(2), 677–688
M.P. 398

239
Composition aux verres et à l'as de trèfle
Composition with Glasses and Ace of Clubs
[1914]
Cut-outs in paper, with pencil
21.5 × 28.4
Z.II², 812; T.l.o.p.(2), 801
M.P. 400

240
Flotteur
Fishing Float
[1914]
Pencil on paper cut-out
9.9 × 3.3
Z.II², 818; T.l.o.p.(2), 803–810
Gift of Paloma Lopez-Picasso
M.P. 1983–6

A corner of the studio at Royan in 1940 (Picasso Archives)

Picture Reliefs

A set of works situated mid-way between plane and volume and best described as *tableaux-reliefs* – picture reliefs – have been grouped under this heading, distinct from painting and sculpture in the accepted sense. This was a requirement that arose from the work of classification involved in the preparation of a catalogue, despite all the conflicts of opinion which it provokes with regard to Picasso's *œuvre*.

Strictly speaking, these objects are not pictures, since the latter are formally defined by their two-dimensional character, while the works in question reach out into space by the third dimension inherent in some of their components. Yet the flat, two-dimensional surface which they retain as the background and foundation for their sculptural elements gives them the appearance of pictures. The organic origin of this ground, whether it be canvas, wood, cardboard or paper, is also relevant, since sculpture traditionally tends to rely on mineral materials such as plaster, stone or bronze. The clearest example of this occurs in the series of 'sanded' reliefs produced at Juan-les-Pins, in which small natural or man-made objects are fastened to the back of small canvases, with the stretcher acting as a frame (cat. 259–262 and 264–266), or when Picasso placed a relief cut-out of tin in a small moulded frame, as though it were a painting (cat. 244).[1] The major contribution made to the general effect by the ground surface in some of these works also helps to make them look like pictures, as in the case of the two large guitars dating from 1926 (cat. 249, 250).

Canvas, stretchers and frames are supplemented by painting, and painting is very often perceived as the dominant element that binds such a picture together. In the Cubist picture reliefs, colour is involved in a subtle interplay with relief, by stressing or opposing it, somewhat on the lines of *trompe-l'œil* work. This is exemplified by the reliefs dating from the summer of 1914, both by those housed in a kind of cigar box (cat. 245–247) and in the *Verre, pipe, as de trèfle et dé* (*Glass, Pipe, Ace of Clubs and Die*) tondo (cat. 248). (The rather unusual format of the latter, incidentally, links it with the whole history of painting since the Renaissance, from Botticelli's Virgins to Ingres's *The Turkish Bath*.) In these works, the relief plays much the same part as that of *papier collé* in a graphic composition, or a collage on canvas embodied in a painted work. Paint as a material in its own right also contributes to the effect of these picture reliefs, as in *Composition au papillon* (*Composition with a Butterfly*, cat. 267) of 1932, where a butterfly, a dead leaf and some fibres have embedded themselves in it: 'The common butterfly immobilized for ever beside a dry leaf . . . .'[2]

Is this painting or sculpture? A number of the works assembled here featured in 1949 in the famous – and first – book devoted to Picasso's sculptures,[3] with a text by Kahnweiler, illustrated by photographs which Brassaï[4] took at Picasso's request in his various studios. These included the sand reliefs of 1930, the *Composition with a Butterfly* of 1932, and the little women made of stitched and painted cardboard originating from Royan in 1940. And, quite recently, all the Musée Picasso's picture reliefs have been included in the revised catalogue of Picasso's sculptures.[5] Inspired scavenging had indeed assembled, stitched or pasted on a background a set of items which impart to these works that third dimension which defines sculpture. This, as Kahnweiler remarked, made it possible 'to remedy the deficiencies of painting when it comes to representing volume'.[6]

Some thirty years earlier, however, Kahnweiler himself had attempted to unravel the problem posed by low relief, lying between painting and sculpture, in an essay entitled 'The

(1) This relief was refurbished in 1979 with a wooden support and a frame on the strength of the photograph published in Zervos II², 852, which shows it in its original state.

(2) A. Breton, 'Picasso dans son élément', *Minotaure*, No. 1, Paris, 1 June 1933, p. 10.

(3) D.-H. Kahnweiler, *Les Sculptures de Picasso*, Paris, 1949. This contains photographs of the following items: cat. 241, 259–261, 263, 264, 266–270. It is surprising that the Cubist reliefs which Picasso had clearly kept, since they were included in the settlement from the estate, are not recorded in this book, except for three items: cat. 241 in its original state and two others, now lost. The latter had probably already been lost or altered by the time of publication, since Brassaï did not photograph them. The three items included in the book originated from the Galerie Leiris archive and not from him.

(4) Brassaï described the circumstances in which he took these first photographs in *Picasso & Co.*, New York, 1966, London, 1967: 'I learned then what my important mission was to be: to photograph the sculptures of Picasso, which were still entirely unknown' (p. 7).

(5) W. Spies, *Picasso, Das plastische Werk*, Stuttgart, 1983 (a catalogue of the output drawn up by C. Piot and W. Spies).

(6) D.-H. Kahnweiler, op. cit.

Essence of Sculpture':[7] '. . . what trips us up here is the question of bas-relief'.[8] As it stands, this description does not meet our purpose because it suggests a surface incised and worked over in such a way that some lightly embossed forms emerge from it: this is hardly adequate as a description of long nails which pierce the canvas and point at the spectator (cat. 250), or of a butterfly stuck on a painted canvas (cat. 267). If, however, the term 'picture relief' is introduced instead – also suggesting that painting is involved – Kahnweiler's analysis becomes more tempting: painting, with imaginary space in fictitious light; sculpture, with real space in real light; and between these, the low relief, restrained by its background from developing freely and fully in real space. In other words, 'any limitation of the field of vision in the direction of the background suppresses real depth and brings imaginary depth into play'.[9] And so the dividing line tends to run between the picture relief and sculpture, rather than between painting and the picture relief: 'The bas-relief makes the resources of sculpture serve its own purpose, which borders on that of painting. . . . Painting and the bas-relief generate their own space. They patently escape from common space.'[10]

The criteria outlined above governed the new classification introduced in this catalogue: a picture-like two-dimensional surface on which some elements stand out in relief and which includes an element of painting.

It may be added that the Musée Picasso owns the most comprehensive collection of such objects: the three 'cigar boxes' (cat. 245–247); eight of the nine small guitars made of cardboard, paper, string and cloth (cat. 251–258) dating from 1926 (these are accurately dated on the back); all eight sand reliefs of 1930 from Juan-les-Pins on record; three of the four little women stitched on cardboard boxes made in Royan in 1940 (the fourth of these was at one time in the Eluard collection). Only the picture reliefs dating from 1937–38[11] are missing.

H.S.

Changes in Dating

Some of the dates put forward in the catalogue of the 1979 Grand Palais settlement exhibition have been altered on the strength of firm evidence, such as a component that can be accurately dated, a bibliographical reference, etc. Others are more tentative, being founded on stylistic considerations. These last are not discussed below.

Cat. 241 (M.P. 246)
The newsprint pasted on to the board refers to 23 April 1913, while the work itself was illustrated in *Les Soirées de Paris*, No. 18 of 15 November 1913. It should be added that the work as it is at present has been altered from its original state: see Kahnweiler's photo (Fig. 1), first published in *Les Soirées de Paris*.

Cat. 242 (M.P. 248)
One of the pieces of newspaper included refers to Tuesday 23 December, and must therefore date from 1913.

Cat. 264 (M.P. 123)
Dated 22 August 1930 in *Cahiers d'Art* special 'Picasso, 1930–1935' issue, Vol. X, Nos. 7–10, 1935, p. 16.

Fig. 1
Guitare et bouteille de Bass (*Guitar and Bottle of Bass*), original state (Photo Galerie Louise Leiris)

(7) D.-H. Kahnweiler, 'Das Wesen der Bildhauerei', *Feuer*, Weimar, Vol. 1, No. 2–3, Nov.–Dec. 1919, reprinted under the title 'L'essence de la sculpture' in *Confessions esthétiques*, Paris, 1963, pp. 84ff.

(8) D.-H. Kahnweiler, op. cit., p. 88.

(9) D.-H. Kahnweiler, op. cit., p. 95.

(10) D.-H. Kahnweiler, op. cit., pp. 88 and 93.

(11) Spies, Nos. 168, 169, 170, 178, 179.

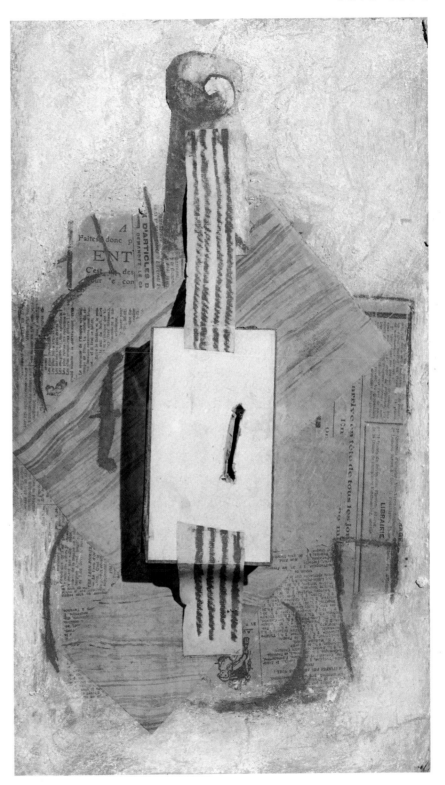

242   Violin

241
Guitare et bouteille de Bass
Guitar and Bottle of Bass
[Spring–autumn] 1913
Paris
Partly painted pinewood components, pasted
paper, strokes of charcoal and nails on
wooden backing
89.5 × 80 × 14
Original state: Z.II², 575; T.l.o.p.⁽²⁾, 621;
D.R. 630; S. 33a. Present state: S. 33b
M.P. 246

242
Violon
Violin
Late December 1913–early 1914
Paris
Cardboard box, pasted papers, gouache,
charcoal and chalk on cardboard
51.5 × 30.4
Z.II², 784; T.l.o.p.⁽²⁾, 618; D.R. 652; S. 32
M.P. 248

243
Bouteille de Bass
Bottle of Bass
Spring 1914
Paris
Oil, charcoal, strokes of crayon, wooden
components and nail on canvas pasted to
wood panel
23.5 × 10.5 × 1.3
Z.XXIX, 45; Duncan, p. 208; D.R. 687; S. 53 A
M.P. 43

244
Verre, journal et dé
Glass, Newspaper and Die
Spring 1914
Paris
Cut-out and painted tin, sand and wire
(wooden base and frame reconstructed)
20.6 × 19 × 9.5
Z.II², 852; T.l.o.p.⁽²⁾, 797; D.R. 750; S. 51
M.P. 251

245
Verre, journal et dé
Glass, Newspaper and Die
Summer 1914
Avignon
Painted wooden and cut-out tin components,
wire on an oil-painted wooden base
17.4 × 13.5 × 3
Z.II², 838; T.l.o.p.⁽²⁾, 787; S. 42
M.P. 45

246
Verre, journal et dé
Glass, Newspaper and Die
Summer 1914
Avignon
Painted wooden components and sand on
base painted in oils
17.5 × 15.2 × 3
Z.II², 847; T.l.o.p.⁽²⁾, 706; D.R. 790; S. 50
M.P. 46

247
Verre et journal
Glass and Newspaper
Summer 1914
Avignon
Painted wooden components and crayon
strokes on wooden base painted in oils
15.4 × 17.5 × 3
D. on back: *A AVIGNON/1914*
Z.II², 846; T.l.o.p.⁽²⁾, 705; D.R. 789; S. 49
M.P. 47

248
Verre, pipe, as de trèfle et dé
Glass, Pipe, Ace of Clubs and Die
Summer 1914
Avignon
Painted wooden and metal components on
wooden base painted in oils
34 (diameter) × 8.5
S. on back: *Picasso*
Z.II², 830; T.l.o.p.⁽²⁾, 783; D.R. 788; S. 45
M.P. 48

249
Guitare
Guitar
Spring 1926
Paris
Canvas, wood, rope, nails and tacks on a
painted panel
130 × 96.5
Duncan, p. 210; S. 65 G
M.P. 86

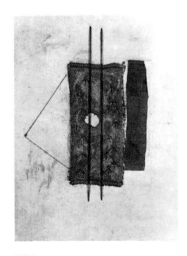

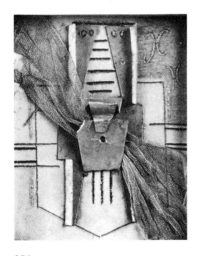

250
Guitare
Guitar
Spring 1926
Paris
Ropes, newsprint, hessian and nails on
painted canvas
130 × 96
Z.VII, 9; Duncan, p. 211; S. 65 H
M.P. 87

251
Guitare
Guitar
29 April 1926
Paris
Cardboard, gauze, string, crayon strokes on
cardboard
12.5 × 10.4
S.D. on back: *Picasso/FECIT/29 Avril 1926*
S. 65 A
M.P. 88

252
Guitare
Guitar
31 [sic] April 1926
Paris
Gauze, ink-painted cardboard, string and
braid on cardboard
14.2 × 9.5
D. on back: *31/Avril/1926*
S. 65 B
M.P. 89

248   Glass, Pipe, Ace of Clubs and Die

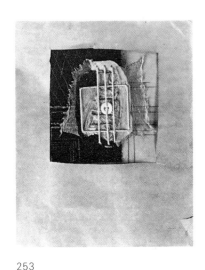

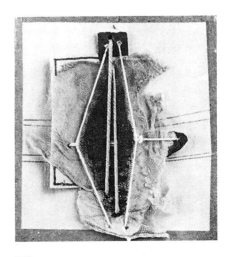

253
Guitare
Guitar
1 May 1926
Paris
String, pieces of cloth, ink-painted cardboard,
button, crayon and ink strokes on cardboard
15.8 × 15.2
D. on back: *1er MAI/ 1926*
S. 65 C
M.P. 90

254
Guitare
Guitar
2 May 1926
Paris
Cardboard, string, gauze, lead shot, ink,
gouache and crayon strokes on cardboard
24.5 × 19.5
D. on back: *2/ MAI/ 1926*
S. 65 D
M.P. 91

255
Guitare
Guitar
May 1926
Paris
Ink-painted cardboard, string, gauze and
crayon strokes on cardboard
13.8 × 12.6
D. on back: *mai/ 1926*
S. 65 E
M.P. 92

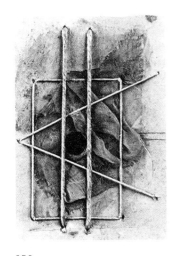

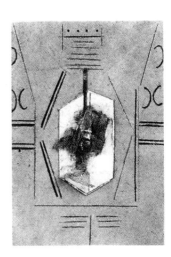

256
Guitare
Guitar
May 1926
Paris
Gauze, string, button and crayon strokes on
cardboard
14 × 10
D. on back: *mai/ 1926*
Z.VII, 21; S. 65
M.P. 93

257
Guitare
Guitar
May 1926
Paris
String, nails, ink and oil-painted cardboard,
button, pieces of cloth, ink and strokes of
crayon on cardboard
24.7 × 12.3
D. on back: *mai/ 1926*
S. 65 F
M.P. 95

258
Guitare
Guitar
April–May 1926
Paris
Paper, lead shot and metal, gauze, string and
crayon strokes on cardboard
14 × 10
D. on back: *1926*
Z.VII, 20; S. 64
M.P. 94

1930

264   Composition with a Glove

259
Baigneuse et profil
Bather and Profile
14 August 1930
Juan-les-Pins
Sand on back of canvas and stretcher;
cardboard and plants stuck and sewn on to
the canvas
27 × 35 × 3
D. on back: *Juan les Pins/le 14 Août/1930/(I)*
S. 76
M.P. 125

260
Visage aux deux profils
Face with Two Profiles
14 August 1930
Juan-les-Pins
Sand, stained in places, on back of canvas
and stretcher; cardboard pasted and sewn on
to the canvas
41 × 33 × 1.5
D. on back: *Juan les Pins/le 14 Août/1930/(II)*
S. 77
M.P. 126

261
Baigneuse debout
Standing Bather
14 August 1930
Juan-les-Pins
Sand on back of canvas and stretcher;
miscellaneous items, cardboard and plants
pasted and sewn on to the canvas
33 × 24.5 × 2
D. on back: *Juan les Pins/le 14 Août 1930/
Villa Bachlyk/Avenue de l'Estérel/(III)*
S. 118
M.P. 124

262
Baigneuse couchée
Reclining Bather
20 August 1930
Juan-les-Pins
Sand, stained in places, on back of canvas
and stretcher; miscellaneous items, string and
cardboard pasted and sewn on to the canvas
24 × 35 × 2
D. on back: *Juan les Pins/20 Août 1930*
S. 118 A
M.P. 127

263
Composition
Composition
21 August 1930
Juan-les-Pins
Sand on canvas; wood and plants pasted and
sewn on to the canvas
35 × 27.5 × 3.5
D. on back: *22* [crossed out] *21 Août 1930/
Juan les Pins/Villa Bachlyk*
S. 119
M.P. 128

264
Composition au gant
Composition with a Glove
22 August 1930
Juan-les-Pins
Sand, stained in places, on back of canvas
and stretcher; glove, cardboard and plants
pasted and sewn on to the canvas
27.5 × 35.5 × 8
S. 75
M.P. 123

265
Objet à la feuille de palmier
Object with a Palm Frond
27 August 1930
Juan-les-Pins
Sand, stained in places, on the back of canvas
and stretcher; plants, cardboard, nails and
miscellaneous items pasted and sewn on to
the canvas
25 × 33 × 4.5
D. on back: *Juan/le 27 Août 1930*
S. 78
M.P. 129

266
Paysage aux bateaux
Landscape with Ships
28 August 1930
Juan-les-Pins
Sand, stained in places, on back of canvas
and stretcher; plants, cardboard and small
ships pasted and sewn on to the canvas
26.5 × 36 × 7
D. on back: *28 AOÛT 1930/JUAN LES PINS*
S. 117
M.P. 130

267
Composition au papillon
Composition with a Butterfly
15 September 1932
Boisgeloup
Cloth, wood, plants, string, drawing pin,
butterfly and oil paint on canvas
16 × 22 × 2.5
D a.: *Boisgeloup*; on l.: *15*;
on r.: *Septembre XXXII*
S. 116
Purchase 1982
M.P. 1982–169

268
Femme assise dans un fauteuil
Woman Seated in an Armchair
1 February 1940
Royan
String and pieces of painted cardboard sewn
on to cardboard painted in oils
17.5 × 15 × 1.5
D.a.r.: *1.2.40.*
S. 182
M.P. 184

269
Femme assise dans un fauteuil
Woman Seated in an Armchair
2 February 1940
Royan
String and pieces of painted cardboard sewn
on to cardboard painted in oils
17.3 × 14.9 × 3.7
D.b.r.: *2.2.40.*
S. 183
M.P. 185

270
Femme assise aux bras levés
Woman Seated with Raised Arms
February 1940
Royan
String and pieces of painted cardboard sewn
on to cardboard painted in oils
15 × 12 × 1
S. 185
M.P. 186

267   Composition with a Butterfly

Vallauris, September 1952 (Photo Robert Doisneau)

Sculptures

It has already been pointed out that no collection in the world will ever be able to match the comprehensive set of sculptures held by the Musée Picasso. Every phase is represented, and often almost the entire output of a particular period, since the artist retained so much of it in his studio. Further acquisitions have come to supplement the original settlement, such as the *Femme se coiffant* (*Woman Dressing her Hair*, cat. 277) of 1906, the *Empreinte de papier froissé* (*Imprint of Crumpled Paper*, cat. 357) of 1933–34 and the three bronzes (cat. 348, 353, 355) specially cast for the museum in 1981 (with the consent of Picasso's heirs) from plaster originals of 1933 which had never been used for fear of damaging them. Many of the paintings and an even larger number of the drawings that the museum is fortunate enough to hold show how Picasso's output developed on a broad front and made use of every technique that came to hand. Some of the sculptures that strike one as most spontaneous in character were preceded, as the collection shows, by an astonishingly large number of preparatory drawings. This also refutes a widely held opinion that Picasso never 'probed'.

In addition to preparatory work, however, there are also drawings and pictures derived from sculptures, at those stages when the latter provided the dominant element in the artist's repertoire. Picasso's inner world of imagery found simultaneous outlets in two- and three-dimensional work. Each separate technique made a contribution of its own and the artist frequently switched from one to another, as in his painted sculptures. His ultimate underlying aim was to 'burst asunder the worlds of painting and of sculpture'.[1]

This is not the place to elaborate on the history of Picasso's sculpture, but rather to signpost those major works and series which lend this collection its importance and reveal the astounding diversity of the techniques employed. These range from the most traditional, such as modelling in clay or plaster of Paris, to the least conventional (assembling, imprinting, cutting out) by way of the wholly rudimentary (direct woodcarving, for instance).

The Wood Sculptures of 1906–1907

Picasso's first wooden sculptures date from 1906. It was a surprising technique for him to use, more or less abandoned by other artists except, of course, for Gauguin, with whose work he had become familiar since 1901 thanks to Paco Durio. The great Salon d'Automne Gauguin retrospective exhibition in 1906 did no more than revive Picasso's interest in the author of *Noa-Noa*, a copy of which he owned. Picasso's first work in wood, as one might expect from a painter, was a carved printing block, on a worthless panel from some old piece of furniture (cat. 274). The works that followed were probably produced during the summer spent at Gosol. One of these, the *Buste de femme* (*Bust of a Woman*, cat. 275) – almost certainly Fernande, to judge by its similarity to the head (cat. 273) produced before he left Paris – has a number of puzzling features. There is an imbalance between the very carefully carved and polished face and the rest of the block, left virtually in the rough: black strokes of paint

(1) A. Malraux (quoting Picasso), *La Tête d'obsidienne*, Paris, 1974, p. 33.

marking the bust and arms suggest that Picasso may well have contemplated further work on this piece, as indicated by drawings in the *Carnet catalan*.[2] Red paint on the face is overlaid by white smudges, possibly the result of an impression taken from it at some stage. The block also bears an inscription, unfortunately blurred and illegible, but which may conceivably refer to painting, since other wooden sculptures, such as the *Nu debout* (*Standing Nude*, cat. 279), were covered in paint. The following year's wood carvings are more primitive in character, both in terms of technique, being crudely carved, and in an approach to design which links them with the major painting of that period, *Les Demoiselles d'Avignon*. Iberian works of art originating from the excavations at Osuna shown at the Louvre in 1906; a first visit, probably in June 1907, to the Musée d'Ethnographie du Trocadéro; and the acquisition – perhaps even at this early date – of primitive art objects, all provide a background for this set of works. The crudest – one might even say the coarsest – of these is the *Figure* (cat. 281), barely indicated in a rough log and endowed with features picked out in red and white paint. Its conception is not unlike that of a Marquesas Islands *tiki* owned by Picasso since 1907, according to Kahnweiler.[3]

Apollinaire and the Marquesas Islands *tiki*.
Boulevard de Clichy studio, 1910–11
(Picasso Archives)

Cubism 1909–1915

During these few years, painting and sculpture came to be more intimately entwined and inevitably interdependent in the artist's output than they had been before and would ever be again, as a result of the Cubist quest for space rendered without resort to illusion.

This period was inaugurated in 1909 by the *Tête de femme (Fernande)* (*Head of a Woman* [*Fernande*], cat. 286), an image constructed from fragments and shattered planes. Such an approach makes perfect sense when dealing with an object in the two dimensions which define a picture surface: a volume must be flattened and this can only be done by breaking it up. It is, however, rather surprising when applied to the three dimensions of real space in sculpture. But be that as it may, this work introduced a new method of using planes in the treatment of volumes. It led to a reinterpretation of concepts such as fullness and emptiness, concavity and convexity, frontal and lateral views, plane and perspective, as the constructions dating from 1912–14 demonstrate. These came into being at the same time as the *papiers collés* and use a variety of components to make up spatial structures. Yet this is not a space freely and frankly employing three dimensions. Most of these items must be viewed from the front and merely differ from picture reliefs by the fact that the background contributes nothing to the object. In fact, *The Glass of Absinthe* of 1914 (New York, The Museum of Modern Art) is the only piece of sculpture dating from this period done genuinely in the round. As for the rest, since Cubism represents a form of realism, a feeling for the object in its own right is revealed in these items by the materials themselves, more often than not consisting of recycled scrap used in its original condition, and by the themes or, more accurately, the single theme of still-life. Examples of this are the *Guitars* (cardboard, string and paper, cat. 287, 288), *Mandoline et clarinette* (*Mandolin and Clarinet*, constructed from partly painted pieces of wood, cat. 289), *Bouteille de Bass, verre et journal* (*Bottle of Bass, Glass and Newspaper*, a tin of powdered milk, labelled *Compagnie française du lait sec*, cut out, folded and painted, cat. 290), the glasses (tin or wood, cat. 291, 292; they also recur in picture reliefs such as *Verre, journal et dé* [*Glass, Newspaper and Die*] housed in a sort of cigar box, cat. 246, and in paintings such as *Verre et paquet de tabac* [*Glass and Packet of Tobacco*] painted on the lid of the same box, cat. 44), and *Violon* (*Violin*, tin cut out, folded and painted, cat. 295). Volume creeps into paintings and picture reliefs, while paint is almost always present in the sculptures. Picasso told Gonzalez that he proposed to dissect paintings and lodge the resulting pieces in space: 'All that would be needed would be to cut up these paintings – since colours are, when all is said and done, no more than indications of different perspectives, of planes tilted in one direction or another – and then to assemble the pieces following the indications provided by the colours in order to find oneself facing a "sculpture".'[4]

(2) Picasso, *Carnet catalan*, facsimile edition, Paris, 1958.

(3) D.-H. Kahnweiler, *Juan Gris, sa vie, son œuvre ses écrits*, Paris, 1946, pp. 155–56, Note 1, quoted by W. Rubin, 'From narrative to iconic in Picasso', *Art Bulletin*, December 1983, Vol. LXV, No. 4, p. 646.

(4) Picasso, quoted by Julio Gonzalez in 'Picasso sculpteur', *Cahiers d'Art*, 1936, Vol. XI, No. 6–7, p. 189.

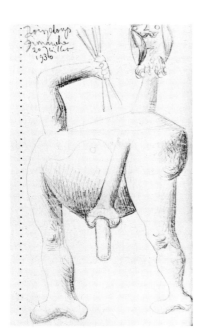

Drawing, Boisgeloup, 20 July 1930
(Artist's Estate)

Picasso's sculpture then went into abeyance until 1928, except for the *Verre et paquet de tabac* (*Glass and Packet of Tobacco*, cat. 300), the large *Guitar* (cat. 301) of 1924 and work done for the stage, in particular the *Parade* ballet costumes.

In Gonzalez's Studio 1928–1930

During a summer spent in Dinard in 1928, Picasso drew in a sketchbook[5] some thread-like figures consisting of lines connecting a series of dots. A small circle with eyes and a mouth topping each of these drawings enables one to guess that these represent women, like the bathers that crowd the rest of this sketchbook. A few weeks later, the figures became small sculptures made of wire, as the drawings suggested. Two such sculptures (cat. 306, 307) were offered – and turned down – as maquettes for a monument to Apollinaire on the tenth anniversary of his death. Picasso produced these wire sculptures in the studio of Julio Gonzalez, an old friend ever since the turn of the century in Barcelona. He thus secured the technical assistance of a specialist who commanded both the essential skills and the requisite materials. Such designs by Picasso called a new form of craftsmanship into being, which in turn launched a formal renewal by the innovative techniques which it introduced. The small cut-out and partly painted metal *Tête* (*Head*, cat. 304), which had been foreshadowed in a series of drawings, was followed by four wire figures (three of which are in the museum, cat. 305–307). These introduced void and transparency as essential ingredients of sculpture, as witness the major creation of this period *La femme au jardin* (*The Woman in the Garden*, cat. 310), a monumental work more than two metres high. The iconography involved – the woman's windswept hair, the table, the vegetative elements, such as the philodendron twigs that also occur in paintings – assembles such elements in accordance with the grammar of Synthetic Cubism. Pieces of iron, stray objects from around the studio and sheet-iron cut out along a drawn outline have been soldered together and covered in white paint to mask the ill-assorted nature of the assemblage and impart unity to this work. It is very closely related in its conception to the *Tête de femme* (*Head of a Woman*, cat. 311), though the latter is rather less sophisticated and makes greater play with the recycling of its components, such as colanders and springs. The counterpart of this work may be seen in the bewhiskered *Tête d'homme* (*Head of a Man*, cat. 312), also produced in Gonzalez's studio, which recurs in drawings dating from the summer of 1930 as the head of a kind of centaur.[6]

The Artist's Own Studio: Boisgeloup 1930–1935

Picasso bought the Château de Boisgeloup in June 1930 and went to live there in May of the following year. It seems likely, however, that he spent some time there from the very start[7] and produced the series of archaistic figures (cat. 313–324) carved with a knife from poorish-quality, probably re-used, pieces of wood. Their elongated shape prompted the creation of small female figures and Picasso carefully preserved the rough patches, knots and fibres in them. At least one of these displays the easily identifiable profile of Marie-Thérèse Walter (cat. 314). Marie-Thérèse, the artist's new mistress, was a well-loved and ubiquitous model. Her strikingly sculptural face – high and projecting cheek-bones, a nose which carried on the line of the forehead, a full mouth with lightly parted lips and a rounded chin – prompted the artist to return to modelling. This resulted in the large heads of 1931 (cat. 337, 339, 340). The pristine

(5) Sketchbook 1044, Dinard, July 1928–Paris, December 1928, published in *Pablo Picasso: Werke aus der Sammlung Marina Picasso*, a catalogue edited by W. Spies, Munich, 1981, pp. 141–55.

(6) See note below for a change in the dating of this work.

(7) See note below for a change in the dating of the cat. 313 item.

whiteness of the plaster originals was so important to Picasso that he was extremely reluctant to allow them to be cast in bronze and only eventually yielded to the entreaties of Sabartés. It is worth pointing out that, in several cases, the Musée Picasso owns both the plaster original and a bronze cast (the latter often unique), as well as a cement copy. The sculptor picked out certain features of the face which he was interpreting – such as the nose, cheek-bones, eyes or hair – and then brought them together again, thereby reassembling a head or bust (cat. 332, 334). 'In the round' is a particularly apt description of these works, all curves and curlicues, as it is also of the *Baigneuses* (*Bathers*, cat. 330, 331). Sculpture was now at the centre of the artist's output to such an extent that it even provided a subject for painting, as in the picture of *Le sculpteur* (*The Sculptor*, cat. 113), or in the series of prints dealing with the sculptor's studio in the *Vollard Suite* of 1933–34. The latter provided a 'parable', in which we see the sculptor, in his classical mask, 'let his lingering gaze sweep back and forth between the eternal feminine model, *whom he also takes time off to caress*, and the block which embodies the infinite possibilities of representation'.[8]

In 1933, while still at Boisgeloup, Picasso tried out a new approach by using plaster of Paris to take impressions of the texture of various materials (such as gratings and corrugated cardboard), or objects (moulds, boxes and leaves). He probably first produced trial pieces, such as the *Empreinte de papier froissé* (*Imprint of Crumpled Paper*, cat. 357, photographed by Brassaï for inclusion in the first book published about Picasso's sculpture in 1949, a sign of the importance which he attached to it).[9] He then conceived human figures consisting of a set of imprints, such as the *Buste d'homme barbu* (*Bust of a Bearded Man*, cat. 354), *Femme accoudé* (*Woman Leaning on her Elbow*, cat. 356) and *La femme à l'orange* (*The Woman with an Orange*, cat. 361). Probably the best known of all these is *La femme au feuillage* (*Woman with Leaves*, cat. 360) which so delighted Malraux. He recalled in connection with it how aware Picasso had been of even the most inconspicuous objects and how he had 'harvested' them for inclusion in his works.[10]

Drawing, 19 April 1937 (M.P. 1190)

1937: *L'orateur* (*The Orator*)

The Orator (cat. 364), one hand raised, came after the figures built up from imprints of textures. It first appeared in two drawings dated 19 April 1937, only a week before the bombing of Guernica, when Picasso was still busy with a first design featuring the artist and his model for the Spanish pavilion at the Paris International Exhibition, which was due to open in June of that year.[11] It is remarkable that this figure should by that time already have carried such a clear political message: the raised arm, now missing in the sculptural version, held the hammer and sickle aloft in a clenched fist.[12]

1942: *Tête de taureau* (*Head of a Bull*)

The *Head of a Bull* (cat. 370) is probably one of the most famous compositions of the twentieth century. It stands out by its economy of materials, the combination of a bicycle saddle and a pair of handlebars picked up from a scrap heap. Picasso arranged to have this assembly cast in bronze, counting on the ability of the metal to impart such a sense of unity to unrelated objects that their real nature would be disguised. What we see here, however, are the actual

(8) A. Breton, 'Picasso dans son élément', *Minotaure*, Paris, No. 1, 1933, p. 21.

(9) D.-H. Kahnweiler, *Les Sculptures de Picasso* (photographs by Brassaï), Paris, 1949, No. 176.

(10) A. Malraux, 1974, p. 33.

(11) This interpretation has been suggested to us by D. Bozo.

(12) See note below for a change in the dating of this sculpture.

components – leather saddle and iron handlebars – brought together and preserving the transitory nature of the original work. Picasso liked to think that the composition might fall apart at any moment and go back to being the saddle and handlebars of a bicycle.

Vallauris, 1950 (Picasso Archives)

1943: *L'homme au mouton* (*Man with a Sheep*)

Man with a Sheep (cat. 375) was heralded – and probably also followed – by a number of drawings. At this stage of the artist's sculptural output, a fully modelled monumental figure may appear surprising. The clay model was produced in the course of a single afternoon in the huge rue des Grands-Augustins studio and cast in plaster on the spot because it was in danger of collapsing: this accounts for the somewhat cursory treatment of the legs and feet, which Picasso lacked time to complete.[13] The size and treatment impart a classicist character to the work, further stressed by the theme: the Good Shepherd (a Christian symbol derived from antiquity) or, more generally still, an image of humanity as a whole. Picasso himself, however, vehemently denied any symbolic intention: 'There's nothing religious about it at all. The man might just as well be carrying a pig, instead of a lamb. There's no symbolism in it. It's merely beautiful. . . . In the *Man with a Sheep* I have expressed a human feeling, a feeling that exists now as it has always existed.'[14]

At Vallauris 1950–1951

Picasso's resumption of intense sculptural activity in 1949 may well have been due to having a large studio at his disposal once more, part of a disused scent factory in the rue du Fournas at Vallauris. Here he introduced yet another technique: a number of the works dating from this time are made up of stray objects picked by the artist on the strength of their shape or texture and assembled by smothering them in plaster, which served as a bond and allowed only such form or texture to show as needed to be seen. Picasso was an inspired scavenger, picking up an assortment of objects which he re-used, as he had earlier done in the constructions of 1914 and in the textural imprints of 1933–34, usually without any preconceived ideas: the *objet trouvé* was to generate the work. Sometimes, however, an idea would come to him and Picasso would then set out to look for objects that might help to embody it. Françoise Gilot reports that this was the case with *La chèvre* (*The Goat*, cat. 383): Picasso no longer had himself driven to his studio, but made his way to it on foot instead, in order to 'do the dustbins' as he went along, and to pick over the rubbish dump![15] In *The Goat*, a palm frond provides the back, an old wicker basket the belly, the legs consist of scrap iron, the udder of two clay pots, the breastbone of a tin can, and the beard and horns are vine-stocks. The animal was thus gradually fashioned in the plaster that held and united these unrelated elements, which nevertheless remained recognizable in all their diversity, and often incompatibility. The charm of the unforeseen, and the consequent pleasure of exploration, vanished once the work had been cast in bronze, as may clearly be seen in the museum, since it owns both the plaster and bronze versions of *The Goat* (cat. 383, 384).

Several monumental sculptures were assembled in the same way, including *La femme à la poussette* (*Woman with a Push Chair*, cat. 382), of which the museum owns a bronze cast, and *Petite fille sautant à la corde* (*Little Girl Skipping*, cat. 381). In the latter, the plaster conceals the component elements more thoroughly than in *The Goat*, but a large number of

(13) See Brassaï, *Picasso & Co.*, New York, 1966, London, 1967, p. 161.

(14) Picasso, in 'Permanence du sacré', *XXe siècle*, December 1964, No. 24, quoted by C. Piot, *Décrire Picasso*, doctoral thesis, Université de Paris I, October 1981, p. 349.

(15) See F. Gilot, C. Lake, *Life with Picasso*, New York, 1964, London, 1965, p. 293.

photographs taken in the studio (as also in the case of *The Goat*) reveal what might appropriately be described as the girl's underwear, since her skirt had once been part of a newspaper. There are also *La grue* (*The Crane*, cat. 386), *La liseuse* (*Woman Reading*, cat. 387), *La petite chouette* (*The Little Owl*, cat. 388), *La guenon et son petit* (*Baboon with Young*, cat. 390) and *L'arrosoir fleuri* (*The Flowering Watering Can*, cat. 391), the original plaster casts of which are in the museum, while those bronzes that have been cast and painted, such as the *Crâne de chèvre, bouteille et bougie* (*Goat's Skull, Bottle and Candle*, cat. 392), vary in their colouring from copy to copy, a practice already adopted by Picasso in 1914 for the six copies of the *Verre d'absinthe* (*Glass of Absinthe*.) The numerous pregnant women who populate the output of this period – announcements of the recent birth of the two children of Picasso and Françoise Gilot, Claude in 1947 and Paloma in 1949 – also deserve a mention. The bronze version of *La femme enceinte* (*The Pregnant Woman*, cat. 385) might suggest that this work had been completely modelled, whereas the belly and breasts in fact originally consisted of earthenware water jugs.

1956: *Les baigneurs* (*The Bathers*)

Picasso made up a cast of six characters (cat. 394–399) in drawings dating from September 1956 and in sketchbooks devoted to a decorative project for UNESCO in 1957 and 1958.[16] The scene was set at the seaside: the woman diver and the man with his hands clasped on the pier, the woman with outstretched arms and the young man on a diving board, and the fountain man and the child in the water. These sculptures (of which the museum owns the bronze casts) were originally made of assembled pieces of wood – planks, often cut to new shapes, picture frames, broomsticks, bed legs – with various anatomical indications carved into the surface, such as facial features, details of torsos, genitals and legs. These are flat pieces of sculpture intended for frontal presentation. They once more confirm Picasso's liking for assembling materials and for the use of found objects.

Design for the decoration of the UNESCO building, 15 December 1957 (M.P. 1518)

From Sheet-iron Cut-outs to Concrete 1954–1962

It was earlier pointed out that the *Tête de femme (Fernande)* (*Head of a Woman* [*Fernande*]) of 1909 (cat. 286) launched a new approach to the treatment of space by means of planes. One of the manifold applications of this invention was the use of sheet-iron, cut out, assembled and/ or folded and set up in space. The first works of this kind were the busts of Sylvette in 1954, followed by the women's heads, which Picasso clearly intended for monumental use (such as that in wood [cat. 401] which he surrounded with small human figures;[17] and that in sheet-iron [cat. 402], which he proposed as a monument at Barcarès). He again obtained technical assistance for his experimental work, this time from Lionel Prejger,[18] whose factory at Vallauris produced tubing by a folding process. Picasso had visited it in 1960 and the sheet-iron cut-outs that now followed in large numbers were manufactured there, including *La chaise* (*The Chair*, cat. 405), *Pierrot assis* (*Seated Pierrot*, cat. 411) and the *Footballers* (cat. 412, 413). Picasso cut out a maquette of paper or cardboard by 'drawing' it, as it were, with his scissors and then shaped it by folding. Such a model might start by being smaller than the projected work and later be enlarged to the proper scale. The sculpture would next be cut out of the metal sheet under the artist's supervision, several copies sometimes being taken from the

(16) Zervos XVII, 160 (*inter alia*) and sketchbooks M.P. 1884 and M.P. 1885.

(17) See note below for a change in the dating of this sculpture.

(18) See L. Prejger, 'Picasso découpe le fer', *L'Œil*, Paris, October 1961, No. 82, pp. 28ff.

same master pattern. The main figure in *Femme à l'enfant* (*Woman and Child*, cat. 410), for instance, reappears in another sculpture, *Femme au plateau et à la sébille* (*Woman with Tray and Bowl*). Finally, the sheet-iron would be painted, normally in white, but here too one may meet with several variously coloured versions of the same figure, such as the four variants of *Femme au chapeau* (*Woman with a Hat*, cat. 408), one of which is polychrome.

Picasso's lifelong hankering after monumental work underlies these endeavours. It was to bear fruit in 1956 when he met a Norwegian artist, Carl Nesjar, who initiated him into the opportunities made available by the use of concrete in sculpture. As a result, the small *Femme aux bras écartés* (*Woman with Outstretched Arms*, cat. 406) cut out of an album page (in which the jagged edges of the paper torn from the spiral wire binding represent the fingers) first evolved into a large cut-out and painted sheet-iron figure (cat. 407) and then into a concrete monument, six metres high, erected in the garden of Kahnweiler's estate at Saint-Hilaire, Essonne.

This accounts for the inclusion in this section of some small cardboard figures, cut out and folded, that were previously classified as drawings (cat. 414–417). They are in fact studies for a monumental *Déjeuner sur l'herbe*, four of which have indeed been carried out in concrete in the garden of the Moderna Museet in Stockholm.

H.S.

Changes in Dating from that given in the 1979 Catalogue

As in the case of the picture reliefs, only fully documented alterations are given below. The majority of these were established in conjunction with Werner Spies and Christine Piot during the preparation of the 'Picasso Plastiken' exhibition, Berlin, Nationalgalerie (7 Oct.–27 Nov. 1983) and Düsseldorf, Kunsthalle (11 Dec. 1983–4 Feb. 1984). A new edition of W. Spies, *Picasso, Das plastische Werk*, Stuttgart, 1971 (*Picasso Sculpture*, London, 1972) was published in this connection in 1983, containing a catalogue of the output compiled by C. Piot and W. Spies.

Cat. 275 (M.P. 233)
Several drawings closely related to this sculpture appear in a sketchbook of the Gosol period, the so-called *Carnet catalan*, published in facsimile by Berggruen et Cie, Paris, 1958; see p. 3 and p. 53).

Cat. 287 (M.P. 244)
The newspaper used in this construction mentions 2 December, thus providing an earliest possible date. Cat. 288 has been dated [December] 1912 by analogy with cat. 287.

Cat. 304 (M.P. 263)
One of the three copies of this sculpture, which differs slightly from that in the museum, was reproduced in *Cahiers d'Art*, Paris, 1929, No. 1, p. 11, and dated October 1928.

Cat. 305 (M.P. 266)
Published in *Cahiers d'Art*, 1929, No. 1, p. 6 and dated October 1928. This allows one to suggest a similar date in autumn 1928 for the other two wire constructions.

Cat. 308 (M.P. 286)
A drawing certainly made after this sculpture and dated 11 May 1929 occurs in a sketchbook held by the Musée Picasso (M.P. 1875). It is reproduced in Spies, p. 129, but wrongly dated.

Fig. 1
Drawing of 6 October 1931
(Artist's Estate)

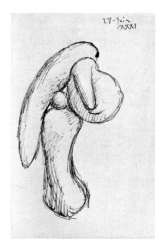

Fig. 2
Drawing of 28 June 1931
(Artist's Estate)

Fig. 3
Drawing of 6 September 1931
(Artist's Estate)

Cat. 309 (M.P. 287)
The same sketchbook (M.P. 1875) contains a drawing on a sheet dated 7–8 May 1929 which was probably made after this sculpture. It is reproduced in Spies, p. 129, but with the same dating error as for cat. 308.

Cat. 311 (M.P. 270)
The first sheets in the sketchbook mentioned above (M.P. 1875), dated 25 February 1929– 12 January 1930, carry a number of studies which comprise some elements of this head. It is reproduced in Spies, p. 114 and p. 117, but wrongly dated.

Fig. 4
Drawing of 13 June 1931
(Artist's Estate)

Fig. 5
La femme à l'orange (*The Woman with an Orange*) in the Boisgeloup studio, *c.* 1934
(Picasso Archives)

Fig. 6
Vallauris, September 1952
(Photo Robert Doisneau)

Cat. 312 (M.P. 269)
A sketchbook (Artist's Estate) contains a series of drawings for this head, some of which are dated July 1930 (ill. p. 143). This work is also reproduced in E. d'Ors, *Pablo Picasso*, Paris, 1930, a reference quoted by W. Rubin in the catalogue of the 'Pablo Picasso: A Retrospective' exhibition, New York, The Museum of Modern Art, 1980, p. 459.

Cat. 313 (M.P. 283)
This small wooden figurine is marked on the underside of its base with a date that had not previously been recorded: '27 [or 29] sptb [septembre] XXX'. The dating of the entire series has been derived from this. Several of the drawings and sketchbooks dating from the summer and autumn of 1930 are marked 'Boisgeloup'. Picasso must therefore have stayed there during that year and probably produced these small sculptures.

Cat. 330 (M.P. 289)
A drawing (Artist's Estate), dated 6 October 1931, shows this sculpture. In fact, it is more likely to represent a drawing after it than a study for it (Fig. 1).

Cat. 331 (M.P. 290)
Drawings closely related to the *Baigneuse allongée* (*Stretched-out Bather*) occur in a sketchbook several pages of which are dated Boisgeloup, September 1931 (Artist's Estate), as well as other drawings (M.P. 1058: Juan-les-Pins, 13 August 1931, reproduced in Spies, p. 144; M.P. 1060 and M.P. 1061: Juan-les-Pins, 16 August 1931) in the museum's collections.

Cat. 332 (M.P. 291)
A sheet dated 28 June 1931 in the sketchbook mentioned above carries a drawing probably made after this sculpture, rather than a study for it (Fig. 2).

Cat. 336 (M.P. 297)
A sheet dated 6 September 1931, Boisgeloup, carries a drawing of this sculpture, once again probably made after it (Fig. 3).

Cat. 338 (M.P. 299)
A sheet dated 13 June 1931, Boisgeloup, from the same sketchbook shows this sculpture in position in the studio (Fig. 4).

Cat. 339 (M.P. 300)
See cat. 338.

Cat. 340 (M.P. 301)
Several drawings in the museum's collections (M.P. 1065–1067) and dated 5 December 1931 should be related to this sculpture (reproduced in C. Lichtenstern, *Picasso, Tête de Femme*, Städelsches Kunstinstitut, Frankfurt-am-Main, 1980, p. 25, and in Spies, p. 150).

Fig. 7
Vallauris, September 1952
(Photo Robert Doisneau)

Fig. 8
Tête de femme (*Head of a Woman*).
Design for a monument
(Photo David Douglas Duncan)

Fig. 9
Drawing of 13 June 1957 (M.P. 1516)

Fig. 10
Paper pattern for *La femme à l'enfant*
(*Woman and Child*), 2 February 1961
(Artist's Estate)

Fig. 11
Drawing of 9 March 1961
(M.P. 1527)

Fig. 12
Paper pattern for *Tête de femme* (*Head
of a Woman*), 9 November 1962
(Artist's Estate)

Cat. 342 (M.P. 296)
This sculpture can be seen in one of the
photographs taken by Brassaï at Boisgeloup
(published in *Minotaure*, No. 1, Paris, 1 June
1933, p. 15 and p. 28, under the title *La
génisse* (*The Heifer*). According to Brassaï's
own statement (*Picasso & Co.*, New York,
1966, London, 1967, pp. 17–18), these
photographs were taken in December 1932.

Cat. 343 (M.P. 323)
The hand can be seen in a photograph taken
by Brassaï in December 1932 at Boisgeloup
(*Minotaure*, No. 1, 1933, p. 17).

Cat. 358 (M.P. 309)
Reproduced in *Cahiers d'Art*, Vol. X, Nos.
7–10, 1935, p. 34 (this refers to the special
number, published in addition to the previous
issue, under the title 'Picasso 1930–1935')
and dated 1934. Cat. 360 has also been dated
in that year, for reasons of similarity.

Cat. 361 (M.P. 327)
An amateur snapshot (Picasso Archives,
Fig. 5) of the Boisgeloup studio shows the
complete sculpture. This picture was most
probably taken before the summer of 1935,
the last Picasso spent there before he was
forced to hand over the Château de
Boisgeloup to Olga. The work can be dated
1934 on the strength of other works in its
vicinity.

Cat. 364 (M.P. 318)
This sculpture appears in a set of two
drawings dated *19.A[vril].37.* which may
represent either an early suggestion for it or
a study after it for use elsewhere. Both are
in the museum's collections (M.P. 1177,
M.P. 1190, ill. p. 144).

Cat. 370 (M.P. 330)
The photograph of the bronze version was
published as *Objet* (*Object*) and dated 1942
on the cover of *La conquête du monde par
l'image*, Paris, April 1942. The handlebars and
saddle were found separately when the
inventory of the estate was drawn up and
were combined in 1984, using the bronze as a
guide.

Cat. 371 (M.P. 325)
A photograph taken by Doisneau at Vallauris
in September 1952 (Musée Picasso
Document) shows this head as having already
been painted by that date (Fig. 6).

Cat. 375 (M.P. 331)
A series of drawings on the theme of a man
carrying a sheep was made between July
1942 and March 1943 (see Zervos XII in
several places). The sculpture had been
completed by the time Françoise Gilot met
Picasso in May 1943 (see F. Gilot, C. Lake,
Life with Picasso, New York, 1964, London,
1965, p. 17). According to Brassaï, the work
was produced in the course of an afternoon
(*Picasso & Co.*, p. 161). See A. Bowness,
'Picasso's Sculpture', in *Picasso in Retrospect*,
New York, 1980, p. 97 and p. 192, note 42.

Cat. 390 (M.P. 342)
This carries a date and all similar sculptures
(cat. 386–389 and 391) have been dated by
analogy with it.

Cat. 391 (M.P. 329)
This work appears, as yet unfinished, in a
photograph by Doisneau in September 1952
(Musée Picasso Document). See cat. 390
above.

Cat. 392 (M.P. 341)
A series of photographs taken by Doisneau in
September 1952 (Musée Picasso Document)
shows the bronze cast being unpacked at the
Vallauris studio before it was painted (Fig. 7).

Cat. 394–399 (M.P. 352–357)
The first drawings definitely made after
Les baigneurs (*The Bathers*) are dated
8 September 1956 (Zervos XVII, 161–65;
see W. Spies, *Pablo Picasso, Werke aus der
Sammlung Marina Picasso*, Munich, 1981,
pp. 260–61).

Cat. 401 (M.P. 350)
Photographs taken by Duncan, most probably
in 1957 before the publication of his book,
show this sculpture surrounded by a set of
smaller figures (Fig. 8), a confirmation that
this was indeed a design for a monument
(D.D. Duncan, *The Private World of Pablo
Picasso*, New York, 1958, pp. 142–43).
Cat. 400 is a maquette for this sculpture.

Cat. 402 (M.P. 351)
Several drawings dated 13 June 1957 (M.P.
1516 [Fig. 9] among them) show studies
done either for or after this sculpture.

Cat. 404 (M.P. 358)
A drawing made after this sculpture (Zervos
XVIII, 252) is inscribed 'bois. donnée [?] le
10.6.58' (wood. presented [?] 10.6.58).

Cat. 410 (M.P. 361)
The paper pattern for the female figure is
dated 2 February 1961 (Artist's Estate,
Fig. 10).

Cat. 411 (M.P. 364)
A drawing either for or after this sculpture is
dated 9 March 1961 (M.P. 1527, Fig. 11).

Cat. 432 (M.P. 366)
The cut-out paper pattern for the woman's
head is dated 9 November 1962 (Artist's
Estate, Fig. 12).

271
Femme assise
Seated Woman
1902
Barcelona
Unfired clay
14.5 × 8.5 × 11.5
On underside, illegible inscription: *PIC* (?)
S. 1(I)
M.P. 230

272
Le fou
The Jester
1905
Paris
Bronze
41.5 × 37 × 22.8
S. on back: *PICASSO*
Z.I. 322; T.l.o.p.[1], 175 A; S. 4
M.P. 231

273
Tête de femme (Fernande)
Head of a Woman (Fernande)
1906
Paris
Bronze
35 × 24 × 25
S. on back: *PICASSO*
Z.I. 323; S. 6
M.P. 234

274
Tête de femme
Head of a Woman
1906
[Paris]
Carved and inked fir
(for a print: G.I, 212)
56 × 38.5
S. 6 A
M.P. 3541

275
Buste de femme (Fernande)
Bust of a Woman (Fernande)
Summer 1906
Gosol
Shaped boxwood with traces of red paint and
features traced in black paint
77 × 15.5 × 15
Illegible inscription in black paint on the right
of the bust and on the back, also in red paint
on the back
S. 6 C
M.P. 233

276
Nu aux bras levés
Nude with Raised Arms
[Summer 1906]
[Gosol]
Shaped and engraved boxwood
46.5 × 4.5 × 6.5
S. 6 B
M.P. 232

277
Femme se coiffant
Woman Dressing her Hair
1906
Paris
Bronze
42.2 × 26 × 31.8
b.r.: *9/10*, on l., stamp:
CIRE PERDUE C. VALSUANI
Z.I, 329; S. 7
Gift of MM. Pellequer and Colas, 1981
M.P. 1981-3

278
Tête de femme
Head of a Woman
1906–1907
Paris
Bronze
11 × 8 × 9
S. on back: *PICASSO*
Z.II², 574; T.l.o.p.[2], 73; S. 12
M.P. 235

279
Nu debout
Standing Nude
1907
Paris
Carved and painted fruit wood
31.8 × 8 × 3
On back: carved birds painted with gouache
(for two prints: G.I, 213 and 214)
Z.II², 667; T.l.o.p.[2], 69; S. 17
M.P. 236

280
Figure
Figure
1907
Paris
Shaped boxwood bearing traces of crayon;
top of head painted
35.2 × 12.2 × 12
Z.II², 668; T.l.o.p.[2], 70; S. 15
M.P. 237

281
Figure
Figure
1907
Paris
Shaped oak with painted highlights
80.5 × 24 × 20.8
Z.II², 607; T.l.o.p.[2], 65; S. 19
M.P. 238

282
Figure debout
Standing Figure
1907
Paris
Shaped and painted fir
31.5 × 6 × 6
S. 20 A
M.P. 239

280   Figure

286   Head of a Woman (Fernande)

283
Trois nus
Three Nudes
1907
Paris
Carved beech, with engraved edge and crayon
stroked on edge and back
32 × 15.4 × 3.2
S. 17 A
M.P. 240

284
Nu assis
Seated Nude
1908
Paris
Bronze
11 × 9 × 10.5
On back: *P/8/9*
Stamp, b.r.: *CIRE PERDUE C. VALSUANI*
T.l.o.p.[(2)], 193; S. 23
M.P. 241

285
Pomme
Apple
1909
Paris
Plaster
11.5 × 10 × 7.5
Z.II[2], 718–719; T.l.o.p.[(2)], 345; S. 26
M.P. 242

286
Tête de femme (Fernande)
Head of a Woman (Fernande)
Autumn 1909
Paris
Bronze
40.5 × 23 × 26
S.b.r.: *Picasso*
Z.II[2], 573; T.l.o.p.[(2)], 296; S. 24
M.P. 243

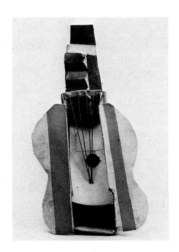

287
Guitare
Guitar
December 1912
Paris
Construction: cardboard cut-out, pasted
paper, cloth, string, oil and traces of crayon
33 × 18 × 9.5
Z.II[2], 770; T.l.o.p.[(2)], 528; D.R. 555; S. 30
M.P. 244

288
Guitare
Guitar
[December] 1912
Paris
Construction: cardboard cut-out, pasted
paper, cloth, string and crayon strokes
22 × 14.5 × 7
Z.II[2], 779; T.l.o.p.[(2)], 530; D.R. 556; S. 29
M.P. 245

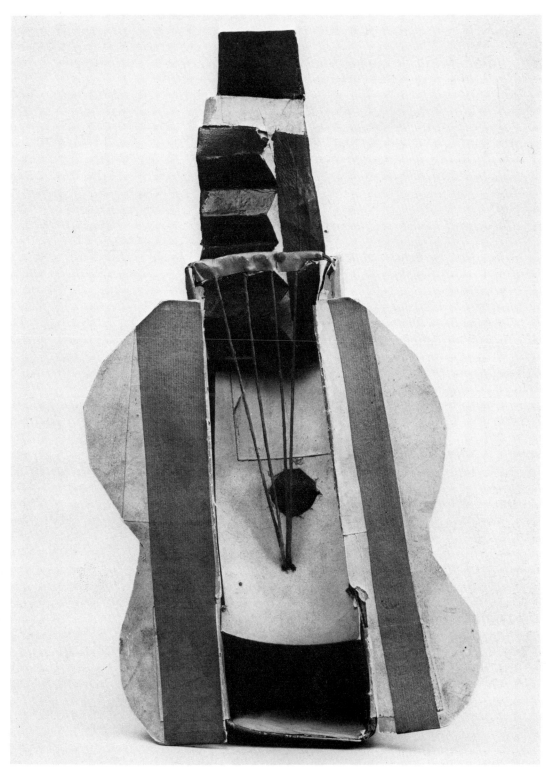

287 Guitar

289   Mandolin and Clarinet

290   Bottle of Bass, Glass and Newspaper

289
Mandoline et clarinette
Mandolin and Clarinet
[Autumn 1913]
Paris
Construction: fir components with paint and crayon strokes
58 × 36 × 23
Z.II², 853; T.l.o.p.(²), 784; D.R. 632; S. 54
M.P. 247

290
Bouteille de Bass, verre et journal
Bottle of Bass, Glass and Newspaper
Spring 1914
Paris
Construction: cut-out and painted tin, sand, wire and paper
20.7 × 14 × 8.5
Z.II², 849; T.l.o.p.(²), 795; D.R. 751; S. 53
M.P. 249

291
Verre
Glass
Spring 1914
Paris
Construction: cut-out and painted tin, nails and wood
15 × 23 × 10
Z.II², 848; T.l.o.p.(²), 794; D.R. 752; S. 52
M.P. 250

292
Verre et dé
Glass and Die
Spring 1914
Paris
Construction: painted pine components
17 × 16.2 × 5.5
Z.II², 840; T.l.o.p.(²), 788; D.R. 748; S. 46
M.P. 252

293
Violon et bouteille sur une table
Violin and Bottle on a Table
[Autumn] 1915
Paris
Construction: fir components, string, nails, with paint and charcoal strokes
45 × 41 × 23
Z.II², 926; T.l.o.p.(²), 857; D.R. 833; S. 57
M.P. 253

294
Bouteille d'anis del Mono et compotier avec grappe de raisin
Bottle of Anis del Mono and Fruit Bowl with a Bunch of Grapes
[Autumn] 1915
Paris
Construction: fir and pine components, tin, nails and strokes of charcoal
35.5 × 27.5 × 26
Z.II², 927; T.l.o.p.(²), 856; D.R. 834; S. 58
M.P. 254

294   Bottle of Anis del Mono and Fruit Bowl with a Bunch of Grapes

295   Violin

295
Violon
Violin
[1915]
Paris
Construction: cut-out, folded and painted
sheet-iron, and wire
100 × 63.7 × 18
Z.II², 580; T.l.o.p.(2), 781; D.R. 835; S. 55
M.P. 255

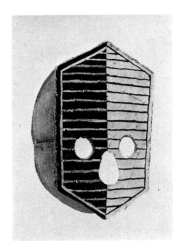

296
Masque
Mask
1919
[Paris]
Cut-out and painted cardboard, and thread
22.5 × 17.5 × 6
Z.XXIX, 465; S. 61 A
M.P. 256

297
Compotier et guitare
Fruit Bowl and Guitar
1919
Paris
Construction: cut-out and painted cardboard,
and cloth
21.5 × 35.5 × 19
Z.III, 414; T.l.o.p.(2), 934; S. 61 D
M.P. 257

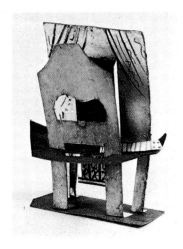

298
Table et guitare devant une fenêtre
Table and Guitar in front of a Window
1919
Paris
Construction: cut-out and painted cardboard,
paper and crayon strokes
12 × 10.5 × 4
Z.III, 415; Z.XXIX, 459; T.l.o.p.(2), 935; S. 61 B
M.P. 258

299
Masque de Pulcinella
Pulcinella Mask
Early 1920
Paris
Painted wood, paper and cloth
17 × 14.5 × 21.5
S. 61 E
M.P. 1790

300
Verre et paquet de tabac
Glass and Packet of Tobacco
1921
Paris
Cut-out, folded and painted sheet-iron, and
wire
14.7 × 49.2 × 16.3
Z.IV, 368; T.l.o.p.(2), 961; S. 62
M.P. 259

301
Guitare
Guitar
1924
Paris
Construction: painted, cut-out and folded
sheet-iron, tin box and wire
111 × 63.5 × 26.6
Z.V, 217; S. 63
M.P. 260

302
Métamorphose I
Metamorphosis I
1928
Paris
Bronze (unique cast)
22.8 × 18.3 × 11
S. 67 (II)
M.P. 261

303
Métamorphose II
Metamorphosis II
1928
Paris
Plaster original
23 × 18 × 11
S. 67 A (I)
M.P. 262

304
Tête
Head
October 1928
Paris
Painted brass and iron
18 × 11 × 7.5
S. 66 A
M.P. 263

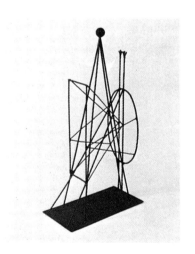

305
Figure
Figure
October 1928
Paris
Wire and sheet-iron
37.5 × 10 × 19.6
S. 71
M.P. 266

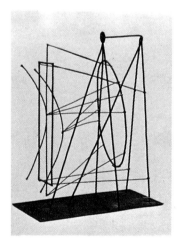

306
Figure
Figure
(suggested as design for a monument to
Guillaume Apollinaire)
Autumn 1928
Paris
Wire and sheet-iron
59.5 × 18.5 × 40.8
S. 68
M.P. 264

307
Figure
Figure
(suggested as design for a monument to
Guillaume Apollinaire)
Autumn 1928
Paris
Wire and sheet-iron
60.5 × 15 × 34
S. 69
M.P. 265

308
Femme assise
Seated Woman
Spring 1929
Paris
Bronze (unique cast)
80.5 × 20 × 22
S. on edge of base plate, back r.: *Picasso*
S. 104 (II)
M.P. 286

309
Femme assise
Seated Woman
Spring 1929
Paris
Bronze (unique cast)
42.5 × 16.5 × 25
S. on the back: *picasso*
S. 106 (II)
M.P. 287

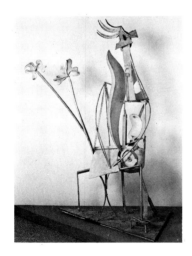

310
La femme au jardin
The Woman in the Garden
1929–1930
Paris
Soldered and painted iron
206 × 117 × 85
S. 72 (I)
M.P. 267

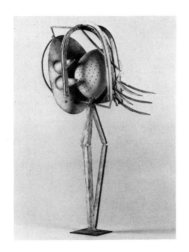

311
Tête de femme
Head of a Woman
1929–1930
Paris
Painted iron, sheet-iron, springs and
colanders
100 × 37 × 59
S. 81
M.P. 270

312
Tête d'homme
Head of a Man
1930
Paris
Iron, brass and bronze
83.5 × 40.5 × 36
S. 80
M.P. 269

311   Head of a Woman

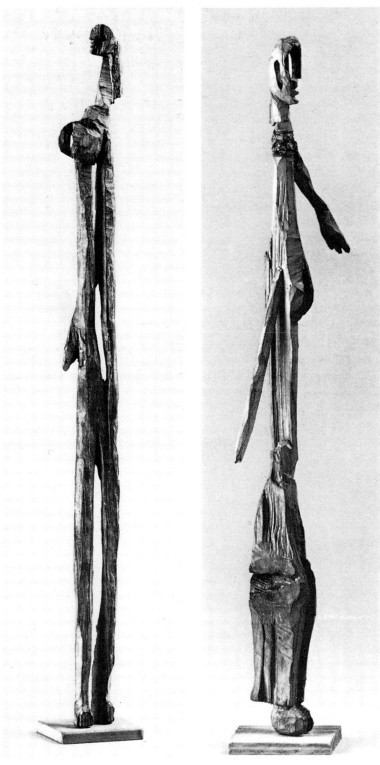

317 Standing Woman   320 Standing Woman   321 Standing Woman

313
Femme debout
Standing Woman
27 (29 ?) September 1930
Boisgeloup
Shaped fir
20.3 × 3.4 × 4
D. underneath base plate in blue ink:
27 [29?] Sptb/XXX
S. 101 (I)
M.P. 283

314
Femme assise
Seated Woman
Autumn 1930
Boisgeloup
Shaped fir
55.7 × 2.5 × 6
S. 86 (I)
M.P. 272

315
Femme debout
Standing Woman
Autumn 1930
Boisgeloup
Shaped fir
51 × 2.3 × 4.4
S. 88 (I)
M.P. 273

316
Femme debout
Standing Woman
Autumn 1930
Boisgeloup
Shaped fir
31.5 × 2.3 × 3.5
S. 89 (I)
M.P. 274

317
Femme debout
Standing Woman
Autumn 1930
Boisgeloup
Shaped fir
48 × 3 × 5
S. 90 (I)
M.P. 275

318
Femme debout
Standing Woman
Autumn 1930
Boisgeloup
Shaped fir
19.5 × 4.5 × 2.3
S. 91 (I)
M.P. 276

319
Femme debout
Standing Woman
Autumn 1930
Boisgeloup
Shaped fir
49.5 × 2.3 × 2.2
S. 93 (I)
M.P. 277

320
Femme debout
Standing Woman
Autumn 1930
Boisgeloup
Shaped fir and wire
47.5 × 5 × 7.5
S. 94 (I)
M.P. 278

321
Femme debout
Standing Woman
Autumn 1930
Boisgeloup
Shaped fir
49 × 5.5 × 2.8
S. 95 (I)
M.P. 279

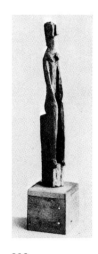

322
Femme assise
Seated Woman
Autumn 1930
Boisgeloup
Shaped fir
17.8 × 2.1 × 2.5
.S. 92 (I)
M.P. 280

323
Femme assise
Seated Woman
Autumn 1930
Boisgeloup
Shaped fir
17.2 × 4.5 × 3.5
S. 99 (I)
M.P. 281

324
Femme assise
Seated Woman
Autumn 1930
Boisgeloup
Shaped fir
15.9 × 3 × 2.9
S. 100 (I)
M.P. 282

325
Buste de femme
Bust of a Woman
[1930]
Boisgeloup
Shaped pine
13 × 5 × 2.5
S. 102 (I)
M.P. 284

326
Couple
Couple
[1930]
Boisgeloup
Shaped lime
10.5 × 3.5 × 2.2
S. 103 (I)
M.P. 285

327
Tête
Head
1931
[Boisgeloup]
Tinted plaster, wood, iron and nails
57 × 48 × 23.5
S. 79
M.P. 268

328
Figure
Figure
1931
[Paris? Boisgeloup?]
Iron and wire
26 × 12.5 × 11.1
S. 84
M.P. 271

329
Femme assise
Seated Woman
1931
Boisgeloup
Plaster original
35 × 23.2 × 30.5
S. 105 (I)
M.P. 288

330
Baigneuse
Bather
1931
Boisgeloup
Bronze (unique cast)
70 × 40,2 × 31.5
Stamped on base plate: *CIRE PERDUE C. VALSUANI*
S. 108
M.P. 289

330   Bather

331
Baigneuse allongée
Stretched-out Bather
1931
Boisgeloup
Bronze (unique cast)
23 × 72 × 31
S. 109 (II)
M.P. 290

332
Tête de femme
Head of a Woman
1931
Boisgeloup
Plaster original
71.5 × 41 × 33
S. 110 (I)
M.P. 291

333
Tête de femme
Head of a Woman
1931
Boisgeloup
Bronze (unique cast)
71.5 × 41 × 33
Stamped on edge of base plate:
CIRE PERDUE, PARIS, E. ROBECCHI
S. 110 (II)
M.P. 292

334
Buste de femme
Bust of a Woman
1931
Boisgeloup
Plaster original
62.5 × 28 × 41.5
S. 111 (I)
M.P. 293

335
Buste de femme
Bust of a Woman
1931
Boisgeloup
Bronze (unique cast)
62.5 × 28 × 41.5
Stamped b.r.: *CIRE PERDUE, PARIS, E. ROBECCHI*
S. 111 (II)
M.P. 294

336
**Tête de femme de profil
(Marie-Thérèse)**
*Head of a Woman in Profile
(Marie-Thérèse)*
1931
Boisgeloup
Bronze (unique cast)
68.5 × 59 × 8
S. 130 (II)
M.P. 297

332   Head of a Woman

337   Bust of a Woman

337
Buste de femme
Bust of a Woman
1931
Boisgeloup
Bronze (unique cast)
78 × 44.5 × 54
S. 131 (II)
M.P. 298

338
Buste de femme
Bust of a Woman
1931
Boisgeloup
Cement
78 × 44.5 × 50
S. 131 (III)
M.P. 299

339
Tête de femme
Head of a Woman
1931
Boisgeloup
Bronze
86 × 32 × 48.5
S. 132 (IIa)
M.P. 300

340
Tête de femme
Head of a Woman
1931
Boisgeloup
Plaster original: plaster and wood
128.5 × 54.5 × 62.5
S. 133 (Ia)
M.P. 301

341
Tête de femme
Head of a Woman
1931
Boisgeloup
Bronze (unique cast)
128.5 × 54.5 × 62.5
S. 133 (II)
M.P. 302

342
Tête de taureau
Head of a Bull
1931–1932
Boisgeloup
Bronze (unique cast)
35 × 55 × 53
S. 127 (II)
M.P. 296

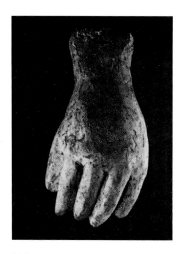

343
Main
Hand
1931–1932
Boisgeloup
Plaster
37 × 19.5 × 11
S. 222
M.P. 323

344
Baigneuse
Bather
1931–1932
Boisgeloup
Plaster original
40.5 × 13.2 × 30.5
S. 113 (I)
M.P. 303

345
Baigneuse aux bras levés
Bather with Raised Arms
1931–1932
Boisgeloup
Bronze (unique cast)
32.5 × 14.7 × 15.5
Stamped on edge of base plate:
CIRE PERDUE C. VALSUANI
S. 114 (II)
M.P. 304

346
Baigneuse
Bather
1931–1932
Boisgeloup
Bronze (unique cast)
56 × 28.5 × 20.5
Stamped on edge of base plate:
CIRE PERDUE, PARIS, E. ROBECCHI
S. 115
M.P. 305

347
Tête de femme
Head of a Woman
1932
Boisgeloup
Plaster original
65 × 43 × 22
S. 120 (I)
M.P. 295

348
Tête de femme
Head of a Woman
1932
Boisgeloup
Bronze (unique cast 21 May 1981)
64.3 × 42.5 × 22
Stamped on edge, b.: *F.C.* [Fondation
Coubertin]; © *Succession Picasso; MNP
épreuve unique*
S. 120 (II)
M.P. 1980–111

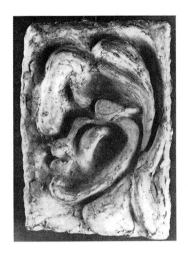

349
Tête de femme de profil
Head of a Woman in Profile
1933
Boisgeloup
Plaster
32.5 × 23 × 7.5
S. 138
M.P. 306

350
Tête de femme de profil
Head of a Woman in Profile
1933
Boisgeloup
Plaster
19 × 16 × 4.5
S. 141
M.P. 307

351
Tête de femme de trois-quarts
Head of a Woman in Three-quarter Profile
1933
Boisgeloup
Plaster
15 × 20.5 × 7
S. 144
M.P. 308

352
Personnage
Character
1933
Boisgeloup
Plaster original
70 × 29 × 15
S. 151 (I)
M.P. 311

353
Personnage
Character
1933
Boisgeloup
Bronze (unique cast, 12 June 1981)
70 × 29 × 15
Stamped on back, b.: *F.C.* [Fondation Coubertin]; *MNP/épreuve unique*; © *succession/Picasso*
S. 151 (II)
M.P. 1980–112

354
Buste d'homme barbu
Bust of a Bearded Man
1933
Boisgeloup
Plaster original
85.5 × 47 × 31
S. 152 (I)
M.P. 312

1934

360   The Woman with Leaves

355
Buste d'homme barbu
Bust of a Bearded Man
1933
Boisgeloup
Bronze (unique cast, 21 May 1981)
85.5 × 47 × 31
Stamped on back, b.: *F.C.* [Fondation
Coubertin]; *MNP/épreuve/unique*; ©
succession Picasso
S. 152 (II)
M.P. 1980–113

356
Femme accoudée
Woman Leaning on her Elbow
1933
Boisgeloup
Bronze (unique cast)
62.2 × 42.5 × 28.9
S. 153 (II)
M.P. 313

357
Empreinte de papier froissé
Imprint of Crumpled Paper
1933–1934
Boisgeloup
Plaster
11 × 31.5 × 24
S. 246
Gift of Marina Ruiz-Picasso, 1983
M.P. 1983–2

358
Visage
Face
1934
Boisgeloup
Plaster
12 × 24.8 × 6.5
S. 148
M.P. 309

359
Masque
Mask
1934
Boisgeloup
Plaster
12.5 × 21.5 × 4
S. 149
M.P. 310

360
La femme au feuillage
The Woman with Leaves
1934
Boisgeloup
Bronze (unique cast)
37.9 × 20 × 25.9
Stamped on base plate on back, l.:
CIRE PERDUE C. VALSUANI
S. 157 (II)
M.P. 314

361
La femme à l'orange
or **La femme à la pomme**
The Woman with an Orange
or *The Woman with an Apple*
1934
Boisgeloup
Bronze (unique cast)
180.5 × 75 × 67.5
S. 236 (II)
M.P. 327

362
La porteuse de jarre
The Jar Carrier
1935
[Paris? Boisgeloup?]
Painted wood, nails and miscellaneous
components on a cement and wood base
plate
59.5 × 14 × 18.4
S. 162
M.P. 315

363
Figure
Figure
1935
[Paris? Boisgeloup?]
Assemblage: ladle, claws, wood, string and
nails
112 × 61.5 × 29.8
S. 165
M.P. 316

364
L'orateur
The Orator
1937
[Paris]
Bronze and stone (unique cast)
183.5 × 66 × 27
S. 181 (II)
M.P. 318

365
Pleureuse
Weeping Woman
[1937]
[Paris]
Plaster
9.5 × 8 × 4
S. 171 A
M.P. 317

366
Main droite de Picasso
Picasso's Right Hand
[1937]
[Paris]
Plaster cast
20.5 × 14.2 × 3.4
S. 220
M.P. 321

367
Main de Picasso
Picasso's Hand
[1937]
[Paris]
Plaster cast (plaster, wood and metal)
9.2 × 28.5 × 10
S. 221
M.P. 322

368
Minotaure blessé
Wounded Minotaur
[1941]
[Paris]
Carved plaster
29.2 × 43.6 × 3.3
S. 194
M.P. 319

369
Homme debout
Standing Man
1942
Paris
Bronze (unique cast)
19.3 × 7 × 5
S. 208
M.P. 320

370
Tête de taureau
Head of a Bull
Spring 1942
Paris
Original components: bicycle saddle and
handlebars (leather and metal)
33.5 × 43.5 × 19
S. 240 (I)
M.P. 330

371
Tête
Head
(for *The Woman in a Long Dress*)
1942–1952
Paris
Painted bronze on wooden pedestal
42.5 × 25 × 28.3
S. 238 A (II)
M.P. 325

372
Chat
Cat
1943
Paris
Bronze
36 × 17.5 × 55
Stamped on the edge of the base plate:
CIRE PERDUE C. VALSUANI
S. 278 (II)
M.P. 324

373
Tête de mort
Death's Head
1943
Paris
Bronze and copper
25 × 21 × 31
S. 219 (II)
M.P. 326

374
Buste de femme
Bust of a Woman
1943
Paris
Cardboard, string, wire, paper and crayon
strokes
28 × 5.6 × 10
S. 277
M.P. 328

375
L'homme au mouton
Man with a Sheep
February or March 1943
Paris
Bronze
222.5 × 78 × 78
Stamped on back of base plate, r.:
CIRE PERDUE C. VALSUANI
S. 280 (II)
M.P. 331

376
Femme
Woman
1948
Vallauris
Bronze
18 × 14.5 × 7.5
Stamped on the back, a.:
E. GODARD CIRE PERDUE
S. 334 (II)
M.P. 332

377
Petite femme enceinte
Small Pregnant Woman
1948
Vallauris
Bronze
32.5 × 9 × 7
Stamped on back of left leg:
E. GODARD CIRE PERDUE
S. 335 (II)
M.P. 333

378
Femme enceinte
Pregnant Woman
1949
Vallauris
Bronze
130 × 37 × 11.5
Stamped on middle of back:
CIRE PERDUE C. VALSUANI
S. 347
M.P. 334

375   Man with a Sheep

1950

379
Arlequin dansant
Dancing Harlequin
[*c.* 1950?]
Lino cut-out
15.8 × 7
M.P. 803

380
Arlequin
Harlequin
[*c.* 1950?]
Lino cut-out
20.8 × 9.5
M.P. 804

381
Petite fille sautant à la corde
Little Girl Skipping
1950
Vallauris
Plaster original (osier basket, cake mould, shoes, wood, iron, pottery and plaster)
152 × 65 × 66
S. 408 (I)
M.P. 336

382
La femme à la poussette
Woman with a Push Chair
1950
Vallauris
Bronze
203 × 145 × 61
S. 407 (II)
M.P. 337

383
La chèvre
The Goat
1950
Vallauris
Plaster original (osier basket, pots, palm frond, metal, wood, cardboard and plaster)
120.5 × 72 × 144
S. 409 (I)
M.P. 339

384
La chèvre
The Goat
1950
Vallauris
Bronze
120.5 × 72 × 144
Stamped on the base plate:
CIRE PERDUE C. VALSUANI
S. 409 (II)
M.P. 340

381   Little Girl Skipping

385
La femme enceinte
The Pregnant Woman
(second state)
1950–1959
Vallauris
Bronze
109 × 30 × 34
On back of base plate: D.r.: *15.3./5 [9]*;
stamped, l.: *CIRE PERDUE C. VALSUANI*
S. 350 (II)
M.P. 338

386
La grue
The Crane
1951
Vallauris
Plaster original (spade, forks, metal items, tap,
sprig of osier and plaster on wooden base
plate)
76.5 × 29 × 43.5
S. 461 (I)
M.P. 343

387
La liseuse
Woman Reading
1951
Vallauris
Plaster original (wood, metal items, nails,
screws and plaster)
16.4 × 36 × 13.5
S. 462 (I)
M.P. 344

388
La petite chouette
The Little Owl
1951
Vallauris
Plaster original (tools, metal items, nails,
screws and plaster)
26.5 × 18.5 × 14.5
S. 475 (I)
M.P. 347

389
Bouquet de fleurs
Bunch of Flowers
1951
Vallauris
Bronze
60 × 49.5 × 34
Stamped on edge of base plate:
CIRE PERDUE C. VALSUANI
S. 470 (II)
M.P. 348

390
La guenon et son petit
Baboon with Young
October 1951
Vallauris
Plaster original (pottery, two model cars,
metal and plaster)
56 × 34 × 71
D. on base plate: *10.51*
S. 463 (I)
M.P. 342

382   Woman with a Push Chair

392   Goat's Skull, Bottle and Candle

391
L'arrosoir fleuri
The Flowering Watering Can
1951–1953
Paris
Plaster original (watering can, pieces of metal,
nails, wood and plaster)
85.5 × 42 × 38
S. 239 (I)
M.P. 329

392
Crâne de chèvre, bouteille et bougie
Goat's Skull, Bottle and Candle
1951–1953
Vallauris
Painted bronze
79 × 93 × 54
Stamped (illegibly) on r. edge of base plate:
CIRE PERDUE C. VALSUANI
S. 410 (IIa)
M.P. 341

393
Pigeon
Pigeon
1953–1954
Vallauris
Bronze
12.5 × 27 × 12
S. 498 (II)
M.P. 349

394
Les baigneurs: La plongeuse
The Bathers: The Woman Diver
Summer 1956
Cannes
Bronze
264 × 83.5 × 83.5
Stamped on back of base plate, l.:
CIRE PERDUE C. VALSUANI
S. 503 (II)
M.P. 352

395
**Les baigneurs:
L'homme aux mains jointes**
The Bathers: The Man with Clasped Hands
Summer 1956
Cannes
Bronze
213.5 × 73 × 36
Stamped on r. of base plate:
CIRE PERDUE C. VALSUANI
S. 504 (II)
M.P. 353

396
Les baigneurs: L'homme-fontaine
The Bathers: The Fountain Man
Summer 1956
Cannes
Bronze
228 × 88 × 77.5
Stamped on back of base plate:
CIRE PERDUE C. VALSUANI
S. 505 (II)
M.P. 354

394 The Bathers: 396 The Bathers: 398 The Bathers:
     The Woman Diver   The Fountain Man   The Woman with Outstretched Arms

     395 The Bathers: 399 The Bathers:
          The Man with Clasped Hands   The Young Man

               397 The Bathers:
                    The Child

397
Les baigneurs: L'enfant
The Bathers: The Child
Summer 1956
Cannes
Bronze
136 × 67 × 46
Stamped on front of base plate, r.:
CIRE PERDUE C. VALSUANI
S. 506 (II)
M.P. 355

398
Les baigneurs: La femme aux bras écartés
The Bathers: The Woman with Outstretched Arms
Summer 1956
Cannes
Bronze
198 × 174 × 46
Stamped on back of base plate, l.:
CIRE PERDUE C. VALSUANI
S. 507 (II)
M.P. 356

399
Les baigneurs: Le jeune homme
The Bathers: The Young Man
Summer 1956
Cannes
Bronze
176 × 65 × 46
Stamped on front of base plate, r.:
CIRE PERDUE C. VALSUANI
S. 508 (II)
M.P. 357

400
Tête de femme
Head of a Woman
1957
Cannes
Thick pastel and pencil on cut-out cardboard (four assembled components)
72.5 × 31.5 × 27
Inscr. (several times): instructions for colouring; *blanc, noir* and for assembly: *A, B, C*
S. 640
M.P. 1828 (1 to 4)

401
Tête de femme
Head of a Woman
(design for a monument)
1957
Cannes
Cut-out and painted wood
78.5 × 34 × 36
S. 493
M.P. 350

402
Tête de femme
Head of a Woman
(design put forward for a monument at Barcarès)
1957
Cannes
Cut-out and painted sheet-iron
87 × 27.5 × 45
S. 495 (2)
M.P. 351

403
Buste de femme
Bust of a Woman
1957
Cannes
Pencil on cut-out and folded cardboard (three
assembled components)
34.7 × 14.6 × 18
S. 496
M.P. 1829 (1 to 3)

404
Tête
Head
10 June 1958
Cannes
Bronze
50.5 × 21.8 × 19.5
Stamped r.b.: *CIRE PERDUE C. VALSUANI*
S. 539 (II)
M.P. 358

405
La chaise
The Chair
1961
Cannes
Cut-out, folded and painted sheet-iron
111.5 × 114.5 × 89
S. 592 (2)
M.P. 359

406
Femme aux bras écartés
Woman with Outstretched Arms
1961
Cannes
Cut-out and folded paper (sheet from an
album)
36.5 × 37
S. 594 (1)
M.P. 1830

407
Femme aux bras écartés
Woman with Outstretched Arms
(design for a monument carried out at Saint-
Hilaire, Chalo St Mars, Essonne)
1961
Cannes
Painted, cut-out and folded sheet-iron, and
grille
183 × 177.5 × 72.5
S. 596
M.P. 360

408
Femme au chapeau
Woman with a Hat
1961
Cannes
Cut-out, folded and assembled sheet-iron,
painted white
127 × 74 × 40
S. 626 (2b)
M.P. 365

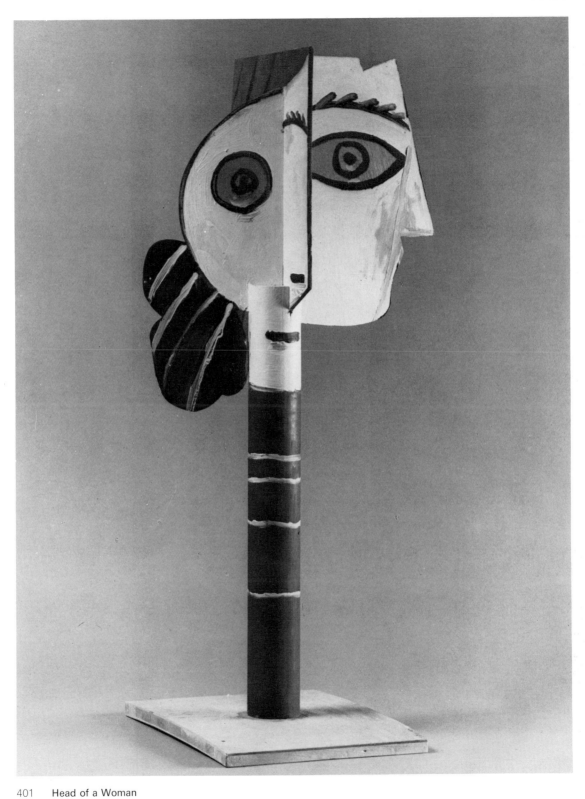

401   Head of a Woman

409
Visage de femme
Face of a Woman
1961
Cannes
Pencil on cut-out and folded paper
22.5 × 15
S. 612 (1)
M.P. 1827

410
Femme à l'enfant
Woman and Child
Early 1961
Cannes
Cut-out, folded, assembled and painted
sheet-iron
128 × 60 × 35
S. 599 (2)
M.P. 361

411
Pierrot assis
Seated Pierrot
Spring 1961
Cannes
Cut-out, folded, assembled and painted
sheet-iron
134.5 × 57 × 57
S. 604 (2)
M.P. 364

412
Footballeur
Footballer
Spring 1961
Cannes
Cut-out and folded sheet-iron, painted in
several colours
58.3 × 47.5 × 14.5
S. 605
M.P. 362

413
Footballeur
Footballer
Spring 1961
Cannes
Cut-out and folded sheet-iron, painted and
decorated with soft crayon
58 × 48 × 24
S. 606 (2)
M.P. 363

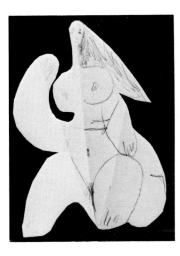

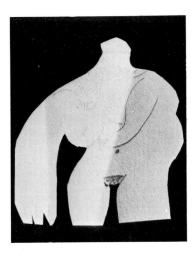

414
Le déjeuner sur l'herbe: Femme assise
Le Déjeuner sur l'Herbe: Seated Woman
(put forward as part of a design for a
monumental set of figures at the Moderna
Museet, Stockholm)
26 August 1962
Mougins
Pencil on both sides of cut-out and folded
cardboard
34.3 × 25
D. on back of raised arm: *26.8.62*
S. 652b (1)
M.P. 1831

415
Le déjeuner sur l'herbe: Femme au bain
Le Déjeuner sur l'Herbe: Woman at the Bath
(put forward as part of a design for a
monumental set of figures at the Moderna
Museet, Stockholm)
26 August 1962
Mougins
Pencil on both sides of cut-out and folded
cardboard
23 × 21.5
D. on back, c.: *26.8.62*
S. 652c (1)
M.P. 1834

416
**Le déjeuner sur l'herbe: Homme assis
accoudé**
*Le Déjeuner sur l'Herbe: Seated Man Leaning
on his Elbow*
(put forward as part of a design for a
monumental set of figures at the Moderna
Museet, Stockholm)
27 August 1962
Mougins
Pencil on both sides of cut-out and folded
cardboard
28 × 37.5
D. on back, c.: *27.8.62*
S. 642 and 652a (1)
M.P. 1841

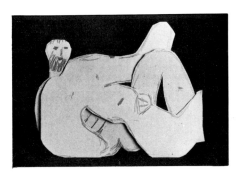

417
**Le déjeuner sur l'herbe: Homme assis
accoudé**
*Le Déjeuner sur l'Herbe: Seated Man Leaning
on his Elbow*
(put forward as part of a design for a
monumental set of figures at the Moderna
Museet, Stockholm)
31 August 1962
Mougins
Pencil on both sides of cut-out and folded
cardboard
25 × 32
D. on back, b.l.: *31.8.62*
S. 652d (1)
M.P. 1847

418
**Le déjeuner sur l'herbe: Homme assis
accoudé**
*Le Déjeuner sur l'Herbe: Seated Man Leaning
on his Elbow*
26 August 1962
Mougins
Pencil on both sides of cut-out and folded
cardboard (two assembled components)
21.5 × 27
D. on back: *26.8.62*
M.P. 1832 (1 and 2)

419
**Le déjeuner sur l'herbe: Homme assis
accoudé**
*Le Déjeuner sur l'Herbe: Seated Man Leaning
on his Elbow*
26 August 1962
Mougins
Pencil on both sides of cut-out cardboard
21.5 × 26
D. on back, c.a.: *26.8.62*
M.P. 1833

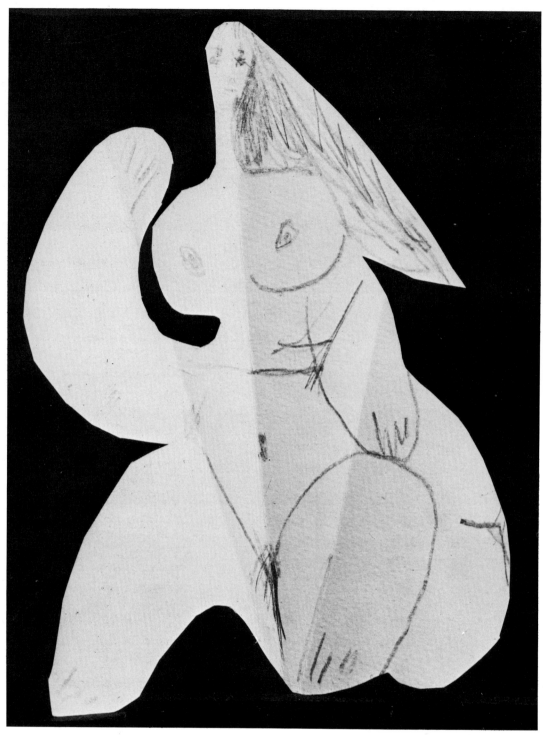

414   Le Déjeuner sur l'Herbe: Seated Woman

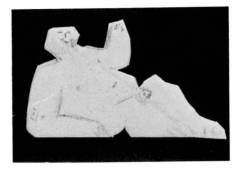

420
Le déjeuner sur l'herbe: Homme assis accoudé
Le Déjeuner sur l'Herbe: Seated Man Leaning on his Elbow
26 August 1962
Mougins
Pencil on both sides of cut-out and folded cardboard
21.5 × 25.5
D. on back, c.: *26.8.62*
M.P. 1835

421
Le déjeuner sur l'herbe: Homme assis accoudé
Le Déjeuner sur l'Herbe: Seated Man Leaning on his Elbow
26 August 1962
Mougins
Pencil on both sides of cut-out cardboard
10.5 × 17
D. on back: *26.8.62*
M.P. 1836

422
Le déjeuner sur l'herbe: Homme assis accoudé
Le Déjeuner sur l'Herbe: Seated Man Leaning on his Elbow
26 August 1962
Mougins
Pencil on both sides of cut-out and folded cardboard
13 × 17.5
D. on back: *26.8.62*
M.P. 1837

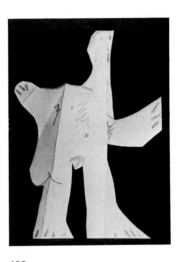

423
Le déjeuner sur l'herbe: Femme assise
Le Déjeuner sur l'Herbe: Seated Woman
27 August 1962
Mougins
Pencil on both sides of cut-out and folded cardboard
26.2 × 20
D.b.r.: *27.8.62*
M.P. 1838

424
Homme debout
Standing Man
27 August 1962
Mougins
Pencil on both sides of cut-out and folded cardboard
23.5 × 12.5
D. on back, b.r.: *27.8.62*
M.P. 1839

425
Homme debout
Standing Man
27 August 1962
Mougins
Pencil on both sides of cut-out and folded cardboard
36.5 × 27.5
D. on back, b.r.: *27.8.62*
M.P. 1840

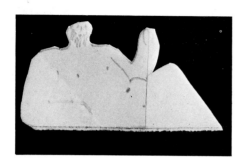

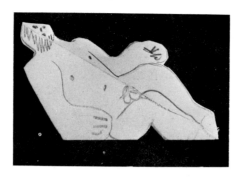

426
**Le déjeuner sur l'herbe: Homme assis
accoudé**
*Le Déjeuner sur l'Herbe: Seated Man Leaning
on his Elbow*
27 August 1962
Mougins
Pencil on both sides of cut-out and folded
cardboard
8.5 × 17
D. on back: *27/8/62*
M.P. 1842

427
**Le déjeuner sur l'herbe: Homme assis
accoudé**
*Le Déjeuner sur l'Herbe: Seated Man Leaning
on his Elbow*
27 August 1962
Mougins
Pencil on cut-out and folded cardboard
9 × 14.5
D. on back, b.r.: *27.8.62*
M.P. 1843

428
**Le déjeuner sur l'herbe: Homme assis
accoudé**
*Le Déjeuner sur l'Herbe: Seated Man Leaning
on his Elbow*
(put forward as part of a design for a
monumental set of figures carried out at the
Moderna Museet, Stockholm, but not
included in it)
28 August 1962
Mougins
Pencil on both sides of cut-out and folded
cardboard
20 × 26
D. on back, b.r.: *28.8.62*
M.P. 1844

429
**Le déjeuner sur l'herbe: Homme assis
accoudé**
*Le Déjeuner sur l'Herbe: Seated Man Leaning
on his Elbow*
28 August 1962
Mougins
Pencil on both sides of cut-out cardboard
24.5 × 33
D. on back, b.c.: *28.8/62*
M.P. 1845

430
**Le déjeuner sur l'herbe: Homme assis
accoudé**
*Le Déjeuner sur l'Herbe: Seated Man Leaning
on his Elbow*
28 August 1962
Mougins
Pencil on both sides of cut-out and folded
cardboard
22 × 34
D. on back, b.r.: *28.8.62*
M.P. 1846

431
**Le déjeuner sur l'herbe: Homme assis
accoudé**
*Le Déjeuner sur l'Herbe: Seated Man Leaning
on his Elbow*
August 1962
Mougins
Pencil on cut-out cardboard (three assembled
components)
20 × 29
M.P. 1848 (1 to 3)

432
Tête de femme
Head of a Woman
End of 1962
Mougins
Sheet-iron, cut-out and folded, and wire, both
painted in several colours
32 × 24 × 16
S. 631 (2)
M.P. 366

433
Tête de femme
Head of a Woman
4 December 1962
Mougins
Pencil on both sides of cut-out paper from an
album sheet
42 × 26.5
D. vertically, b.r.: *4.12.62*
M.P. 1850

Vallauris, September 1952 (Photo Robert Doisneau)

Ceramics

The breed of artists who followed a variety of disciplines simultaneously and were at once painters, sculptors, engravers, perhaps also potters and sometimes architects, had become extinct since the Renaissance, or so it might have seemed. Since then, the creative artist had turned into a 'specialist'. He might be basically a painter, or primarily a sculptor, each trying to cope with the problems arising specifically within his own technique. Picasso, however, resurrected the ancient tradition of the all-round artist who explored the whole range of painting, sculpture, graphic art, engraving – and ceramics. He turned enthusiastically to the last towards the end of the 1940s, unfailingly intrigued by any new techniques that offered themselves to him, eager to master a new line of knowledge and a novel 'trade'. This was a tall order when it came to ceramics: he was faced with a new material – fired or unfired clay – new kinds of colours, metallic oxides, washes or slips, trial by fire and the surprises it might have in store. Sabartés was surprised, even mildly uneasy, to hear Picasso resorting to the technical vocabulary of the professional potter he was becoming: 'When I travelled to Vallauris, intending to view what Picasso had achieved at the Céramiques Madoura factory, I could not but be shocked by the language he used to the Ramié couple as soon as they touched on questions of the craft: "Perhaps the glaze should have been matt. . . . That's on account of the flux. . . . Just with an ordinary lead slip. . . . Engobes. . . . Oxides. . . . Colour slip on biscuit. . . . Fired . . . unfired . . . matt tin glaze. . . . Silicate . . . lead glaze. . . . Sulphite. . . . High-temperature firing. . . . Open hearth. . . . Forced-draft kilns." '[1]

Chance played a part in his adoption of this new craft. Picasso had been staying at Golfe-Juan during the summer of 1946. He went to look at an exhibition of local artefacts in Vallauris and met Georges and Suzanne Ramié who ran the Madoura workshop, a ceramics factory, there. He was invited to visit it and modelled a few small figures just for the fun of it. The following year he was back in Golfe-Juan again and returned to Madoura. This time he brought some sketches for pieces of pottery, not unlike the somewhat later ones of October 1947 for two female-shaped vases (cat. 441, 442), and set to work in earnest. So he went on for several years, further stimulated by moving to Vallauris itself in 1948. Picasso remained there until he moved to La Californie in Cannes in 1955. Vallauris was not far away and he went on working as a potter, turning out items in Cannes which were then taken for firing to Madoura. Two vases from an earlier period in the museum's collection deserve a mention: they date from 1929, are additionally signed by Jean Van Dongen (the brother of Kees, the painter), who was Maillol's assistant, and they bear witness to Picasso's latent interest in this technique.

Picasso played havoc with all established procedures in pottery work, took a hand at every stage of production – from the material itself to its decoration and its firing – and indulged in extremely unorthodox practices. As the Ramié couple used to say, 'an apprentice who operated like Picasso would soon find himself out of a job'.[2]

The objects produced were sometimes very traditional indeed: plates, long or rectangular dishes, Spanish platters with a deep border and convex inner field, pitchers – gothic or otherwise – vases, stamped or thrown Madoura ware in series production, which Picasso would snatch away and decorate to his own taste. He would enlist even more utilitarian items which were not intended for decoration at all, such as *pignates*, the twin-handled cooking pots (cat. 463–465) which were then still turned out in large numbers in the South of France, even though they were not entirely safe for culinary purposes, because the glaze used for lining

Drawing, 21 October 1947, for *Femme à l'amphore* (*Woman with an Amphora*, cf. cat. 442) (Artist's Estate)

(1) J. Sabartés, 'Picasso à Vallauris', *Cahiers d'Art*, No. 1, Paris, 1948, p. 81.

(2) S. and G. Ramié, quoted by Sabartés, 1948, p. 83.

them contained lead oxide. He also resorted to *tomettes*, the small hard-baked clay slabs traditionally used in that part of the country as flooring material, to tiles of various sizes and even to bricks. The use made by Picasso of kiln furniture (on which items for firing are stacked) was even odder, indeed somewhat startling to any professional potter who would immediately recognize it for what it was. Among these were the *gazelles*, kiln props shaped rather like elongated Roman roof-tiles, on which he set about painting tall figures (cat. 466–468). Some of these props carry a regular pattern of small triangular notches (cat. 470, 471) which receive the terracotta stilts that connect the props and support the load in the kiln. These *gazelles* had been fired again and again in the course of their 'humble and hard-worked existence as kiln-chargers',[3] before they turned from being items of technical equipment into works of art. As a result, they had acquired a highly characteristic grey colouring, but – a mark of their lowly origin – the clay used for making them was low-grade and the lumps of limestone they contained reacted to damp, so that the body tended to chip. Finally, there were rejects salvaged when the kiln was emptied. Picasso set great store by them and endowed them with a new identity in masterly fashion: *pignate* sherds turned into comic masks (cat. 473–475) and a few touches of colour transformed broken bricks into women's faces (cat. 519, 520).

Frequently, however, he was not content simply to decorate the objects he used as he found them, whether ordinary potter's ware or the more unlikely things that he had picked out for their shape, colour or texture – the gritty body of the *tomette* tiles provides an instance of the latter. He would pounce on unfired clay objects before they were dry and reshape them, bend them, hollow them out, stick them together and cut them up. The transformations he wrought were astounding and the potter now became a sculptor. There were *tanagras*, so called because of their resemblance to classical statuettes, small female figures which had begun life as vases or bottles with a closed neck, and in which he stressed a volume that became a breast or a belly (cat. 461), pressed out a hollow for the waist or the back of a knee (cat. 453), or stuck on an arm, or bent the figure until it was kneeling (cat. 477). There were large female heads (cat. 451, 456), made up of a number of pieces that had been thrown, reshaped and stuck together until they were unrecognizable; vases filled with flowers (cat. 445, 446); and pigeons and doves (cat. 489, 493), fashioned out of bottles or slabs of raw clay which Picasso bent, folded, concertinaed with his nimble hands. Cocteau used to say about these things that 'by wringing their necks, you endow them with life'.[4] And there were also a great many little Hellenistic figurines – fauns (cat. 483), flute players (cat. 476), nymphs or bacchantes (cat. 462) which Picasso first left as the original biscuit under a white slip, then decked in colour – small antique and naked folk dwelling in the shade of the vines.[5]

New difficulties arose for Picasso when it came to colour. Here was a painter driven to dealing with colours of a deceptive kind. Firing alone reveals the potter's palette and the effect of the metallic-oxide-based materials applied to a piece of pottery can only be assessed in the mind's eye. Worse still, Picasso made empirical, indeed anarchic, use of the means at his disposal. He combined slips (colours carried in diluted clay) with tin glazes, pastels and vitreous glazes (the coating normally used for ceramic ware), as well as burnishing (only used where glazes are absent). He engraved the surfaces and scraped away the overlay to reveal the colour of the body beneath. His daring technical experiments sometimes led to 'lapses' of such beauty that he might well be forgiven for an oxide fired to excess (cat. 439) or for a glaze that has shrunk (cat. 446).

The decoration sometimes conforms to the shapes it covers and sometimes contrasts with them. It is not merely a matter of colour: Picasso incised and cut, sometimes deep into the body, by carving sardines in a dish (cat. 439) or making owls stand out on the side of a vase (cat. 509). He added extraneous decorative elements which he had modelled, such as the fauns that decorate the four sides of a square jug (cat. 486), or he simply scavenged; for example, the head of a faun (cat. 457), built up from kiln cockspurs and lumps of fired clay, or the laughing and bearded face of another faun, made from coils of red clay and pieces of clinker (cat. 458).

The iconographic vocabulary of Picasso's pottery is pretty well defined: representations of the sun and heads of fauns occupy the centre of round and rectangular dishes; bullfight scenes fill long dishes; still-life motifs quite naturally take up space in other dishes and plates; the *tomette* tiles carry scenes of bacchanals in which drinkers, sileni, double-flute players and

Femme agenouillée (*Kneeling Woman*, cat. 477) before colouring (Photo Robert Picault), published in *Faunes et nymphes de Pablo Picasso* by André Verdet

(3) G. Ramié, 'Céramiques', *Verve*, Vol. VII, Nos. 25 and 26, Paris, 1951.

(4) J. Cocteau, quoted by D.-H. Kahnweiler in *Picasso-Keramik*, Hanover, 1957, p. 27.

(5) See the photographs published in A. Verdet, *Faunes et nymphes de Pablo Picasso*, Geneva, 1952.

dancers take part. These also mingle and cavort on the bellies of the *pignate* cooking pots, as remote relatives of Greek black-figure vases. The owl and the bull, the favourites in Picasso's bestiary, crop up everywhere. The extent to which the themes of Mediterranean antiquity are represented in this equally Mediterranean and ancient form of art is striking. Subjects borrowed from painting, such as *Las Meninas* (cat. 510), have also been brought into play.

Ceramic work is often treated as a minor art form. There is a touch of condescension in all the ways of describing it, such as 'applied' and 'decorative art'. It might therefore seem surprising that Picasso should have been so obviously drawn to it at the peak of his career as a painter. Closer inspection, however, reveals that he reached out beyond traditional ceramic work, especially when dealing with volumes, and achieved what he had so long sought after – the merging of painting and sculpture. He had, in fact, earlier attempted to paint volumes in his Cubist phase, when he produced the six different versions of the painted bronze *Verre d'absinthe* (*Glass of Absinthe*), or wood and sheet-iron constructions that were also coloured. Ceramic work implies the use of immutable colours which cannot be further modified once they have been fired. Such an offer of immortality must inevitably have seduced the painter: 'Picasso has never painted as much as he has done since he took to potting.'[6] A number of problems inherent in painting fall away as soon as the support is no longer limited to two dimensions: colour is no longer responsible for rendering light and shade effects because the volume itself is available. Picasso as a potter told the sculptor Laurens how carried away he was: 'You ought to work in ceramics. It is splendid. . . . I did a head. Well, you can look at it from any side you like – and it is *flat*. It's the painting, of course, that makes it flat – because it is painted. I have fixed it so that the colour should make it look flat from every angle. What one looks for in a picture is depth and the greatest possible amount of space. As to a sculpture, one must try to make it flat for the onlooker, seen from everywhere. I have also done other things: I have painted on curved surfaces. I have painted things as round as a ball.'[7]

One might mention in passing – quite incidentally – that some pottery items have contributed to the creation of sculptures made from assembled elements. Thus, the udder of *La chèvre* (*The Goat*, cat. 383) consists of two glazed pots, terracotta jars provide the breasts and belly of *La femme enceinte* (*The Pregnant Woman*) in the plaster version of the work (cat. 385) and the belly of the baboon (cat. 390) is a large rounded vase whose two handles make the shoulders, while kiln props provide the legs.

The eighty-eight ceramic items taken into the collection as part of the settlement from the estate are one-off versions. That is true even of those (cat. 514, 515) which carry the *Edition Picasso* mark, because these were pieces produced as part of a series and taken back by Picasso in order to paint them himself.

Finally, something must be said about the pottery series produced by Madoura. These are either '*répliques authentiques*' (authentic replicas) made by duplicating shapes and decoration on the basis of an original model, and marked *Edition Picasso*; or '*empreintes originales*' (original impressions), which involve Picasso's engraved ceramics: in these, the subject was incised by the artist in a hardened plaster matrix and then transferred by pressing it to plaques of clay called *lastres*. These works were marked '*Empreinte originale de Picasso*'.

H.S.

(6) S. and G. Ramié, *Céramiques de Picasso*, Paris, 1948, p. 18.

(7) Picasso to Laurens, 8 July 1948, quoted in D.-H. Kahnweiler, 'Entretiens avec Picasso', *Quadrum*, No. 2, Brussels, November 1956, p. 76.

Technical Note

All works have been catalogued as 'Ceramics' which involve fired clay, including three items (cat. 472, 484, 485) which could equally well have been classified as 'Sculptures', since they were cast after a plaster original from which a mould had been taken, in much the same way as a bronze cast is derived from a plaster original.

Unless otherwise stated, all the ceramics were produced at Vallauris. From 1955 on, when Picasso moved to La Californie in Cannes, he painted a number of pieces there, which were then taken to be fired by Madoura at Vallauris: this is documented by photographs, such as those showing cat. 504 and 506, in D.D. Duncan, *The Private World of Pablo Picasso*, New York, 1958, p. 43; cat. 496 is dated 'Cannes 1957'. From 1955 on, the place of production might be described as Cannes-Vallauris and, from June 1961, as Mougins-Vallauris, when Picasso moved to Notre-Dame-de-Vie. The information provided by M. Yvan Oreggia has been decisive in the drawing up of this catalogue.

Fig. 1
Drawing for *Chouette* (*Owl*)
(Artist's Estate)

Fig. 2
Ceramics by Picasso at the 'De Palissy à Picasso' exhibition, Vallauris, 1949
(Picasso Archives)

Dating

Documentation has made it possible to attribute dates to items which are not themselves dated. Dating based on stylistic considerations is not explained here.

Cat. 439 (M.P. 3678)
Reproduced in *Cahiers d'Art*, 1948, Paris, No. 1, p. 191, together with cat. 436 and 437, which are dated 1947.

Cat. 440 (M.P. 3687)
Reproduced in *Cahiers d'Art*, 1948, No. 1, p. 102.

Cat. 441 (M.P. 3679)
Drawings dated 21 October 1947 for this piece were reproduced in the 'Picasso' exhibition catalogue, New York, Pace Gallery, 16–23 October 1982, p. 57 (ill. p. 199).

Cat. 442 (M.P. 3680)
There are drawings dated 21 October 1947 for this piece (see cat. 441). It was reproduced in *Cahiers d'Art*, 1948, No. 1, p. 99.

Cat. 443 (M.P. 3722)
Two drawings in the artist's estate, one of which is dated 15 August 1947, represent designs for this item (Fig. 1), from which an edition was made in 1953 (R. 705).

Cat. 444 (M.P. 3688)
Suzanne and Georges Ramié mention in *Céramiques de Picasso*, Paris, September 1948, 'ball-shaped items resting on a pedestal' (p. 17). An identical piece featured in the exhibition 'De Palissy à Picasso', Vallauris, 1949 (see photograph in the Picasso Archives, Fig. 2).

Fig. 3
Drawing with *Chouette en colère* (*Angry Owl*), 13 March 1950
(Private Collection)

Cat. 445 (M.P. 3755)
Cat. 446 (M.P. 3756)
The text mentioned above (see cat. 444) also describes the following items: '. . . flower vases consisting of a pot topped by a bunch of flowers. This bouquet is most ingeniously represented by a feature shaped like an oblong cone, which was then modelled and painted to represent flowers' (p. 17). These vases were shown at the exhibition in Vallauris mentioned above.

Cat. 472 (M.P. 335)
A drawing dated 13 March 1950 (private collection, Fig. 3) includes studies for the head of *Chouette en colère* (*Angry Owl*). A copy shown at The Museum of Modern Art, New York, in 1967 (*The Sculpture of Picasso*, catalogue by Roland Penrose, plate on p. 140) carries a different pattern of decoration from that in the museum and is dated 1953.

434
Vase décoré de baigneuses
Vase with Bathers
May 1929
[Paris]
White body; cast; red (burnished) and black
slip, with white tin glaze
47 × 32.5 (diameter)
S.D. on base in black slip:
MAI/XXIX/Picasso;
incised: *Jean Van Dongen*
M.P. 3673

435
**Vase globulaire décoré de mains tenant
des poissons**
Globular Vase with Hands Grasping a Fish
30 June 1929
[Paris]
Reddish body; cast; painted in slips and white
tin glaze
22 × 27.5 (diameter)
S.D. on base in black slip: *Picasso/ 30.6.XXIX*;
incised: *Jean Van Dongen*
M.P. 3674

436
**Plat rectangulaire décoré d'une tête de
faune**
Dish with Head of a Faun
20 October 1947
White body; pressed; slips, white tin glaze and
incised patterns, the whole dipped in glaze
32 × 38.2 × 3.5
On underside, D. in blue slip: *20.10.47.II*;
stamp: *PLEIN FEU MADOURA*
M.P. 3675

437
**Plat rectangulaire décoré d'une nature
morte: verre, couteau et pomme**
Dish with Still-life: Glass, Knife and Apple
28 October 1947
White body; pressed; slips, incised pattern and
white tin glaze, the whole dipped in glaze
32.2 × 38 × 4.3
On underside, D. in blue slip: *28.10.47.VI*;
stamp: *PLEIN FEU MADOURA*
M.P. 3676

438
**Plat rectangulaire décoré d'une tête de
faune; on underside: taureau**
Dish with Head of a Faun; on underside: Bull
30 October 1947
White body; pressed; applied and incised
design; slips and white tin glaze under
brushed glaze; on underside, design in
coloured slips under brushed glaze
31.5 × 38.5 × 4.8
On underside, D. in blue slip: *30.10.47.IX*;
stamp: *PLEIN FEU MADOURA*
M.P. 3677

438 (underside)

439
Plat rectangulaire aux sardines
Sardine Dish
1947–1948
White body; pressed; incised, manganese
decoration
31 × 37.5 × 4
M.P. 3678

440
Assiette portant couteau, fourchette,
pomme coupée en deux et épluchures
Plate with Knife, Fork, Halved Apple and Peel
1947–1948
White body; thrown; modelled, applied and
slipped design, partly glazed
33 (diameter) × 4.5
Stamp on underside: *PLEIN FEU MADOURA*
M.P. 3687

441
Vase: Femme à l'amphore
Vase: Woman with an Amphora
October 1947–1948
White body; thrown, modelled and assembled
components; decorated with slips and white
tin glaze, incised, burnished after firing
42.5 × 32.5 × 15.5
M.P. 3679

442
Vase: Femme à l'amphore
Vase: Woman with an Amphora
October 1947–1948
White body; thrown and modelled; decorated
with slips and incised
49 × 26.5 × 18
M.P. 3680

443
Chouette
Owl
1947–1953
White body; thrown and assembled
components; decorated with slips and incised
30 × 18 × 27
M.P. 3722

444
Sphère décorée d'une nature morte
Ball with Still-life
1948
White body; thrown; decorated with slips and
incised
34 (diameter)
M.P. 3688

445
Vase de fleurs
Flower Vase
1948
White body; two thrown, modelled and joined components; decorated with slips, white tin glaze, partially brush-glazed, reserved areas burnished with red slip, incised
56 × 33.5 × 25.5
M.P. 3755

446
Fleurs dans un vase
Flowers in a Vase
1948
White body; three thrown and assembled components, one of them remodelled; decorated with slips, white tin glaze, incised, irregular brushed-on glaze and burnished black slip
55 × 32.5 × 32
M.P. 3756

447
Plat rectangulaire décoré d'une tête de faune barbu
Dish with Head of a Bearded Faun
21 January 1948
White body; pressed; white tin-glaze decoration, slips under irregular brushed-on glaze, burnished with highly diluted Indian ink after firing
38.3 × 32 × 4
On underside: D. in black and red slip: *21.1.48.III*; stamp: *PLEIN FEU MADOURA*
M.P. 3681

448
Pichet gothique décoré de 2 oiseaux en cage
Gothic Pitcher with Two Birds in a Cage
4 February 1948
White body; thrown and modelled; black slip under brushed glaze in places; incised and burnished with Indian ink
37 × 35 × 24
D. inside neck: *4.2.48.*
M.P. 3682

449
Lastre décorée d'une tête de femme
Plaque with Head of a Woman
4 March (or 4 May?) 1948
Red body; colour slips, white tin glaze added to body, under brushed glaze
27 × 19.5 × 0.8
D. on back in black slip: *4.M.48.*
M.P. 3684

450
Plat rectangulaire décoré d'une tête de faune; on underside: **décor de fleurs**
Dish with Head of a Faun; on underside: *Flower Pattern*
12 March 1948
White body; pressed; incised, slips under brushed glaze; on underside, slips under glaze
38.5 × 32.5 × 4
On underside: D., incised: *12.3.48.*;
stamp: *PLEIN FEU MADOURA*
M.P. 3683

450 (underside)

451
Tête de femme à la résille
Head of a Woman with a Hairnet
30 April 1948
White body; two thrown, modelled and joined
elements; decorated with slips and incised
40 × 34.5 × 32
D. on back, incised: *30.4.48.*
M.P. 3685

452
**Plat rectangulaire décoré d'une grappe
de raisin et de ciseaux**
Dish with a Bunch of Grapes and Scissors
[1948]
White body; pressed; painted in blue slip,
incised and finger-marked, then retouched
with slips and white tin glaze, all under
brushed glaze; on underside, slips, partly
glazed, burnished with grey slip
31 × 37.2 × 4
On underside, stamp: *PLEIN FEU MADOURA*
M.P. 3689

452 (underside)

453
Bouteille: Femme debout
Bottle: Standing Woman
[1948]
White body; thrown and modelled
47 × 13 × 10.5
M.P. 3694

454
**Lastre ovale décorée d'une tête de
femme**
Oval Plaque with Head of a Woman
[1948–1949]
White body; slips under brushed glaze
46.2 × 35.4 × 1
M.P. 3727

451   Head of a Woman with a Hairnet

455
Lastre ovale décorée d'un visage
Oval Plaque with a Face
[1948–1949]
White body; slips and white tin glaze under brushed glaze
46 × 35.4 × 1
M.P. 3728

456
Tête de femme à la résille
Head of a Woman with a Hairnet
[1948–1950]
White body; two thrown, modelled and joined elements; slips, white tin glaze and incised, covered with brushed glaze
37 × 27 × 24.5
M.P. 3706

457
Plat décoré d'une tête de faune
Dish with Head of a Faun
5 February 1949
White body; thrown; white tin glaze and slips; applied cockspurs and pieces of red terracotta; the whole partly covered with glaze; burnished after first firing with grey slip or Indian ink
40.5 (diameter) × 5
D. incised on front: *5.2.49.*;
stamp on underside: *PLEIN FEU MADOURA*
M.P. 3690

458
Plat rectangulaire décoré d'une tête de faune
Dish with Head of a Faun
7 February 1949
White body; pressed; applied coils of red clay and clinker partly brushed with glaze; burnished with slips or Indian ink
38.5 × 32.5 × 4
D. on lower border in slip under glaze:
7.2.49.;
stamp on underside: *PLEIN FEU MADOURA*
M.P. 3691

459
Chouette
Owl
30 December 1949
White body; thrown; slips, white tin glaze and incised, all under brushed glaze
19 × 18 × 22
D. under base plate, incised: *30.12.49.*
R. 81
M.P. 3692

460
Vase: Femme
Vase: Woman
[1949]
White body; thrown and modelled; black slip
47 × 16.5 × 11
M.P. 3693

459   Owl

1949–1950

461
Vase: Femme à la mantille
Vase: Woman with a Mantilla
[1949]
White body; thrown and modelled; painted with slips
47 × 12.5 × 9.5
M.P. 3695

462
Femme nue debout
Nude Standing Woman
20 July 1950
Red body; modelled; painted with slips and incised
17 × 5.8 × 6.2
D. incised on base: *VALLAURIS/ 20 juillet/ 50*
M.P. 3696

463
Pignate à bord droit décorée d'un taureau et de trois femmes courant
Straight-edged Cooking Pot with a Bull and Three Running Women
4 August 1950
Red fire-proof body; thrown; slips
18 × 28 × 21.5
D. underneath base in black slip:
VALLAURIS/4 AOÛT/1950
M.P. 3697

463 (back)

464
Pignate décorée d'une chèvre et d'un buste d'homme tenant une coupe
Cooking Pot with a Goat and Head and Shoulders of a Man Holding a Cup
5 August 1950
Red fire-proof body; thrown; painted with black slip
19.7 × 27 × 24.5
D. vertically in black slip: *VALLAURIS 5.8.50.*; stamp close to upper rim: *VALLAURIS*
M.P. 3698

464 (back)

210 Ceramics

465

Pignate décorée d'une farandole et de personnages portant une colombe géante
Cooking Pot with a Round Dance and Figures Carrying a Giant Dove
11 August 1950
Red fire-proof body; thrown; painted with black slip
20 × 27.5 × 25.5
D. underneath base in black slip:
VALLAURIS/ 11.8.50/ IV
M.P. 3699

465 (back)

466

Gazelle de four décorée d'une femme nue
Kiln Prop with Nude Woman
18 September 1950
Reddish grogged clay; painted with black slip
102 × 22.3 × 9
S.D. inside, in black slip:
VALLAURIS 18.9.50/ PICASSO;
initials scratched into the surface: *RP*
M.P. 3700

467

Gazelle de four décorée d'une femme nue se coiffant
Kiln Prop with Nude Woman Dressing her Hair
19 September 1950
Reddish grogged clay; painted with black slip
102.3 × 22.5 × 8.5
S.D. inside, in black slip:
VALLAURIS 19.9.50/ PICASSO;
initials scratched into the surface: *RP*
M.P. 3701

468

Gazelle de four décorée d'un buste d'homme au tricot rayé
Kiln Prop with Head and Shoulders of a Man in a Striped Jersey
23 September 1950
Reddish grogged clay; painted with slips
101.5 × 22.7 × 8
S.D. a. in black paint:
VALLAURIS 23.9.50. PICASSO
R. 105
M.P. 3702

469

Brique réfractaire décorée de deux profils de Françoise Gilot
Firebrick with Two Profiles of Françoise Gilot
4 October 1950
Reddish clay; painted with slips
22 × 11 × 4.7
S. on one edge in black slip: *Picasso*;
D. on the other: *VALLAURIS 4.10.50.*
M.P. 3703

461   Vase: Woman with a Mantilla

477   Bottle: Kneeling Woman

470
Gazelle de four décorée d'un torse d'homme nu
Kiln Prop with Head and Torso of a Nude Man
8 October 1950
Grogged grey clay notched for stilts; painted with slips
91 × 23 × 8
D. inside in black slip: *8.10.50.IV*
M.P. 3704

471
Gazelle de four décorée d'un enfant à la colombe
Kiln Prop with a Child Holding a Dove
Autumn 1950
Grogged red clay notched for stilts; painted with slips
59 × 23 × 7.5
M.P. 3705

4/2
Chouette en colère
Angry Owl
1950–[1953]
White body; cast; painted with red slip under glaze; burnished with black slip after firing
28.5 × 30 × 32
S. on plinth in red slip: *PICASSO*
S. 404 (IIIa)
M.P. 335

473
Fragment de pignate décoré d'un visage
Fragment of Cooking Pot with a Face
[1950]
Red body; crayon design
16.5 × 21 × 6.5
M.P. 3707

474
Fragment de pignate décoré d'un visage
Fragment of Cooking Pot with a Face
[1950]
Red body; crayon design
19.5 × 19 × 9
M.P. 3708

475
Fragment de pignate décoré d'un visage
Fragment of Cooking Pot with a Face
[1950]
Red body; crayon design
14 × 12 × 4.5
M.P. 3709

476
Musicien assis
Seated Musician
[1950]
Sheet of white body; cut out and modelled;
painted with slips and incised
14.8 × 8 × 6.5
M.P. 3710

477
Bouteille: Femme agenouillée
Bottle: Kneeling Woman
[1950]
White body; thrown and modelled; oxides on
white tin glaze
29 × 17 × 17
R. 133
M.P. 3720

478
**Assiette décorée d'une scène de tournoi:
cavalier en armure et page**
*Plate with Jousting Scene: Knight in Armour
and Page*
26 January 1951
White body; thrown; black slip, very lightly
engraved
23.5 (diameter) × 2.5
On underside: D. in black slip:
VALLAURIS/le 26 janvier 1951;
stamp: *PLEIN FEU MADOURA*
M.P. 3711

479
**Assiette décorée d'une scène de tournoi:
cavalier en armure**
Plate with Jousting Scene: Knight in Armour
29 January–1 February 1951
White body; thrown; painted with slips and
incised
22.5 (diameter) × 2.5
On underside: D. in black slip:
29.1.51/1er.2.51;
stamp: *PLEIN FEU MADOURA*
M.P. 3712

480
**Assiette décorée d'une scène de tournoi:
cavalier en armure;** on underside: **décor
avec une colombe**
Plate with Jousting Scene: Knight in Armour;
on underside: *Pattern with a Dove*
30 January 1951
White body; thrown; painted with black slip;
underside painted with black slip
22 (diameter) × 2.5
On underside: D. in black slip:
VALLAURIS/le 30.1.51.;
stamp: *PLEIN FEU MADOURA*
M.P. 3713

480 (underside)

481
Rondeau d'enfournement décoré d'une femme lisant
Kiln Disc with a Woman Reading
8 March 1951
Red body; painted with slips; irregularly glazed
22.5 (diameter) × 1.3
D.a.r.: *8.3.51.*
M.P. 3724

482
Plaque décorée d'une nature morte
Plaque with Still-life
13 March 1951
Grogged red body; painted with slips
18 × 49 × 2.5
D. on back, in black paint: *VALLAURIS/13.3.51.*
M.P. 3714

483
Faune
Faun
18 March 1951
White body; figure modelled and applied; painted with slips
20.4 × 8
S.D. on back in black slip:
VALLAURIS/peinte le 18.3.51/Picasso
M.P. 3715

484
**Chouette à tête d'homme
(Couple Carnaval)**
Man-faced Owl (Carnival Couple)
1951–27 February 1953
White body; cast; painted with slips
33.5 × 34.5 × 25
D. under plinth: *27.2.53.*;
inscr. on plinth in chalk: *Carnaval*
S. 403 (IIIa)
M.P. 345

485
**Chouette à tête de femme
(Couple Carnaval)**
Woman-faced Owl (Carnival Couple)
1951–27 February 1953
White body; cast; painted with slips and pastel
33.5 × 34.5 × 25
D. under plinth, in black slip: *27.2.53.*;
inscr. on plinth in red pastel: *Carnaval*
S. 403 (IIIb)
M.P. 346

486
Pichet décoré de faunes
Pitcher with Fauns
[1951]
Red body; thrown and modelled; reliefs moulded and applied; painted with slips
26 × 22.5 × 16
Stamp underneath base: *PLEIN FEU MADOURA*
M.P. 3723

486   Pitcher with Fauns

487
Lastre décorée d'une tête de femme
Plaque with Head of a Woman
[1952]
White body; painted with slips and incised
56.5 × 32.5 × 1
M.P. 3686

488
Tête de femme
Head of a Woman
29 January 1953
White body; elements thrown and assembled;
painted with black slip
50 × 32.5 × 35
D. scratched into bottom of neck: *29.1.53.*
M.P. 3716

489
Colombe aux œufs
Dove with Eggs
29 January 1953
White body; thrown (as a bottle) and
modelled on a base; painted with slips
22 × 26 × 14.5
D. incised into l. wing: *29.1.53.*
R. 142; S. C3
M.P. 3746

490
Pichet gothique décoré d'arums
Gothic Pitcher with Arum Lilies
20 April 1953
Thrown and modelled; painted with slips and
incised
28.3 × 27.7 × 17
D., incised on side: *20.4.53.*;
stamp underneath base: *PLEIN FEU MADOURA*
M.P. 3717

491
Coupe
Bowl
5 June 1953
Grogged red body; thrown; painted with
pastels and black slip, partly under brushed
glaze; thick transparent enamel in bottom of
bowl
13.5 × 30 (diameter)
D. on outside in charcoal:
VALLAURIS 5 juin 1953
M.P. 3718

492
**Pichet décoré de 3 médaillons: paysage,
couple, femme au singe**
*Pitcher with Three Medallions: Landscape,
Couple and Woman with a Monkey*
4 July 1953
Grogged red body; thrown; painted with slips,
partly brush-glazed
27 × 21 × 17.5
D. on base in black slip:
VALLAURIS 4 juillet 1953;
stamp on back: *PLEIN FEU MADOURA*
M.P. 3719

493
Colombe
Dove
[1953]
White body; modelled slab; painted with slips and incised
14.5 × 26.3 × 13
R. 141
M.P. 3721

494
Carreau décoré d'une tête d'enfant laurée
Tile with a Child Wearing a Laurel Wreath
8 August 1956
Pastel under glaze
30.5 × 25.5 × 2
D.a.l.: *8.8.56.*
M.P. 3725

495
Carreau décoré d'une bacchanale: un silène assis et un buveur debout; on back: **12 caricatures**
Tile with Bacchanal: Seated Silenus and Standing Drinker; on back: *Twelve Caricatures*
14 December 1956
White body; very lightly scraped black slip background, with brush strokes of black slip and white tin glaze; back painted with black slip
30.5 × 25.5 × 2
D.a.l.: *14.12.56.*
M.P. 3726

496
Carreau décoré de deux personnages dont un musicien
Tile with Two Characters, One of Them a Musician
16 January 1957
Grogged red body; pastel and black slip under glaze
20 × 19.5 × 4
D.a.l.: *16.1.57.*;
on back, in black slip: *Cannes/16.1.57.*
M.P. 3729

497
Tomette hexagonale décorée de trois personnages: musicien, danseur et spectateur
Hexagonal Floor Tile with Three Characters: Musician, Dancer and Onlooker
28 January 1957
Grogged red body; pastel under brushed glaze
19.5 × 38.8 × 4
D. on lower edge in black slip: *28.1.57.*
M.P. 3730

498
Assiette décorée d'un petit visage central et de feuilles stylisées
Plate with a Small Central Face and Stylized Leaves
19 February 1957
Red body; thrown; painted with slips, incised and partly glazed with brush
23.5 (diameter) × 2
On underside: D. in black slip: *19.2.57.*;
stamp: *PLEIN FEU MADOURA*
M.P. 3731

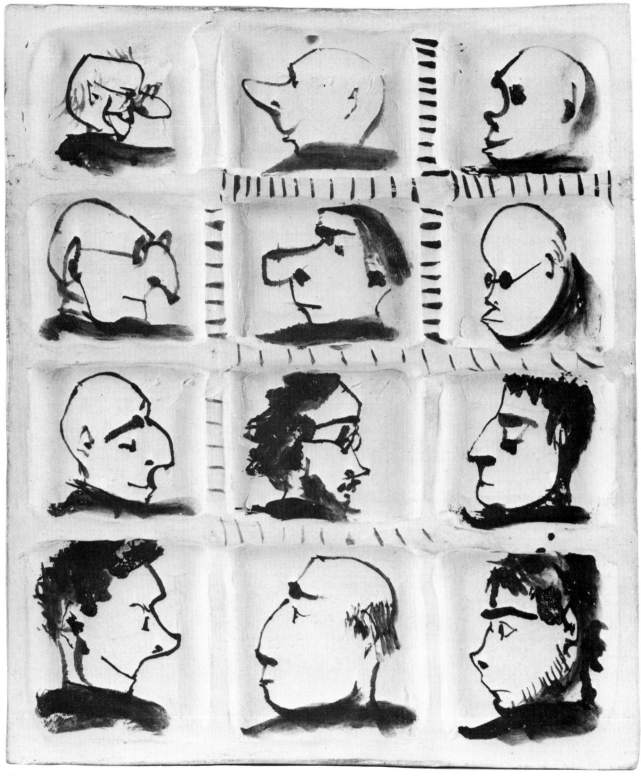

495 (back)   Twelve Caricatures

499
Tomette décorée de trois personnages: musicien, danseur et spectateur; on the back: **musicien et danseur avec une chèvre**
Floor Tile with Three Figures: Musician, Dancer and Onlooker; on the back: *Musician and Dancer with a Goat*
26 February 1957
Grogged red body; painted with pastel and slip under glaze; on reverse: design in black slip
20 × 33.5 × 4
D. on lower edge in black slip: *26.2.57.*
M.P. 3732

499 (reverse)

500
Assiette décorée de musiciens
Plate with Musicians
27 February 1957
Red body; thrown; painted with slips, scored areas under glaze, incised
23 (diameter) × 2
On underside: D. in black slip: *27.2.57.*; stamp: *PLEIN FEU MADOURA*
M.P. 3733

501
Tomette décorée d'une bacchanale: musicien, danseur et buveur
Floor Tile with Bacchanal: Musician, Dancer and Drinker
6 March 1957
Grogged red body; painted with slips
19.5 × 39.5 × 4
S.D. on back in black slip: *6.3.57./I Picasso*
M.P. 3734

502
Tomette hexagonale décorée d'un danseur et d'un musicien
Hexagonal Floor Tile with a Dancer and a Musician
6 March 1957
Red body; painted with slips
20 × 39.2 × 4
S.D. in black slip: *6.3.57.III/PICASSO*
M.P. 3735

503
Tomette découpée et décorée en forme de chouette
Floor Tile in the Form of an Owl
16 March 1957
Grogged red body; painted with slips and incised, all under brushed glaze
33.5 × 20 × 4
S.D. on the edge, below owl's feet: *16.3.57. PICASSO*
M.P. 3736

504

Plat espagnol décoré d'une chouette;
on underside: **trois taureaux en médaillons**
Spanish Dish with an Owl; on underside:
Three Bulls in Medallions
27 March 1957
Red body; thrown; dipped in white slip,
painted with black slip, incised and scored
surface, under glaze brushed on in parts;
incised pattern on underside
47.5 (diameter) × 6.5
D. incised on underside: *27.3.57.*
M.P. 3737

504 (underside)

505

Plat espagnol décoré d'une chouette;
on underside: **6 chouettes**
Spanish Dish with an Owl; on underside:
Six Owls
29 March 1957
Red body; thrown; dipped in white slip,
painted with black slip and incised; on back,
painted with black slip, incised and scored
surfaces
45 (diameter) × 7
D. incised on underside of rim: *29.3.57.*
M.P. 3738

505 (underside)

506

Plat espagnol décoré d'un taureau;
on underside: **3 têtes de taureaux et motifs**
Spanish Dish with a Bull; on underside:
Three Bulls' Heads and Various Patterns
30 March 1957
Red body; thrown; dipped in white slip,
painted with black slip, incised and scored
surfaces; on underside, blue slip, incised
45 (diameter) × 7.5
D. on underside, incised in centre: *30.3.57.*
M.P. 3739

506 (underside)

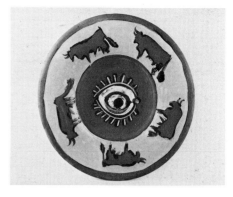

507
Coupe décorée d'un faune aux cymbales; on underside: **2 personnages**
Bowl with a Faun Holding Cymbals;
on underside: *Two Figures*
10 May 1957
White body; thrown; sprayed with iron-oxide primer and matt white glaze; painted with metal oxide, incised and scored
29 (diameter) × 8
D. incised on underside: *10.5.57.;*
stamp under base: *PLEIN FEU MADOURA*
M.P. 3740

507 (underside)

508
Plat espagnol décoré d'un œil et de taureaux; on underside: **tête de taureau**
Spanish Dish with an Eye and Bulls;
on underside: *Head of a Bull*
20 May 1957
Red body; thrown; painted with slips, incised and partly glazed with brush; on underside, incised black slip under glaze
40 (diameter) × 5.5
D. on underside in black slip: *20.5.57.*
M.P. 3741

508 (underside)

509
Vase globulaire décoré de hiboux
Globular Vase with Owls
15 November 1957
Red body; thrown; incised with a knife; blue slip partly covered with brushed glaze, runs of glaze, burnished with black slip
30 × 35 (diameter)
D. incised on front: *15.11.57.*
M.P. 3742

510
Plaque décorée d'une Infante (Les Ménines)
Plaque with an Infanta (Las Meninas)
Second half of 1957
White body; white tin glaze and metal oxides under glaze
24 × 19.2
M.P. 3743

507   Bowl with a Faun Holding Cymbals

509   Globular Vase with Owls

511
Joueur de flûte debout
Standing Flute Player
[1958]
Grogged reddish body (set of fifteen tiles);
painted with slips
213 × 83 × 2
M.P. 3744

512
Joueur de diaule assis
Seated Twin-pipe Player
[1958]
Grogged reddish body (set of twelve tiles);
painted with slips; scored areas and incised
126.5 × 125.5 × 2
M.P. 3745

513
**Vase à 2 anses décoré d'une tête de
faune et d'une chouette**
*Two-handled Vase with a Faun's Head and an
Owl*
14 February 1961
White body; thrown and assembled
components; painted with slips and incised
57.5 × 45 × 40
D. incised on front of foot: *14.2.61.*;
stamp inside neck: *PLEIN FEU MADOURA*
R. 584; S. C4
M.P. 3747

514
**Vase de forme ovoïde décoré d'une tête
de femme**
Egg-shaped Vase with Head of a Woman
21 February 1961
White body; thrown; painted with slips;
incised and scored areas
31.5 × 21 (diameter)
D. above left ear of figure, incised and traced
in blue slip: *21.2.61.*; two stamps under base:
PLEIN FEU MADOURA; EDITION PICASSO
M.P. 3748

515
**Vase à 2 anses décoré de têtes (1 face,
1 profil) et de 2 chouettes**
*Two-handled Vase with Heads (one frontally,
the other in profile) and Two Owls*
24 February 1961
White body; thrown and assembled
components; painted with slips
57 × 47 × 38
D. incised on foot of vase, at the back:
24.2.61.; two stamps inside neck:
EDITION PICASSO; PLEIN FEU MADOURA
M.P. 3749

516
Plat espagnol décoré d'un soleil;
on underside: **feuillage**
*Spanish Dish with Sun Pattern; on underside:
Leaf Pattern*
25 February 1961
Red body; thrown; dipped in white slip,
painted with slips, incised and scored
surfaces, all under brushed glaze; on
underside, incised black slip
37.5 (diameter) × 5.5
D. in black slip at centre of underside:
25.2.61.; stamp: *PLEIN FEU MADOURA*
M.P. 3750

516 (underside)

517
Carreau industriel décoré au verso d'une tête de faune
Mass-produced Tile with a Faun's Head on the Back
11–12 March 1961
Red body; painted with slips and partly covered with brushed glaze
20.5 × 20.3 × 0.8
D.a.r. in black slip: *11-12.61.*; on back, in black slip: *11.3.61.*
M.P. 3752

518
Carreau industriel décoré au verso d'une tête de faune
Mass-produced Tile with a Faun's Head on the Back
12 March 1961
Red body; painted with slips and partly covered with brushed glaze
15 × 15 × 0.8
D.a.r., in varnish: *12.3.61.*
M.P. 3751

519
Fragment de brique décoré d'un visage de femme
Piece of Brick with Face of a Woman
12 July 1962
White body; painted with slips
22 × 7.5 × 13
D. on inner side of brick, in black slip: *12.7.62.*
R. 592; S. C6
M.P. 3753

520
Fragment de brique: tête de femme
Piece of Brick with Head of a Woman
12 July 1962
White body; painted with black slip, partly covered with brushed glaze
22 × 16.5 × 8.5
D. on back in black slip: *12.7.62.*
R. 628; S. C5
M.P. 3754

521
d'après Picasso
Plaque rectangulaire décorée d'un faune musicien
After Picasso: Rectangular Plaque with a Faun Musician
White body; painted with slips
35.3 × 27
M.P. 3757

Picasso, Mougins, April 1965 (Musée Picasso Document, photo A. Gomes)

Picasso's Personal Collection

Picasso's exceptional importance in terms of twentieth-century art as a whole suggested that it would be appropriate to exhibit, as an integral part of the museum, the works of other artists – his masters or his contemporaries – as well as those objects of primitive art which particularly interested him and which, as we know, played a significant part in the evolution of Cubism. Throughout his life, Picasso sought inspiration in the art of the past. He drew upon world art for themes and images which he then reinterpreted in his own pictorial idiom. As contacts and opportunities arose, he also built up a personal art collection which is doubly interesting, both in what it reveals about the owner's personality and by its intrinsic worth. These works throw light on the painter's aesthetic universe, his tastes, his affinities and his friendships. The recollections of those who knew him intimately, as well as a host of photographs, point to the prominent position which these items occupied in his successive dwellings and how much Picasso was attached to them.

This additional section therefore covers, regardless of the techniques employed, not only those works by other artists now included in the Musée Picasso collections thanks to the 1973 gift, which had been on show in the Pavillon de Flore of the Louvre from 1978 to 1984 and have now been transferred to the Hôtel Salé, but also the settlement from the artist's estate in 1979 and other works made available through generous gifts and bequests since that date.

The outstanding importance of the original gift was stressed by Jean Leymarie in a publication dated 1978.[1] Among its most important items are works by Cézanne and Rousseau, from whom Cubism derived much of its inspiration, and by the artist's contemporaries – Braque, Derain, Matisse – the latter being represented by one of his masterpieces, the *Nature morte aux oranges* (*Still-life with Oranges*, cat. T.50) of 1912, bought by Picasso in 1944. The highly significant selection of Old Masters also requires a mention – Le Nain, Chardin, Corot, Courbet – because it reveals his taste for a particular French pictorial tradition. In the course of time, Picasso was to paraphrase Le Nain's *Le retour du baptême* (*The Return from the Christening*, cat. 51) and Courbet's *Les demoiselles des bords de Seine* (*Young Women on the Banks of the Seine*). In addition, there are works which suggested themes, such as Degas's monotypes for the *Maison Tellier* series (cat. T.19–T.30) – brothel scenes and voyeuristic views which Picasso took up again in his many *Suite 347* prints – and the Renoirs which immediately put one in mind of Picasso's large bathers of the 1920s.

Only one younger artist, Balthus, is represented in the collection by a painting (cat. T.3) purchased in 1941. Picasso also owned two pictures by his fellow-countryman Miró which plainly show the realist beginnings of this artist when he first reached Paris in 1919: a *Self-portrait* (cat. T.54) of 1919 and *Portrait d'une danseuse espagnole* (*Portrait of a Spanish Dancer*, cat. T.55) of 1921.

(1) *Donation Picasso, La collection personnelle de Picasso*, Paris, 1978.

The Settlement

Among the works acquired as part of the settlement in lieu of death duties, Derain's *Baigneuses* (*Bathers*, cat. T.31) of 1908 deserves a mention, if only as a token of the original contribution made to Cubism by this artist. It also acts as a reminder of the close ties linking the two painters at this time, of which Derain's 1908 drawing of Picasso (cat. T.32) provides further evidence. Drawings by Max Jacob, André Salmon and Guillaume Apollinaire, as well as a picture by Marie Laurencin, speak of the friendships of those heady days at the Bateau-Lavoir and the links with the poets of that time. The *Portrait of Alfred Jarry* by Hermann-Paul (cat. T.39) serves to confirm Picasso's interest in this writer.[2] A Bakst watercolour for *The Good Tempered Ladies* ballet (cat. T.2) recalls the work he did for the Ballets Russes.

A number of these works represent gifts and tributes by other artists, such as the portrait by Victor Brauner (cat. T.6) and the gouache cut-out by Matisse (cat. T.53), warmly dedicated to Picasso. The latter provides evidence of the far-ranging contacts linking the two main artistic poles in twentieth-century art and bears witness to the extent of the mutual respect involved.

There are also works by Dali, Ernst, Giacometti and Fernandez, evidence of Picasso's links with Surrealist circles and of the interest in him displayed by that group. The inventory of the estate brought to light a hitherto unpublished album of metaphysical drawings and some writings by Giorgio de Chirico (cat. T.18-1–T.18-23).[3] They had belonged to Paul Eluard, who had bought them during his trip to Italy in 1922, had had them mounted and bound in 1925 with the help of André Breton, and had then sold them to Picasso at some time between 1936 and 1940. The somewhat belated and chance inclusion of these drawings among Picasso's belongings nevertheless provides new material for a study of the complex and fleeting relations between him and De Chirico.

Finally, some of the works involved, such as the magnificent drawings by Seurat (cat. T.73–T.77) personally acquired by him at a Hôtel Drouot sale in 1942, represent deliberate purchases by Picasso.

The Artist's Dining Room, Montrouge, 1917 (M.P. 795)

Primitive Art

Although the museum does not have the whole of the artist's personal collection of primitive art at its disposal, all that is available here is of outstanding interest. It provides a check on the items actually present in his studio, gives some idea of his tastes and preferences in this area and makes it possible to study how these objects may have influenced some of his works, especially in the run-up to Cubism. Picasso's interest in African art went back to 1906, and was thus contemporaneous with that of Matisse, Vlaminck and Derain, but his real encounter with it – the aesthetic revelation – occurred in June 1907, during his now famous visit to the Musée du Trocadéro.

A list of these works shows that Picasso was less interested in their quality and intrinsic value than in their power of suggestion and formal invention. 'We bought these sculptures as works of art', pointed out D.-H. Kahnweiler. 'It was not merely their appearance, but an understanding of their intention which influenced Cubism.'[4] Among the earliest of such objects given house room by Picasso were the two carved roof posts from New Caledonia (cat. T.88, T.89), as a photograph of his studio taken in 1908 shows. The characteristic modelling of the legs, the way in which each body can be inscribed in a rectangle, the stocky and massive look of the crudely carved figures are reflected in some drawings and wood figurines dating from 1907. The actual provenance of these objects is not always perfectly clear. It is certain, however, that one of the finest pieces in the collection – the New Guinea sculpture (cat. T.83) – had belonged to Georges de Miré and was bought by Picasso at a sale on 7 May 1931 (Hôtel Drouot, No. 295). The Benin head (cat. T.81) was bought from Louis Carré in 1944. The

(2) A link noted by Ron Johnson in 'Picasso's "Demoiselles d'Avignon" and the theatre of the absurd', *Arts Magazine*, Vol. 55, No. 2, October 1980, pp. 102–13.

(3) Published by M. Fagiolo dell'Arco in *Cahiers du musée national d'art moderne*, Centre Georges Pompidou, No. 13, 1984, pp. 44–73.

(4) D.-H. Kahnweiler, *Confessions esthétiques*, Paris, 1963, p. 222.

The 'Nevinbumbaau' headdress (cat. T.80) in Picasso's studio at La Californie in Cannes (Picasso Archives)

The painter Ramon Pichot in Picasso's studio in the boulevard de Clichy in 1910–11. On the wall, the Punu mask (cat. T.84) (Picasso Archives)

Nimba mask from Guinea (cat. T.82) had been in his studio since 1931. (One is tempted to see a resemblance between this and the monumental heads of Marie-Thérèse in which one finds the same protuberant nose, a sexual symbol of fertility, and the way of treating each part of the face – the nose, the forehead, the skull – as separate volumes.) The Grebo (formerly called Wobe) mask (cat. T.90) was, according to Kahnweiler, actually the starting point for the upheaval which Picasso's sculpture underwent in 1912. He wrote that 'beneath a very high forehead curved slightly backwards, the Wobe masks display the lower part of the face as a flat surface on which the triangular nose, the parallelepiped mouth and the cylindrical eyes jut out. . . . The "true" shape of the face, represented as it is seen, is modelled to the front of the actual mask, at the end of the cylinder-eyes. The eyes are therefore seen as "hollows".' He remarks further on that 'the creation of imaginary signs, which is one of the characteristics of Negro masks, has made it possible to liberate sculpture from the block in which it is cut and thus make it transparent, in other words to display the inner space of a volume.'[5]

Picasso owned at least two Grebo masks.[6] It is obvious that the mask drawn on the wall of his Montrouge studio (M.P. 795) in 1917 was different from that now in the museum, since it is pictured without horns and with a longer beard. The 'Nevinbumbaau' headdress from the New Hebrides (cat. T.80) was a special gift from Matisse in 1947. Françoise Gilot relates that Matisse told Picasso: 'I've got something that's much better suited to you. It's from New Guinea. It's a full-sized human figure that's completely savage. It's just right for you. . . . ' 'That New Guinea thing frightens me', Picasso later confided to Françoise. 'I think it probably frightens Matisse too and that's why he's so eager to get rid of it. He thinks I'll be able to exorcise it better than he can.'[7]

Lastly, Picasso owned a Punu mask (cat. T.84), which can be seen on the wall of the boulevard de Clichy studio in 1911, and which also hangs on the right of the *Portrait of Kahnweiler*. Fernande Olivier mentioned this object in her memoirs: 'Picasso was specially fond of a small mask of a woman; the white paint on its face contrasted with the wood-coloured hair and produced a strangely gentle expression.'[8]

(5) D.-H. Kahnweiler, op. cit., p. 233.

(6) The second mask is reproduced in W. Spies, *Picasso, Das plastische Werk*, Stuttgart, 1983, p. 55.

(7) F. Gilot, C. Lake, *Life with Picasso*, New York, 1964, London, 1965, pp. 247 and 249.

(8) F. Olivier, *Picasso et ses amis*, Paris 1933, p. 170.

Head of a Man. Iberian sculpture
(Musée des Antiquités Nationales
de Saint-Germain-en-Laye)

Head of a Woman. Iberian sculpture
(Musée des Antiquités Nationales
de Saint-Germain-en-Laye)

Iberian Statuettes

The influence of Iberian art on Picasso's output in 1906[9] and its role in the elaboration of the initial part of *Les Demoiselles d'Avignon* are well enough known. Picasso had no doubt already seen Iberian works in Spain, but he was only able to confirm his impressions and study the stylistic features of these sculptures from the winter of 1905–1906 on, when the collection of reliefs from Osuna[10] was on exhibition at the Louvre. He also personally owned two Iberian stone heads, which he had acquired with the help of Apollinaire in 1907.[11]

The set of bronzes included in the settlement covers a different category of such works: *ex-votos* representing petitioners (cat. T.91–T.93, T.95, T.97–T.101) and dating from the fifth to the third centuries BC.

No document or witness exists to establish the date at which these pieces became part of Picasso's collection. It is known, however, that very similar pieces from the sanctuary of Despenaperros, brought back and catalogued by Lantier, formed part of the Louvre's collection in 1906, and that one of them had been stolen. An exhibition of Iberian art had also been held in Barcelona in 1903, and many Spanish artists, Picasso's close friend Santiago Rusiñol among them, also owned collections of these small bronzes. It therefore seems likely that Picasso may have been able to buy them at a very early stage, during the very period when he was interested in Iberian art, since they were fairly easy to come by in the open market. A number of replicas and copies were also made and sold locally soon after the excavations had taken place. This may help to explain the somewhat dubious character of some of the pieces in Picasso's collection (cat. T.93, T.95). Whatever the date of acquisition, however, it is easy enough to see what could have attracted Picasso in this type of work: the pronounced schematization of the faces, the monolithic and extended outlines of some of these statuettes (which one may trace, for instance, in the wooden figurines from Boisgeloup) and the forming of the arms into a geometrical figure. This is particularly marked in cat. T.92 and is closely related to some drawings of 1907, themselves representing variations on the theme of African statues. These formal features, characteristic of all archaic work, are supplemented by the Iberian origins of this primitive art, thus creating objects to which Picasso as a Spaniard could not fail to respond.

M.-L. B.-B.

Bibliography

J. Adhémar, F. Cachin, *Degas, gravures et monotypes*, Paris, 1973.
F. Cachin, A. Ceroni, *Tout l'œuvre peint de Modigliani*, Paris, 1972.
F. Daulte, *Auguste Renoir, catalogue raisonné de l'œuvre peint*, Vol. 1: *Figures, 1860–1890*, Lausanne, 1971.
J. Dupin, *Joan Miró*, Paris, 1961.
C. de Hauke, *Seurat et son œuvre*, Paris, 1961.
P.-A. Lemoisne, *Degas et son œuvre* (4 vols.), Paris, 1957–1959.
N. Mangin de Romilly, *Catalogue de l'œuvre de Georges Braque*, Paris, 1942–47.
A. Robaut, *L'œuvre de Corot*, Vol. 2, Paris, 1905.
D. Vallier, *Tout l'œuvre peint d'Henri Rousseau*, Paris, 1970.
L. Venturi, *Paul Cézanne, son art, son œuvre* (2 vols.), Paris, 1936.
A. Vollard, *Tableaux, pastels et dessins de P.-A. Renoir* (2 vols.), Paris, 1918, new ed. 1954.
N. Worms de Romilly, J. Laude, *Braque, le cubisme, fin 1907–1914*, Paris, 1982.

Iberian Bronzes

F. Alvarez-Ossorio, *Catálogo de los exvotos de bronce ibéricos*, Madrid, 1941 (ref.: A.O.)
G. Nicolini, *Les Ibères, Art et Civilisations*, Paris, 1973.
G. Nicolini, *Les bronzes figurés des sanctuaires ibériques*, Paris, 1969 (ref.: Nicolini, *Les bronzes*).
G. Nicolini, *Bronces ibéricos*, Barcelona, 1977 (ref.: Nicolini, *Bronces ibéricos*).

(9) P. Daix, *La vie de peintre de Pablo Picasso*, Paris, 1977, pp. 43–44; J. Golding, *Le cubisme*, Paris, 1962, p. 43; J.J. Sweeney, 'Picasso and Iberian Sculpture', *Art Bulletin*, No. 3, 1941.

(10) Excavations in 1903 by Paris and Engel.

(11) These heads had been stolen from the Musée du Louvre by Géry-Piéret, a Belgian adventurer who had been his secretary for a time. They were returned in 1911 through the intermediation of *Paris-Journal*.

Apollinaire (Guillaume)
1880–1918

T.1
Les oiseaux chantent avec les doigts
The Birds Sing with their Fingers
1916
Watercolour over pencil
16 × 10.8
Inscr. a.r.: *Les oiseaux chantent avec les doigts*; on back: *Guillaume Apollinaire, 1916, à P. Picasso*
Settlement
M.P. 3588

Bakst (Léon)
1866–1924

T.2
Portrait de dame
Portrait of a Lady
1917
Pencil, watercolour, gold paint on papier Ingres, mounted on pale-green cardboard with a gold stripe
49 × 33
S.D.b.l.: *Bakst, 1917*; inscr. a.r.: *Dames de bonne humeur, 'Constanza'*
Settlement
M.P. 3589

Balthus (Balthazar Klossowski de Rosa, called)
1908

T.3
Les enfants Hubert et Thérèse Blanchard
The Children Hubert and Thérèse Blanchard
1937
Oil on canvas
125 × 130
On back: Inscr. a.l.: *Les enfants Hubert et Thérèse Blanchard*
S.D.r.: *Balthus, 1937*
Picasso Gift
R.F. 1973–56

Braque (Georges)
1882–1963

T.4
Nature morte à la bouteille
Still-life with Bottle
1910–1911
Oil on canvas
55 × 46
On back: *Braque*; on stretcher: *Galerie Kahnweiler, 28, rue Vignon*
N.W. de Romilly, J. Laude, n° 78
Picasso Gift
R.F. 1973–58

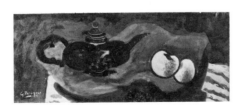

T.5
Théière et pommes
Teapot and Apples
1942
Oil on canvas
26 × 65
S.b.l.: *G. Braque*
N.M. de Romilly, p. 78
Picasso Gift
R.F. 1973–57

Brauner (Victor)
1902–1966

T.6
Pour Picasso, grand initiateur
For Picasso, The Great Initiator
Vallauris, 1953
Indian ink, watercolour and wax on paper
31 × 22
Dedication, S.b.r.: *Pour Picasso grand initiateur homme de la libertée son admirateur et son ami Victor Brauner*, D.b.l.: *Vallauris, 28.6.1953*
Settlement
M.P. 3617

Cézanne (Paul)
1839–1906

T.7
Cinq baigneuses
Five Bathers
1877–1878
Oil on canvas
45.8 × 55.7
L. Venturi, n° 385
Picasso Gift
R.F. 1973–61

T.8
La mer à l'Estaque
The Sea at l'Estaque
1878–1879
Oil on canvas
73 × 92
L. Venturi, n° 425
Picasso Gift
R.F. 1973–59

T.9
Château Noir
Château Noir
1905
Oil on canvas
74 × 94
L. Venturi, n° 795
Picasso Gift
R.F. 1973–60

Chardin (Jean-Baptiste-Siméon)
(?)
1699–1779

Corot (Jean-Baptiste-Camille)
1796–1875

T.10
Paysage: la cathédrale d'Aix
Landscape: Aix Cathedral
1904–1906
Watercolour over pencil
34 × 48
Picasso Gift
R.F. 35794

T.11
Table de cuisine et ustensiles avec un carré de mouton
Kitchen Table and Utensils with a Rack of Mutton
c. 1740
Oil on canvas
34 × 46
Picasso Gift
R.F. 1973–62

T.12
L'Italienne Maria di Sorre
The Italian Maria di Sorre
[1825–1828]
Paper pasted on cardboard
26.2 × 18
b.r.: stamp of Corot sale
A. Robaut, II, n° 64
Picasso Gift
R.F. 1973–66

Corot

T.13
M. Edouard Delalain
Mr Edouard Delalain
[1845–1850]
Oil on canvas
28.5 × 25
S.(?)b.r.: *Corot*
A. Robaut, II, nº 594
Picasso Gift
R.F. 1973–65

Corot (?)

T.14
La petite Jeannette
Little Jeannette
c. 1848
Paper on canvas
30 × 27
Picasso Gift
R.F. 1973–63

T.15
Paysage
Landscape
Oil on canvas
22 × 30.2
S.b.l.: *COROT*
Picasso Gift
R.F. 1973–64

Courbet (Gustave)
1819–1877

T.16
Tête de chamois
Head of a Chamois
Oil on canvas
38 × 46
S.b.l.: *G. Courbet*
Picasso Gift
R.F. 1973–67

Dali (Salvador)
1904

T.17
Dessin préparatoire pour 'La mémoire de la femme-enfant'
Preparatory Drawing for 'The Memory of the Child-Woman'
1932
Indian ink, pencil and crayon on papier Ingres
watermarked WBW
35.2 × 28
Inscr. b.c.: *La mémoire de la femme-Enfant*
Settlement
M.P. 3591

De Chirico (Giorgio)
1888–1978

T.18
Giorgio De Chirico: 12 tavole in fototipia, con vari giudizi critici (Twelve collotype plates, with various critical remarks), Rome, Edizioni di 'Valori Plastici', 1919. Not paginated, 24.5 × 19. Green half-morocco binding.

This copy had belonged to Paul Eluard and contains his ex-libris. It is supplemented at the start by the catalogue of the 'G. de Chirico' exhibition, Paris, Paul Guillaume, March–April 1922, 4 pages, and at the end by 15 pages, on which 8 original drawings have been mounted, and 11 manuscript sheets (including 1 drawing) mounted on guards, as well as by 18 manuscript pages from a notebook (including 1 drawing) mounted on guards, similarly by De Chirico. This copy is also accompanied by 14 original drawings and 12 manuscript pages by this artist.
M.P. 3590

De Chirico

T.18–1
L'énigme d'une journée
The Enigma of a Day
1913
Indian ink on lined paper mounted on a
bound album sheet
22 × 17.5
Inscr. b.r.: *l'énigme d'une journée*
Settlement
M.P. 3590–1

T.18–2
Sans titre [Place d'Italie, vue de haut]
Untitled [Italian Piazza, Seen from Above]
1914–1915
Ink and pencil on paper mounted on a bound
album sheet
11.5 × 15.7
Settlement
M.P. 3590–2

T.18–3
**Sans titre [Jeune fille devant une place
d'Italie]**
Untitled [Girl in front of an Italian Piazza]
1914
Ink on paper mounted on a bound album sheet
14.5 × 11.5
On back, inscription by the artist on a printed
form for exhibition at the Salon des
Indépendants, 1914:
1. *La nostalgie de l'infini*
2. *Les jours et les énigmes d'une heure
   étrange*
3. *L'énigme d'une journée*
Settlement
M.P. 3590–3

T.18–4
L'énigme de la fatalité
The Enigma of Fatality
Preparatory sketch
1914
Crayon on paper (back of mourning notice)
mounted on a bound album sheet
17.5 × 10.9
Inscr. a.r.: *L'énigme de la Fatalité*
Settlement
M.P. 3590–4

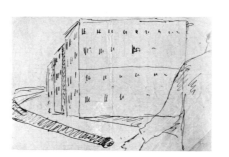

T.18–5
**Sans titre [Place d'Italie avec statue et
cheminée]**
*Untitled [Italian Piazza with Statue and
Chimney]*
1914
Indian ink on squared paper mounted on a
bound album sheet
13.1 × 20.8
Settlement
M.P. 3590–5

T.18–5 (back)
Etude de gant
Study of a Glove
Indian ink

De Chirico

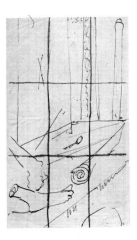

T.18–6
Esquisse pour 'Le mystère et la mélancolie d'une rue'
Sketch for 'The Mystery and Melancholy of a Street'
1914
Indian ink on squared paper mounted on a bound album sheet
12 × 21
Settlement
M.P. 3590–6

T.18–6 (back)
Esquisse pour 'Composition métaphysique'
Sketch for 'Metaphysical Composition'
1913
Indian ink and soft pencil

T.18–7
Sans titre [Jardins de Versailles]
Untitled [Gardens of Versailles]
1913
Pencil on lined paper mounted on a bound album sheet
15 × 20.5
On back, in the artist's hand: *Ce que doit être l'Impressionnisme...*
Settlement
M.P. 3590–7

T.18–8
Sans titre [Place d'Italie avec bananes]
Untitled [Italian Piazza with Bananas]
1913–1914
Pencil on lined paper mounted on a bound album sheet
21.3 × 16.4
On back, in the artist's hand: *Mélancolie*
Settlement
M.P. 3590–8

T.18–9
Esquisse pour 'Mélancolie d'une belle journée'
Sketch for 'Melancholy of a Fine Day'
1912–1913
Ink on lined paper
16.2 × 27
On back, in the artist's hand: *deuxième partie, le sentiment de la préhistoire*
Settlement
M.P. 3590–9

T.18–10
Sans titre [wagon, locomotive et statue]
Untitled [Railway Carriage, Engine and Statue]
1914
Pencil on green paper
13.9 × 18
On back: *Study of a Railway Carriage*
Settlement
M.P. 3590–I

T.18–11
**Etude pour 'Les joies et les énigmes
d'une heure étrange'**
*Study for 'The Joys and the Enigmas of a
Strange Hour'*
1913–1914
Ink and blue crayon on squared paper
13.5 × 20.8
Settlement
M.P. 3590–II

T.18–12
Sans titre [Place d'Italie]
Untitled [Italian Piazza]
[1913]
Pencil on paper
13.6 × 21.7
On back: writing paper headed 'Gustave
Dreyfus' addressed to *Madame la Baronne de
Chirico*; dated 30 June 1913
Settlement
M.P. 3590–III

T.18–13
La grande place mystérieuse
The Great Mysterious Square
1913–1914
Ink on squared paper
13.2 × 20.9
Inscr. b.r.: *La grande place mystérieuse*
Settlement
M.P. 3590–IV

T.18–14
Sans titre [Place d'Italie, vue de haut]
Untitled [Italian Piazza, Seen from Above]
1914
Ink on paper
13.7 × 15.3
Settlement
M.P. 3590–V

T.18–15
Esquisse pour 'L'après-midi d'Ariane'
Sketch for 'Ariadne's Afternoon'
1913
Pencil on paper
18 × 14
Settlement
M.P. 3590–VI

T.18–16
**Sans titre [Composition métaphysique
avec livre, œuf, main et flèche]**
*Untitled [Metaphysical Composition with
Book, Egg, Hand and Arrow]*
1914
Ink on lined paper
22 × 17
Settlement
M.P. 3590–VII

De Chirico

T.18–17
Sans titre [Statue entre deux arcades]
Untitled [Statue between Two Arcades]
1914
Soft pencil on squared paper
21.3 × 13.7
On back: part of a letter in purple ink
Settlement
M.P. 3590–VIII

T.18–18
Esquisse pour 'Nature morte: Turin printanier'
Sketch for 'Still-life: Turin in Springtime'
1914
Ink on squared paper
18.3 × 13.4
Settlement
M.P. 3590–IX

T.18–19
Sans titre [Composition avec tours gothiques, main et boulets de canon]
Untitled [Composition with Gothic Towers, Hand and Cannon-balls]
1914–1915
Pencil on paper, a piece of a Mussorgsky concert programme
16.7 × 9.2
Settlement
M.P. 3590–X

T.18–20
Etude pour 'Le mystère et la mélancolie d'une rue'
Study for 'The Mystery and Melancholy of a Street'
1914
Pencil on mauve paper
14.2 × 18.5
Settlement
M.P. 3590–XI

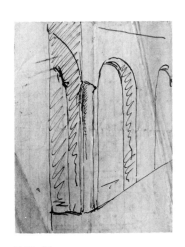

T.18–21
Etudes d'arcades
Studies of Arcades
1913–1914
Ink on lined paper
19.7 × 15
Settlement
M.P. 3590–XII

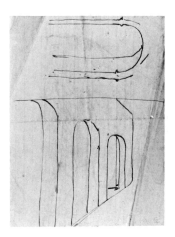

T.18–21 (back)
Etudes d'arcades
Studies of Arcades

De Chirico

T.18–22
Le vainqueur (Etude pour 'La Conquête du Philosophe')
The Victor (Study for 'The Philosopher's Conquest)'
1913–1914
Pencil on cardboard
13.7 × 10.5
Inscr. b.r.: *Le vainqueur*
Settlement
M.P. 3590–XIII

T.18–23
Etude de cheval pour 'L'énigme du cheval'
Study of a Horse for 'The Enigma of the Horse'
August 1913
Pencil on back of envelope
12.5 × 8.5
Settlement
M.P. 3590–XIV

Degas (Hilaire-Germain-Edgar de Gas, called) 1834–1917

T.19
Pianiste et chanteur
Pianist and Singer
[1877]
Monotype in black ink, highlighted in watercolour and pastel
16 × 12
P.A. Lemoisne, nº 437
Picasso Gift
R.F. 35789

T.20
Dans l'omnibus
In the Omnibus
[1877–1878]
Monotype in black ink on white paper
28 × 29.7
J. Adhémar, F. Cachin, nº 33
Picasso Gift
R.F. 35792

T.21
La fête de la patronne
The Party for the Madame
[1878–1879]
Monotype in black ink touched up with pastel
26.6 × 29.6
P.A. Lemoisne, nº 549
Picasso Gift
R.F. 35791

T.22
Repos sur le lit
A Rest on the Bed
[1878–1879]
Monotype in black ink on rice paper
12.1 × 16.4
Studio stamp on back, b.l.
J. Adhémar, F. Cachin, nº 102
Picasso Gift
R.F. 35783

Degas

T.23
Trois filles assises de dos
Three Seated Prostitutes from the Back
[1879]
Monotype in black ink on white paper,
touched up with pastel
16 × 22
P.A. Lemoisne, no 548
Picasso Gift
R.F. 35790

T.24
L'attente
The Wait
[1879]
Monotype in black ink on rice paper
12.1 × 16.4
Studio stamp on back, b.l.
J. Adhémar, F. Cachin, no 86
Picasso Gift
R.F. 35784

T.25
Au salon
In the Salon
[1879]
Monotype in black ink on thick white paper
16.4 × 21.5
Studio stamp on back, b.l.
J. Adhémar, F. Cachin, no 87
Picasso Gift
R.F. 35785

T.26
L'attente (second version)
The Wait (second version)
[1879]
Monotype in black ink on rice paper
21.6 × 16.4
Studio stamp on back, b.l.
J. Adhémar, F. Cachin, no 94
Picasso Gift
R.F. 35786

T.27
Repos
Rest
[1879]
Monotype in black ink on rice paper
16.4 × 21.6
Studio stamp on back, b.l.
J. Adhémar, F. Cachin, no 113
Picasso Gift
R.F. 35787

T.28
Le client
The Client
[1879]
Monotype in black ink on white paper
22 × 16.4
Studio stamp on back, b.l.
J. Adhémar, F. Cachin, no 95
Picasso Gift
R.F. 35788

Degas

T.29
Sur le lit
On the Bed
[1880]
Monotype in black ink on rice paper
16 × 11.7
Studio stamp on back, b.l.
Settlement
M.P. 3592

T.30
Femme vue en buste, 'La bonne'
Head and Shoulders of a Woman, 'The Maid'
1880
Monotype in black ink
8.7 × 7.9
J. Adhémar, F. Cachin, nº 37
Picasso Gift
R.F. 35782

T.31
Baigneuses
Bathers
1908
Oil on cardboard
24 × 32.5
Settlement
M.P. 3593

Ernst (Max)
1891–1976

T.32
Portrait de Picasso
Portrait of Picasso
1908
Brushed ink on paper (album page)
21.5 × 16.9
Inscr. b.r. by Picasso: *Mon portrait fait par
André Derain*
Settlement
M.P. 3594

T.33
Portrait de jeune fille
Portrait of a Girl
1914
Oil on canvas
61 × 50
Picasso Gift
R.F. 1973–68

T.34
L'oiseau forestier
The Forest Bird
[1927–1928]
Oil on paper pasted on cardboard
31 × 22
S.b.r.: *max ernst*
Settlement
M.P. 3595

Fernandez (Louis)
1900–1973

T.35
Composition érotique
Erotic Composition
[1936]
Pencil on two sheets of paper
107.5 × 65.5
Settlement
M.P. 3596

T.36
Composition érotique
Erotic Composition
[1936]
Pencil on paper
107.5 × 65.5
Settlement
M.P. 3597

Gauguin (Paul) (?)
1848–1903

T.37
Paysage
Landscape
Oil on canvas
65 × 50
Picasso Gift
R.F. 1973–69

Giacometti (Alberto)
1901–1966

T.38
Portrait d'Innocent X d'après Vélasquez
Portrait of Innocent X after Velázquez
1942
Pencil on paper
25.5 × 20.5
S.b.r.: *Alberto Giacometti*
Settlement
M.P. 3599

Hermann-Paul
1874–1950

T.39
Portrait d'Alfred Jarry
Portrait of Alfred Jarry
[1901–1905]
Pencil, ink, crayon and gouache on paper
pasted on cardboard
53 × 34
Dedicated, S.a.l.: *à Alfred Jarry, Hermann Paul*
Settlement
M.P. 3598

Jacob (Max)
1876–1944

T.40
Portrait de Picasso
Portrait of Picasso
[1903]
Indian ink on paper
26 × 17.5
Inscr. a.r.: *retrato hecho por Max Jacob*
Settlement
M.P. 3600

Jacob

T.41
Portrait de Manolo
Portrait of Manolo
[1903]
Pencil, purple ink and crayons on paper
23 × 15.8
Inscr. a.r.: *De Manolo*
Settlement
M.P. 3601

T.41 (back)
Tête de Manolo
Head of Manolo

Laurencin (Marie)
1885–1956

T.42
La songeuse
The Dreamer
[1910–1911]
Oil on canvas
91 × 73
S.a.l.: *Marie Laurencin*
Settlement
M.P. 3602

Le Nain (?) Louis (?)

T.43
La halte du cavalier
The Horseman's Rest
Oil on canvas
57 × 67
Picasso Gift
R.F. 1973–70

Master of the Procession of the Ram (follower of the Le Nain brothers)

T.44
La procession du bœuf gras, also called
La fête du vin
The Procession of the Fatted Ox, also called
The Wine Feast
108 × 166
Picasso Gift
R.F. 1973–71

Maar (Dora)
(wrongly attributed ?)

T.45
Picasso et son modèle
Picasso and his Model
Pencil on paper
19.6 × 20
Inscr. in Picasso's hand a.l.:
Dessin de Dora Maar
Settlement
M.P. 3604

Matisse (Henri)
1869–1954

T.46
Les Alpes de Savoie
The Savoy Alps
c. 1901
Oil on canvas pasted on cardboard
36 × 48
S.b.r.: *Henri Matisse*
Picasso Gift
R.F. 1973–76

T.47
Les Aiguilles Vertes et la Croix de Javernaz
The Aiguilles Vertes and the Croix de Javernaz
c. 1901
Oil on canvas pasted on cardboard
36 × 48
Picasso Gift
R.F. 1973–75

T.48
Bouquet de fleurs dans la chocolatière
Bunch of Flowers in a Chocolate Pot
[1902]
Oil on canvas
64 × 46
S.b.l.: *Matisse H.*
Picasso Gift
R.F. 1973–73

T.48 (back)
Etude de nature morte
Study for Still-life

T.49
Marguerite
Marguerite
1907
Oil on canvas
65 × 54
Inscr. a.l.: *Marguerite*
Picasso Gift
R.F. 1973–77

T.50
Nature morte aux oranges
Still-life with Oranges
1912
Oil on canvas
94 × 83
S.b.l.: *Henri Matisse*
Picasso Gift
R.F. 1973–72

Matisse

T.51
Jeune fille assise, robe persane
Seated Girl in a Persian Dress
1942
43 × 56
S.D.b.r.: *Henri Matisse 12/42*
Picasso Gift
R.F. 1973–78

T.52
Tulipes et huîtres sur fond noir
Tulips and Oysters on a Black Background
1943
Oil on canvas
61 × 73
D.S.b.r.: *2/43, Henri Matisse*
Picasso Gift
R.F. 1973–74

T.53
Papier découpé
Paper Cut-out
December 1947
Gouache, cut out and pasted on paper
40.5 × 26
Dedicated, S.D.b.r.: *à Picasso,
affectueusement H. Matisse, déc. 47*
Settlement
M.P. 3605

Miró (Joan)
1893–1983

T.53 (back)
Visage de femme
Face of a Woman
Pencil on paper

T.54
Autoportrait
Self-portrait
1919
Oil on canvas
73 × 60
S.D.a.l.: *Miró 1919*
J. Dupin, n° 67
Picasso Gift
R.F. 1973–79

T.55
Portrait d'une danseuse espagnole
Portrait of a Spanish Dancer
1921
Oil on canvas
66 × 56
S.D.a.r.: *Miró 1921*
J. Dupin, n° 73
Picasso Gift
R.F. 1973–80

Modigliani (Amedeo)
1884–1920

T.56
Jeune fille brune, assise
Brunette Girl, Seated
[1918]
Oil on canvas
92 × 60
S.a.r.: *Modigliani*
F. Cachin, A. Ceroni, nº 86
Picasso Gift
R.F. 1973–81

Ortiz de Zarate (Manuel)
1886–1946

T.57
Portrait de Picasso
Portrait of Picasso
[1920–1925]
Oil on wood panel
41 × 32.7
On back: *retrato de Picasso por Ortiz de Zarate*
Settlement
M.P. 3606

Prévert (Jacques)
1900–1977

T.58
Portrait de Salvadi d'Alors
Portrait of Salvadi d'Alors
[n.d.]
Collage, ink on paper
32.5 × 23.5
Inscr. b.r. *BY*; a.l.: *Portrait de Salvadi d'Alors*
Settlement
M.P. 3607

Prévert (Jacques)
Villers (André)

T.59
Photo-collage 'A Picasso'
Photo-collage 'To Picasso'
[1955–1960]
Paper collage on photograph
23 × 29.5 (with mount: 28 × 44)
Dedicated, S.a.r.: *à Picasso, Jacques*
Settlement
M.P. 3608

T.60
Photo-collage 'A Pablo Picasso'
Photo-collage 'To Pablo Picasso'
[1951]
Paper collage on photograph
34 × 24 (with mount: 45.8 × 32.6)
Dedicated, S.b.r.: *A Pablo Picasso, son ami Jacques Prévert et André Villers*
Settlement
M.P. 3609

Renoir (Pierre-Auguste)
1841–1919

T.61
Mythologie, personnages de tragédie antique
Mythology, Characters from Classical Tragedy
[1895]
Oil on canvas
41 × 24
Studio label b.r.: *Renoir*
Picasso Gift
R.F. 1973–82

Renoir

T.62
Baigneuse assise dans un paysage,
also called **Eurydice**
Bather Seated in a Landscape, also called
Eurydice
[1895–1900]
Oil on canvas
116 × 89
S.b.r.: *Renoir*
F. Daulte, I, n° 392
Picasso Gift
R.F. 1973–87

T.63
La coiffure or **La toilette de la baigneuse**
The Coiffure, or *The Bather's Toilette*
[1900–1901]
Sanguine and white chalk on canvas
145 × 103
Picasso Gift
R.F. 35793

T.64
Paysage méditerranéen, Cagnes
Mediterranean Landscape, Cagnes
[1905–1910]
Oil on canvas
17 × 18
Initialled b.r.: *R*
F. Daulte, II, pl. 123
Picasso Gift
R.F. 1973–86

T.65
Portrait d'enfant
Portrait of a Child
[1910–1912]
Oil on canvas
41 × 33
S.b.r.: *Renoir*
F. Daulte, I, n° 494
Picasso Gift
R.F. 1973–83

T.66
Nature morte aux poissons
Still-life with Fish
1916
Oil on canvas
40 × 50
S.D.b.r.: *Renoir 1916*
A. Vollard, II, pl. 68
Picasso Gift
R.F. 1973–85

T.67
Portrait de modèle en buste
Head and Shoulders Portrait of a Model
1916
Oil on canvas
55 × 46
S.D.b.l.: *Renoir 1916*
F. Daulte, I, n° 194
Picasso Gift
R.F. 1973–84

Rousseau (Henri)
(known as 'Le Douanier Rousseau')
1844–1910

T.68
Portrait de femme
Portrait of a Woman
[1895]
Oil on canvas
160 × 105
D. Vallier, nº 85
Picasso Gift
R.F. 1973–90

T.69
Portrait de l'artiste à la lampe
Portrait of the Artist with a Lamp
[1902–1903]
Oil on canvas
23 × 19
D. Vallier, nº 140A
Picasso Gift
R.F. 1973–88

T.70
**Portrait de la seconde femme de
Rousseau**
Portrait of Rousseau's Second Wife
[1903]
Oil on canvas
23 × 19
D. Vallier, nº 140B
Picasso Gift
R.F. 1973–89

Salmon (André)
1881–1969

Seurat (Georges)
1859–1891

T.71
**Les représentants des puissances
étrangères venant saluer la République
en signe de paix**
*The Representatives of the Great Powers
Arriving to Salute the Republic as a Mark of
Peace*
1907
Oil on canvas
130 × 161
S.D.b.r.: *Henri J. Rousseau 1907*
D. Vallier, nº 194
Picasso Gift
R.F. 1973–91

T.72
Portrait de Monsieur Picasso
Portrait of Señor Picasso
Paris, 1908
Watercolour on paper
20.4 × 16.9
S.D.a.r.: *Portrait de Monsieur Picasso par
André Salmon, Paris 1908*
Settlement
M.P. 3611

T.73
**Etude de jupe pour 'Un dimanche d'été à
la Grande Jatte'**
*Study of Skirt for 'A Sunday in Summer at the
Grande Jatte'*
1884–1885
Conté pencil on paper
30 × 17
de Hauke, nº 624
Settlement
M.P. 3612

Seurat

T.74
Femme de dos (négresse)
Woman from the Back (Negress)
1880–1881
Conté pencil on paper
16.2 × 10.5
Inscr.: *rouge, orangé, jaune, vert*
de Hauke, n° 390
Settlement
M.P. 3613

T.75
Femme assise
Seated Woman
[1881]
Conté pencil on paper
16.2 × 10.6
On back: *Seurat, Vente Hôtel Drouot,*
3-11-1942, n° 55 du catalogue
de Hauke, n° 437
Settlement
M.P. 3614

T.76
Couple assis
Seated Couple
[1881]
Conté pencil on paper
16.2 × 10.5
On back: *Seurat, Vente Hôtel Drouot,*
3-11-42, n° 56 du catalogue
de Hauke, n° 438
Settlement
M.P. 3615

Van Dongen (Kees)
1881–1968

Vuillard (Edouard)
1868–1940

T.77
Femme debout
Standing Woman
[1881]
Conté pencil
16 × 10.5
On back: *Seurat, Vente Hôtel Drouot,*
3-11-1942, n° 54 du catalogue
de Hauke, n° 426
Settlement
M.P. 3616

T.78
La vigne
The Vineyard
[1905]
Oil on canvas
46 × 55
S.a.r.: *V.D.*; Inscr. on back: *la vigne*; Inscr. on
the stretcher: *05 Kees Van Dongen*
Picasso Gift
R.F. 1973–92

T.79
La berceuse
The Cradle Song
[1896]
Lined cardboard on strengthened wooden
panel
28 × 49
Studio label b.r.
Picasso Gift
R.F. 1973–93

Primitive Art

T.80
Coiffure cérémonielle 'Nevinbumbaau'
'Nevinbumbaau' Ceremonial Headdress
Vanuatu (New Hebrides, South Malekula)
Tree ferns and pandanus coated in painted clay
114 × 60 × 92
With chair: 135 × 63 × 92
Settlement
M.P. 3624

T.81
Tête en bronze
Bronze Head
Kingdom of Benin (Nigeria)
Bronze
54 × 39 (diameter)
Settlement
M.P. 3636

T.82
Masque Nimba
Nimba Mask
Baga (Guinea)
Wood and raffia
126 × 59 × 64
Settlement
M.P. 3637

T.83
Sculpture (fragment)
Part of a Sculpture
New Guinea, Lower Sepik
Wood
45.5 × 20 × 17.5
Settlement
M.P. 3638

T.84
Masque Mukuyi
Mukuyi Mask
Punu (Gabon, left bank of N'Gounié River)
Baobab wood and kaolin powder
28 × 16 × 13
Settlement
M.P. 3639

T.85
Masque Tsogho
Tsogho Mask
Gabon
Wood coated with white clay, poso raffia streamers
28 × 18 × 12
Settlement
M.P. 3640

Primitive Art

T.86
Masque du Kono
Kono Mask
Bambara (Mali)
Wood, sacrificially smeared
72.5 × 33.5 × 23.5
Settlement
M.P. 3641

T.87
Masque Bélier (Saga)
Saga Ram Mask
Bozo (Mali)
Wood, metal plate and cloth
30 × 24.5 × 49.5
Settlement
M.P. 3642

T.88
Sculpture masculine: Poteau de faîtage
Male Figure: Roof Post
New Caledonia
Wood
126 × 19
Settlement
M.P. 3643

T.89
Sculpture féminine: Poteau de faîtage
Female Figure: Roof Post
New Caledonia
Wood
118.5 × 16
Settlement
M.P. 3644

T.90
Masque Grebo
Grebo Mask
Grebo (Ivory Coast)
Wood, white paint, plant fibres
64 × 25 × 16; beard: 16
Gift of Marina Ruiz-Picasso
M.P. 1983–7

Iberian Bronzes

T.91
Bronze ibérique: Orante
Iberian Bronze: Female Petitioner
Bronze
12.6 × 3.5 × 2.4
Akin to A.O., n⁰ 60
Settlement
M.P. 3625

T.92
Bronze ibérique: Orant nu
Iberian Bronze: Nude Male Petitioner
Sixth or fifth century BC
Bronze
84 × 3.7 × 1.7
Akin to A.O. n⁰ 2381
Settlement
M.P. 3626

T.93
Bronze ibérique (?): Orante
Iberian Bronze (?): Female Petitioner
Bronze
7.7 × 2.5 × 1.4
Akin to A.O., n⁰ 1575
Settlement
M.P. 3627

T.94
Bronze ibérique: Taureau
Iberian Bronze: Bull
Bronze
5.1 × 2.7 × 7.3
Akin to A.O., n⁰ 1839
Settlement
M.P. 3628

T.95
Bronze ibérique (?): Orant
Iberian Bronze (?): Male Petitioner
Bronze
7.9 × 2.7 × 1.8
Akin to Nicolini, *Bronces ibéricos*, n⁰ 86
Settlement
M.P. 3629

T.96
Statuette en bronze
Bronze Statuette
Provenance unknown
Bronze
10.3 × 4.8 × 1.9
Settlement
M.P. 3630

Iberian Bronzes

T.97
Bronze ibérique: Orant
Iberian Bronze: Male Petitioner
Fourth or third century BC
Bronze
3.6 × 0.3 × 0.3
Nicolini, *Les bronzes*, pp. 252–53
Settlement
M.P. 3631

T.98
Bronze ibérique: Orant
Iberian Bronze: Male Petitioner
Fourth or third century BC
Bronze
5.7 × 0.8 × 0.5
Settlement
M.P. 3632

T.99
Bronze ibérique: Orant
Iberian Bronze: Male Petitioner
Fourth or third century BC
Bronze
8.1 × 1.3 × 1.3
Settlement
M.P. 3633

T.100
Bronze ibérique: Orante
Iberian Bronze: Female Petitioner
Bronze
9.5 × 1.3 × 1.3
Akin to A.O., nos 1387, 1588, 1590
Settlement
M.P. 3634

T.101
Bronze ibérique (?): Orante
Iberian Bronze (?): Female Petitioner
Bronze
10.5 × 1.6 × 1.2
Akin to A.O., no 1388
Settlement
M.P. 3635

New Acquisitions[1]

The task of the Musée Picasso is not merely to make this artist's work generally available. It also involves placing his output within its historical context and bringing together all the documents that relate to the *oeuvre*, to the man himself and to the era with which he is so indissolubly linked. It therefore appeared important to enrich his private collection with works which recall these links and the unique scope of that 'Picasso universe' which touches upon every field of creativity.

This is the perspective which has brought to the museum, thanks to a number of generous gifts and bequests, Matisse's preliminary sketch for the *Still-life with Oranges* (cat. T.105), an engraving by Marcoussis of Gertrude Stein and Alice B. Toklas (cat. T.104) and two portraits of Picasso, by Giacometti (cat. T.102) and by Hoffmeister (cat. T.103).

The Musée Picasso's collection also contains a large number of photographs, by Man Ray, Dora Maar, Henri Cartier-Bresson, Cecil Beaton and others, which have not been listed in this catalogue. They are to form part of a later publication which will deal with all the photographs in the possession of the museum, including those obtained by settlement or gift, and others derived from the Picasso Archives holding.

Similarly, the manuscripts acquired as part of the settlement are not represented here. They will be published in the course of time in works specially devoted to the archives.

M.-L. B.-B.

[1] Other than works by Picasso listed earlier in the present catalogue.

Giacometti (Alberto)
1901–1966

T.102
Hommage à Picasso
Homage to Picasso
1961
Blue ink on paper
32 × 24
D.S. and dedicated: *Pour Picasso. Pourquoi ce dessin si je ne sais pas Stampa 28 juillet 1961 Alberto Giacometti*
Gift of M. and Mme Jean Krugier, 1980
M.P. 1981–1

Hoffmeister (Adolphe)
1902–1973

T.103
Portrait de Picasso
Portrait of Picasso
1958
Ink and collage on paper
31 × 22.1
S.D.b.r.: *A.H. 58/Cannes*
Gift of Mathilde Visser, 1980
M.P. 1980–109

Marcoussis (Louis Markous, called)
1883–1941

T.104
Portrait de Gertrude Stein et Alice B. Toklas
Portrait of Gertrude Stein and Alice B. Toklas
c. 1934
Copper engraving
45.5 × 32.5
Third state
S. on sheet: *Marcoussis*
Gift of Raoul Leven, 1980
M.P. 1980–106

Matisse (Henri)
1869–1954

T.105
Esquisse pour 'Nature morte aux oranges'
Sketch for 'Still-life with Oranges'
1912
Indian ink on paper
26 × 17.1
S.c.: *Tanger, H. Matisse*
Gift of M. Lionel Prejger, 1981
M.P. 1981–2

Exhibitions

Select Bibliography

Chronology

Concordances

Exhibitions

This list is essentially limited to Picasso's one-man exhibitions. However, it also includes group exhibitions up until 1910, as these are not very numerous; and also certain exhibitions devoted to Picasso and one other artist when there is particular significance in the association of the two names.

1900
Picasso, Barcelona, Els Quatre Gats, February 1900.

1901
Picasso, pastels, Barcelona, Sala Parès, June 1901.
Exposition de tableaux de F. Iturrino et de P.R. Picasso, preface by Gustave Coquiot, Paris, Galerie Ambroise Vollard, 25 June–14 July 1901.

1902
Tableaux et pastels de Louis Bernard-Lemaire et de Picasso, preface by Adrien Farge, Paris, Galerie Berthe Weill, 1–15 April 1902.
Peintures, pastels et dessins de MM. Girieud, Launay, Picasso et Pichot, preface by Harlor, Paris, Galerie Berthe Weill, 15 November–15 December 1902.

1904
Exposition de MM. Charbonnier, Clary-Baroux, Dufy, Girieud, Picabia, Picasso, Thiesson, preface by Maurice Le Sieutre, Paris, Galerie Berthe Weill, 24 October–20 November 1904.

1905
Exposition d'œuvres de MM. Trachsel, Gérardin, Picasso, preface by Charles Morice, Paris, Galerie Serrurier, 25 February–6 March 1905.

1910
Picasso, Paris, Galerie Notre-Dame-des-Champs, May 1910.
Braque et Picasso, Munich, Galerie Thannhauser, 1–15 September 1910.

1910–1911
Picasso, Paris, Galerie Ambroise Vollard, December 1910–February 1911.

1911
Pablo Picasso, an Exhibition of Early and Recent Drawings and Watercolors, preface by Marius de Zayas, New York, '291', Little Galleries of the Photo-Secession, 28 March–25 April 1911.

1912
Œuvres anciennes de Picasso, Barcelona, Galeria Dalmau, February 1912.
26 dessins de Picasso, London, Stafford Gallery, April 1912.

1913
Picasso, œuvres de 1901 à 1912, introduction by Justin Thannhauser, Munich, Galerie Thannhauser, February 1913.

1914
Picasso, Dresden, Kunstsalon Emil Richter, January 1914.
Pablo Picasso, Vienna, Galerie Miethke, February–March 1914.

1914–1915
Picasso and Braque. An Exhibition of Recent Drawings and Paintings, New York, '291', Photo-Secession Gallery, 9 December 1914–9 January 1915.

1918
Matisse et Picasso, preface by Apollinaire, Paris, Galerie Paul Guillaume, 23 January–15 February 1918.

1919
Dessins et aquarelles par Picasso, preface by André Salmon, Paris, Galerie Paul Rosenberg, 20 October–15 November 1919.

1920
Picasso, Paris, Galerie Paul Rosenberg, 1920.

1921
Works by Pablo Picasso, introduction by Clive Bell, London, Leicester Galleries, January 1921.
Picasso, Paris, Galerie Paul Rosenberg, May–June 1921.

1922
Picasso, Munich, Galerie Thannhauser, autumn 1922.

1923
Picasso Drawings, Chicago, Arts Club, 1923.
Pablo Picasso, 1906–1913, Munich, Galerie Thannhauser, 1923.
Recent Work, New York, Paul Rosenberg/Wildenstein Gallery, November 1923.

1923–1924
Exhibition of Paintings by Pablo Picasso, introduction by Clive Bell, Chicago, Art Institute, 18 December 1923–21 January 1924.

1924
Œuvres nouvelles de Picasso, Paris, Galerie Paul Rosenberg, 28 March–17 April 1924.
Picasso. Cent dessins, Paris, Galerie Paul Rosenberg, April 1924.

1926
Picasso. Œuvres récentes, Paris, Galerie Paul Rosenberg, 15 June–10 July 1926.

1927
Picasso, Drawings, New York, Wildenstein Galleries, 1927.
Cent dessins par Picasso, Paris, Galerie Paul Rosenberg, 15 June–13 July 1927.
Dessins, aquarelles et pastels de 1902 à 1927, Berlin, Galerie Alfred Flechtheim, 16 October–10 November 1927.

1927–1928
Picasso, Paris, Galerie Pierre, December 1927–February 1928.

1928
Original Drawings by Picasso, loaned by Wildenstein and Co., Chicago, Arts Club, 1928.

1930
Picasso, Paris, Galerie M.G. Aron, 1930.
Picasso et Derain, New York, Reinhardt Galleries, 25 January–2 March 1930.
15 peintures, Chicago, Arts Club, March–April 1930.
22 Drawings and Gouaches (1907–1928), text by Frank Crowninshield, New York, John Becker, 1 October–1 November 1930.

1931
Picasso: Ovid Illustrations, New York, Marie Harriman Gallery, 1931.
Picasso, 15 Etchings for Ovid's Metamorphoses, Cambridge, Harvard Society for Contemporary Art, January 1931.
Abstractions of Picasso, New York, Valentine Gallery, January 1931.
Thirty Years of Pablo Picasso, preface by Gertrude Stein, London, Alex Reid and Lefevre Ltd, June 1931.
Exposition d'œuvres de Picasso, peintures, gouaches, pastels, dessins, d'époques diverses, Paris, Galerie Percier, 23 June–11 July 1931.
Quelques œuvres importantes de Picasso, Paris, Paul Rosenberg, 1–21 July 1931.
Pablo R. Picasso, Paintings, New York, Demotte Inc., December 1931.

1932
Illustrations d'Ovide par Pablo Picasso, Munich, Graphisches Kabinett, 1932.
Illustrations for Ovid's Metamorphoses, Cambridge, Harvard Society for Contemporary Art, 5–27 January 1932.
Radierungen von Pablo Picasso zu den Metamorphosen des Ovid, Berlin, Galerie Flechtheim, 2–30 April 1932.
Picasso, catalogue by Charles Vrancken, Paris, Galerie Georges Petit, 16 June–30 July 1932.
Picasso, catalogue by Charles Vrancken, introduction by W. Wartmann, Zurich, Kunsthaus, 11 September–13 November 1932.

Œuvres de Picasso et de Ramón Casas, Barcelona, Galeria la Pinacoteca, 1–14 October 1932.
Gravures de Picasso et objets de Joseph Cornell, New York, Julien Levy Gallery, 26 November–30 December 1932.

1933
Picasso, preface by Valentine Dudensing, New York, Valentine Gallery, 6 March–1 April 1933.

1934
Pablo Picasso, Hartford, Wadsworth Atheneum, 6 February–1 March 1934.
Picasso, Buenos Aires, Galeria Müller, October 1934.

1935
Picasso. Papiers collés, introduction by Tristan Tzara, Paris, Galerie Pierre, 20 February–20 March 1935.

1936
Picasso, sculptures, Paris, Galerie Cahiers d'Art, 1936.
Picasso, Peintures et dessins 1900–1910, Paris, Galerie Kaete Perls, 1936.
Picasso, Barcelona, ADLAN (Amigos de las Artes Nuevas), Sala Esteva, 13 January–28 February 1936; Bilbao, March 1936; then Malaga and Madrid, 1936.
Picasso. Dessins, Paris, Galerie Renou et Colle, 14–28 February 1936.
28 œuvres de Picasso, Paris, Galerie Paul Rosenberg, 4–31 March 1936.
57 œuvres de Picasso, London, Zwemmer Galleries, 20 May–20 June 1936.
Picasso 1901–1934, Retrospective Exhibition, New York, Valentine Gallery, 26 October–21 November 1936.
Picasso Blue and Rose Periods, 1901–1906, New York, Jacques Seligmann & Co., Inc., 2–26 November 1936.

1937
Watercolors and Gouaches by Picasso, Chicago, Art Institute, 1937.
Picasso: Recent Works, London, Rosenberg and Helft Gallery, 1937.
Fifty Drawings by Pablo Picasso, London, Zwemmer Gallery, 1937.
Picasso, les débuts du cubisme, Paris, Galerie Pierre, 9–24 April 1937.
Drawings, Gouaches and Pastels by Picasso, New York, Valentine Gallery, 12–24 April 1937.
Picasso from 1901 to 1937, New York, Valentine Gallery, November 1937.
Twenty Years in the Evolution of Picasso, 1903–1923, New York, Jacques Seligmann & Co., Inc., 2–20 November 1937.

1938
Picasso: Drawings and Collages, London, London Gallery, 5–31 May 1938.
Picasso's 'Guernica', London, New Burlington Galleries, 4–29 October 1938.
Picasso and Matisse, Boston, Museum of Modern Art, 19 October–11 November 1938.
21 Paintings: 1908 to 1934, New York, Valentine Gallery, 7–26 November 1938.

1939
Drawings by Pablo Picasso loaned by Mr. Walter P. Chrysler, Jr., Chicago, Arts Club, 3–27 January 1939.
Picasso. Natures mortes, Paris, Galerie Paul Rosenberg, 17 January–18 February 1939.
Figure Paintings, Picasso, New York, Marie Harriman Gallery, 30 January–18 February 1939.
32 Recent Works, London, Rosenberg and Helft Gallery, March 1939.
Picasso before 1910, New York, Perls Galleries, 27 March–29 April 1939.
Guernica et études, New York, Valentine Gallery, 5–29 May 1939; Los Angeles, Stendahl Gallery, 10–21 August 1939; then Chicago, Arts Club, and San Francisco, Museum of Art, 1939.
Picasso in English Collections, London, London Gallery, 16 May–3 June 1939.

1939–1941
Picasso: Forty Years of his Art, catalogue by Alfred H. Barr, Jr., New York, Museum of Modern Art, 15 November 1939–7 January 1940; Chicago, The Art Institute, 1 February–3 March 1940. Subsequent travelling exhibition to Saint Louis, Boston, San Francisco, Cincinnati, Cleveland, New Orleans, Minneapolis, Pittsburgh, 1940–1941.

1940
Picasso: Drawings and Watercolors, New York, Buchholz Gallery, 1940.
Aquarelles, gouaches et dessins de Picasso, introduction by Yvonne Zervos, Paris, Galerie Mai, 19 April–18 May 1940.

1941
Picasso: Guernica, Cambridge, Mass., Fogg Museum of Art, 1941.
Picasso, Epochs in his Art, New York, Museum of Modern Art; Utica, Durham, Kansas City, Milwaukee, Grand Rapids, Hanover, Poughkeepsie, 1941.
Picasso, Epochs in his Art, Minneapolis, Institute of Arts, 1 February–2 March 1941.
Picasso, Early and Late, New York, Bignou Gallery, March 1941.

1942
Picasso: Loan Exhibition of Masterpieces, 1918–1926, New York, Paul Rosenberg Gallery, 1942.
Picasso, Wellesley, Wellesley College, 1942.
Picasso oleos y gouaches, Havana, Lyceum, 18 June–4 July 1942.

1943
Picasso, New York, Pierre Matisse Gallery, 1943.
Picasso, New York, Paul Rosenberg Gallery, 1943.

1944
Picasso, Washington, Phillips Memorial Gallery, 20 February–20 March 1944.
Rétrospective Picasso, Mexico, Sociedad de Arte Moderno, June 1944.
Œuvres de Picasso, Paris, Salon d'Automne, 6 October–5 November 1944.

1945
Peintures et dessins d'une collection privée, New York, Buchholz Gallery, 27 February–17 March 1945.
Picasso: Paintings, Sculpture and Drawings, Denver, Art Museum, 12 April–12 May 1945.
Picasso libre. Peintures récentes, Paris, Galerie Louis Carré, 20 June–13 July 1945.
Peintures de Picasso et Matisse, introduction by Christian Zervos, London, Victoria and Albert Museum, December 1945.

1946
Matisse, Picasso, Amsterdam, Stedelijk Museum, April 1946; Brussels, Palais des Beaux-Arts, May 1946.
Picasso. Dix-neuf peintures, Paris, Galerie Louis Carré, 14 June–14 July 1946.

1947
Picasso, Recent Paintings, New York, Samuel M. Kootz Gallery, 27 January–15 February 1947.
Picasso before 1907, New York, M. Knoedler & Co., 15 October–8 November 1947.
Pablo Picasso Lithographs 1945–1947, New York, Buchholz Gallery, 20 October–15 November 1947.
Pablo Picasso, Etsningar och litografier, 1904–1947, Stockholm, Blanch's Konstgalleri, November–December 1947.

1947–1948
Pablo Picasso: Lithographs, 1945–1947, Buffalo, Albright Knox Art Gallery, 31 December 1947–2 February 1948.

1948
Picasso, 43 lithographieën, 1945–1947, Amsterdam, Stedelijk Museum, 1948.
Pablo Picasso: Zweiundfünfzig Lithographien aus den Jahren 1945 bis 1947, Hanover, Kestner-Gesellschaft, 1948.
Pablo Picasso, Lithographs, 1945–1948, introduction by Bernhard Geiser, New York, Curt Valentin Gallery, 1948.
Picasso, New York, Kootz Gallery, 26 January–14 February 1948.
Picasso, Antwerp, Galerie Artes, 6–28 March 1948.
Picasso: Drawings, Gouaches, Paintings from 1913 to 1947, New York, Paul Rosenberg Gallery, 16 March–3 April 1948.
Picasso, New York, Durand-Ruel Galleries, May 1948.
Picasso, 55 Lithographs, 1945–1947, London, Arts Council of Great Britain, September 1948. Subsequent travelling exhibition in several towns in Great Britain.
Picasso, œuvres de Provence, 1945–1948, Paris, Galerie Louise Leiris, 5–20 October 1948.
Picasso, 55 Lithographs 1945–1947, London, Kidderminster Art Gallery, December 1948.
Lithographies de Pablo Picasso pour le Chant des Morts de Pierre Reverdy, Paris, Galerie Louis Carré, 17–31 December 1948.

1948–1949
Poterie et une sculpture de Picasso, Paris, Maison de la Pensée française, 26 November 1948–5 January 1949.
Picasso, Barcelona, Galerias Layetanas, 24 December 1948–7 January 1949.

1949
Picasso, 52 Lithographien aus den Jahren 1945–1947, Berlin, Haus am Waldsee, 1949.
Pablo Picasso: Lithographien aus den Jahren 1945 bis 1947, Frankfurt, Kunstverein, 1949.
Picasso Drawings, Princeton, University, The Art Museum, 10–31 January 1949.
Pablo Picasso, Recent Work, New York, Buchholz Gallery, 8 March–2 April 1949.
Picasso, Toronto, The Art Gallery, April 1949.
Twenty Original Drawings by Pablo Picasso and the Early Chirico, London, The London Gallery Ltd, 10 May–4 June 1949.
Picasso. Œuvres récentes, Paris, Maison de la Pensée française, July 1949.
Picasso: 100 etsningar 1930–1937 editerade av Ambroise Vollard, Stockholm, Galerie Blanche, October–November 1949.
Poteries de Picasso éditées par Madoura, dessins et livres, Paris, Librairie Creuzevault, December 1949.

1950

Picasso, The Figure, New York, Louis Carré Gallery, 9 January–9 February 1950.
Picasso: The Sculptor's Studio, text by William S. Lieberman, New York, Museum of Modern Art, 24 January–19 March 1950.
Picasso, catalogue by E.L.T. Mesens, Knokke-le-Zoute, Grande Salle des Expositions, 15 July–27 August 1950.
Picasso in Provence, London, Arts Council of Great Britain, New Burlington Galleries, 14 November–16 December 1950.

1950–1951

Picasso. Sculptures, dessins, preface by Louis Aragon, Paris, Maison de la Pensée française, November 1950–January 1951.

1951

Picasso, Recent Lithographs, text by Jaime Sabartés, New York, Buchholz Gallery, 29 May–23 June 1951.
Pablo Picasso, Tokyo, Yomiuri Shimbun Nihonbashi, Takashimaya, 27 August–2 September 1951.
Picasso Drawings and Watercolours since 1893, London, The Institute of Contemporary Arts, 11 October–24 November 1951.

1951–1952

P. Picasso, Milan, Galleria del Naviglio, 22 December 1951–4 January 1952.

1952

Picasso: lithographieën, aquatints, bronzen, Amsterdam, Stedelijk Museum, 1952.
Pablo Picasso: Radierungen und Lithographien, 1905 bis 1951, Munich, Nuremberg, Basel, Berlin, Essen, Freiburg, Hamburg, Stuttgart, 1952.
Picasso, His Graphic Art, catalogue by William S. Lieberman, New York, Museum of Modern Art, 14 February–20 April 1952.
Pablo Picasso: Paintings, Sculpture, Drawings, New York, Curt Valentin Gallery, 19 February–15 March 1952.
La Chèvre de Picasso, dessins inédits, Paris, Galerie de Beaune, July 1952.
Pablo Picasso, 1920–1925, New York, Curt Valentin Gallery, 22 September–18 October 1952.
Empreintes céramiques de Picasso, Paris, Galerie La Hune, December 1952.

1953

Pablo Picasso, Radierungen und Lithographien, 1905–1952, text by Daniel-Henry Kahnweiler, Bremen, Düsseldorf, Cologne, Krefeld, Dortmund, Essen, 1953.
Pablo Picasso, lithographieën, aquatints, bronzen, Eindhoven, Stedelijk Museum, 1953.
Picasso, the 'Thirties', New York, Perls Gallery, 5 January–7 February 1953.
Ceramica de Picasso, Madrid, CLAN, 8–30 April 1953.
Picasso (1898–1936), London, Alex Reid and Lefevre, Ltd, 1 May–30 June 1953.
Picasso, catalogue by Lionello Venturi, Rome, Galleria Nazionale d'Arte Moderna, 5 May–5 July 1953.
Œuvres récentes de Picasso, Paris, Galerie Louise Leiris, 19 May–June 1953.
Picasso, texts by Jean Cassou, Daniel-Henry Kahnweiler, Christian Zervos, René Jullian, Marcel Michaud, catalogue by Madeleine Rocher-Jauneau, Lyons, Musée des Beaux-Arts, 1 July–27 September 1953.
Pablo Picasso, catalogue by Franco Russoli, Milan, Palazzo Reale, 23 September–31 December 1953.

Pablo Picasso, 1950–1953, New York, Curt Valentin Gallery, 24 November–19 December 1953.

1953–1954

Rétrospective Picasso, catalogue by Maurice Jardot, São Paulo, Museu de Arte Moderna, 13 December 1953–20 February 1954.

1954

Picasso, l'œuvre graphique, Liège, Musée des Beaux-Arts, 1954.
Picasso, New York, Saidenberg Gallery, 1954.
Picasso in Russia, opere del Museo d'Arte Occidentale di Mosca, Rome, Galleria dell'Obelisco, 27 February–7 March 1954.
Picasso, Basel, Galerie Beyeler, 16 March–17 April 1954.
Picasso: 1938–1953, London, The Lefevre Gallery, May 1954.
Pablo Picasso, Das graphische Werk, Zurich, Kunsthaus, May–June 1954.
Picasso, Dessins 1903–1907, preface by Daniel-Henry Kahnweiler, Paris, Galerie Berggruen, 25 May–24 July 1954.
Picasso. Œuvres des musées de Leningrad et de Moscou, 1900–1914, introduction by Maurice Raynal, Paris, Maison de la Pensée française, June 1954.
Picasso. Deux périodes, 1900–1914 et 1950–1954, preface by Louis Aragon, Paris, Maison de la Pensée française, July 1954.
Pablo Picasso. Tauromachies et œuvres récentes, lithographies, céramiques, Céret, Musée d'Art moderne, July–September 1954.
Picasso, tauromachies, gravures, lithographies, empreintes céramiques originales tirées par Madoura, Paris, Galerie La Hune, July–September 1954.
Picasso; het Graphisch Werk, introduction by Bernhard Geiser, The Hague, Gemeente-Museum, 7 August–4 October 1954.
Picasso, San Antonio, The Marion Koogler McNay Art Institute, 4 November–5 December 1954.

1954–1955

L'Œuvre gravé de Pablo Picasso, texts by Jean Cocteau and Bernhard Geiser, Geneva, Musée Rath, 11 November 1954–31 January 1955.

1955

Pablo Picasso, œuvres des musées de Leningrad et de Moscou, 1900–1914 et de quelques collections parisiennes, Paris, Cercle d'Art, 1955.
Picasso, l'œuvre gravé, Rome, Galleria Le Meduse, 1955.
Picasso Exhibit, Houston, Contemporary Art Association, 14 January–20 February 1955.
Picasso: 12 Masterworks, New York, Museum of Modern Art, 15 March–24 April 1955.
Picasso. The Woman, New York, Chalette Gallery, 16 April–1 June 1955.
Picasso: 63 Drawings 1953–1954, 10 Bronzes 1945–1953, introduction by Rebecca West, London, Marlborough Fine Art, Ltd, May–June 1955.
Picasso. L'œuvre gravé, preface by Julien Cain, introduction by Jean Vallery-Radot, catalogue by Jean Adhémar and Charles Pérussaux, Paris, Bibliothèque Nationale, 13 June–16 October 1955.
Picasso: eaux-fortes, lithographies, 1905–1947, Bern, Galerie Gutekunst und Klipstein, August–September 1955.
Pablo Picasso, Oslo, Kunstnernes Hus, 1 November–31 December 1955.

Mostra di Pablo Picasso, 20 pochoirs, Ferrara, Galleria d'arte Cosme, 15–30 November 1955.

1955–1956

Picasso. Peintures 1900–1955, introduction and catalogue by Maurice Jardot, Paris, Musée des Arts décoratifs, June–October 1955; Munich, Haus der Kunst, 25 October–18 December 1955; Cologne, Rheinisches Museum, 30 December 1955–29 February 1956; Hamburg, Kunsthalle, 10 March–29 April 1956.
Fifty-five Drawings by Pablo Picasso, 1953–1954, text by Daniel-Henry Kahnweiler, New York, Saidenberg Gallery, 5 December 1955–23 January 1956.

1956

Pablo Picasso, Suite Vollard, 1930–1937, Cologne, Eigelsteintorburg, Hamburg, Kunsthalle 1956.
Picasso: 100 Etchings "La Suite Vollard", Los Angeles, Calzell Hatfield Galleries, 1956.
Picasso: Dessins d'un demi-siècle, preface by Maurice Jardot, Paris, Galerie Berggruen, 1956.
Picasso, œuvres récentes, Paris, Galerie Louise Leiris, 1956.
Picasso, New York, Kootz Gallery, 12 March–7 April 1956.
Twenty Recent Drawings and Ten Recent Lithographs by Pablo Picasso, Beverly Hills, Frank Perls Gallery, 20 March–20 April 1956.
Picasso: The Woman; Paintings, Drawings, Bronzes, Lithographs, New York, Chalette Gallery, 16 April–19 May 1956.
Picasso: Guernica, avec 60 études et variantes, Brussels, Palais des Beaux-Arts, May–June 1956; Amsterdam, Stedelijk Museum, July–September 1956; Stockholm, Nationalmuseum, October–November 1956.
Picasso: Fifty Years of Graphic Art, introduction by Philip Brutton James, London, Arts Council of Great Britain, 22 June–5 August 1956.
Picasso. Peintures, dessins 1904–1955, gravures rares, céramiques, preface by Gilberte Duclaud, Cannes, Galerie 65, 14 August–30 September 1956.
Hommage à Picasso: collection Bergengren, Malmö, Museum, 30 September–25 October 1956.
Picasso Himself, London, Institute of Contemporary Arts, October–December 1956.
Picasso, litografías originales, Barcelona, Sala Gaspar, 6–19 October 1956.
Picasso chez Goya, Castres, Musée Goya, November 1956.
Picasso, Oslo, Kunstnernes Hus, 1 November–31 December 1956.
'Pâtes blanches', nouvelles empreintes céramiques originales de Pablo Picasso, éditées par Madoura, Paris, Galerie La Hune, December 1956.

1956–1957

Picasso. Un demi-siècle de livres illustrés, Nice, Galerie Henri Matarasso, 21 December 1956–31 January 1957.

1957

Picasso, Graphic Art, Chicago, The Art Institute, 1957.
Picasso, Graphic Work, 1930–1956, Japan, travelling exhibition, 1957.
Picasso: Ceramics, London, Arts Council, 1957.
Picasso, Sculptures, Part 1, New York, Fine Arts Associates, 15 January–9 February 1957.

Picasso: Sculpture, New York, O'Gerson Gallery, 15 January–9 February 1957.
Picasso. Peintures 1955–1956, introduction by Daniel-Henry Kahnweiler, Paris, Galerie Louise Leiris, 26 March–April 1957.
Picasso Ceramiek, Rotterdam, Museum Boymans, July 1957.
Picasso. Dessins, gouaches, aquarelles, 1898–1957, preface by Douglas Cooper, Arles, Musée Réattu, 6 July–2 September 1957.
'Pâtes blanches', empreintes originales éditées par Madoura, gravures originales rares, Cannes, Galerie 65, 9–31 August 1957.
Picasso, his Graphic Art, Providence, Rhode Island School of Design, 11 September–20 October 1957.
Picasso: collection Bergengren, Lund, Copenhagen, Frederiksberg Radhaus, Kunstforeningen, 28 September–11 October 1957.
Pablo Picasso: Paintings, 1954–1955–1956, New York, Saidenberg Gallery, 30 September–26 October 1957.
Pablo Picasso, Das graphische Werk, Berlin, Nationalgalerie, October–November 1957.
Picasso: Pintura, Escultura, Dibujo, Cerámica, Mosaico, introduction by Jaime Sabartés and Daniel-Henry Kahnweiler, Barcelona, Sala Gaspar, 30 October–29 November 1957.

1957–1958
Picasso: 75th Anniversary Exhibition, by Alfred H. Barr, Jr., New York, Museum of Modern Art, 4 May–8 September 1957; Chicago, Art Institute, 29 October–8 December 1957; Philadelphia, Museum of Art, 6 January–23 February 1958.

1958
Picasso, an Exhibition of Lithographs and Aquatints, 1945–1957, introduction by Daniel-Henry Kahnweiler, Auckland, Dunedin, Wellington and Melbourne, 1958.
Picasso, Copenhagen, Charlottenburg, 1958.
Picasso, preface by Henry Clifford, introduction by Carl Zigrosser, Philadelphia, Museum of Art, 8 January–23 February 1958.
Picasso. Cent cinquante céramiques originales, texts by Hélène Parmelin, Suzanne and Georges Ramié, Paris, Maison de la Pensée française, 8 March–30 June 1958.
Ceramics by Picasso, New York, Museum of the Arts of Decoration, 28 March–10 May 1958.
Picasso, Geneva, Galerie du Perron, 19 April–end of May 1958.
Picasso '100 eaux-fortes et lithographies', Paris, Galerie Marcel Guiot, 29 May–21 June 1958.
Picasso, Liège, Musée d'Art Wallon, July–September 1958.
Picasso. Céramiques, Céret, Musée d'Art moderne, 15 July–15 October 1958.
Picasso: Five Master-works, New York, Kootz Gallery, 30 September–18 October 1958.
A Selection of Works by Picasso in Ten Media, New York, Saidenberg Gallery, 18 November–27 December 1958.

1959
Picasso: the Bathers, New York, Fine Arts Associates, 10 February–7 March 1959; Boston, Museum of Fine Arts, 15 March–15 April 1959.
Picasso Lithographs since 1945, Cincinnati, Art Museum, Contemporary Arts Center, 14 March–12 April 1959.
Picasso from 1907 to 1909, Boston, Museum of Fine Arts, 15 March–15 April 1959.
Picasso, catalogue by Douglas Cooper, Marseilles, Musée Cantini, 11 May–31 July 1959.
Picasso. Les Ménines, 1957, introduction by Michel Leiris, Paris, Galerie Louise Leiris, 22 May–27 June 1959.
Picasso, Stockholm, Svensk-Franska Konstgalleriet, 26 September–18 October 1959.
Picasso, Faces and Figures, 1900 to 1959, New York, Saidenberg Gallery, 10 November–12 December 1959.

1960
Picasso, London, Redfern Gallery, 1960.
Pablo Picasso, Linolschnitte, Vienna, Albertina, 1960.
26 aguatintas originales de Pablo Picasso ilustrando 'la Tauromaquia o arte de torear', Barcelona, Sala Gaspar, 11–16 January 1960.
Picasso. Œuvre gravé, preface by Jean Cocteau, foreword by Madeleine Ferry, Nice, Galerie des Ponchettes, 12 January–15 March 1960.
Picasso, Santa Barbara, Museum of Art, 15 January–7 February 1960.
Picasso, His Blue Period (1900–1905), Collection of Pastels, Watercolors and Drawings also The Complete Set of Small Bronzes of Female Figures 1945–47, New York, Sidney Janis Gallery, 25 April–21 May 1960; London, O'Hana Gallery, 23 June–28 July 1960; Warwickshire, Stoneleigh Abbey, 30 July–14 August 1960; Geneva, Galerie Motte, 23 August–10 September 1960.
Picasso et ses amis. Collection d'un amateur parisien, foreword by Hans Haug, introduction by Albert Châtelet, Strasbourg, Musée des Beaux-Arts, June–July 1960.
Picasso. 45 gravures sur linoléum 1958–1960, introduction by Bernhard Geiser, Paris, Galerie Louise Leiris, 15 June–13 July 1960; Stockholm, Svensk-Franska Konstgalleriet, September 1960.
Œuvre gravé de Picasso, preface by Daniel-Henry Kahnweiler, Mulhouse, Musée des Beaux-Arts, 25 June–30 August 1960.
Picasso, Retrospective, 1895–1959, catalogue by Roland Penrose, London, Tate Gallery, 6 July–18 September 1960.
Picasso: 45 grabados sobre linoleum 1958–1960, originales de Pablo Picasso, Barcelona, Sala Gaspar, 12–30 July 1960.
42 ceramiche originali di P. Picasso, Faenza, Museo Internazionale della ceramiche, 1 August–15 October 1960.
Picasso, pinturas, 30 cuadros ineditos, 1917–1960, Barcelona, Sala Gaspar, November–December 1960.
La Tauromaquia o arte de torear por José Delgado alias Pepe Illo, Geneva, Galerie Gérald Cramer, 8 November–20 December 1960.
P. Picasso: incisione su linoleum, catalogue by Bernhard Geiser, Rome, Galleria Il Segno, 21 November–31 December 1960.
Picasso. Dessins 1959–1960, preface by Michel Leiris, Galerie Louise Leiris, 30 November–31 December 1960.

1961
Picasso, Graphic Work, Haifa, Museum of Modern Art, 1961.
Picasso, Madrid, Museo de Arte Contemporaneo, 1961.
Opere recenti di P. Picasso, Rome, Galleria La Nuova Pera, 1961.
Pablo Picasso. 45 Linoleum Cuts 1958–1960, Cincinnati, Art Museum, 2–24 January 1961.
Dibujos de Picasso, Barcelona, Sala Gaspar, January–February 1961.
Picasso: dibujos, gouaches, acuarelas, text by José Bergamin, Barcelona, Sala Gaspar, April 1961.
Picasso, Bremen, Kunsthalle, 23 June–6 August 1961.
Picasso: Gemälde 1950–1960, Lucerne, Galerie Rosengart, summer 1961.
Picasso grabador, Mexico, Universidad Autonoma, Museo de Ciencias y artes, October 1961.
Hommage à Picasso, Vallauris, October 1961.
Picasso, Les Saltimbanques, le Chef d'Œuvre inconnu, Suite Vollard, 45 gravures en couleurs sur linoléum, lavis, Stockholm, Samlaren, October–November 1961.
'Bonne fête Monsieur Picasso': from Southern California Collectors, preface by Daniel-Henry Kahnweiler, Los Angeles, University of California, Art Gallery, 25 October–12 November 1961.
Picasso cumple ochenta anos 1881, Buenos Aires, Museo Nacional de Bellas Artes, October–November 1961.

1961–1962
Picasso Graphics from the Mr. and Mrs. Fred Grunwald Collection, Berkeley, University of California, Art Gallery, 29 November 1961–7 January 1962.
Pablo Picasso: Keramik aus der Manufaktur Madoura, introduction and text by André Verdet, Düsseldorf, Kunsthalle, 5 December 1961–21 January 1962.

1962
Picasso, his Later Works, 1938–1961, Worcester, Art Museum, 25 January–25 February 1962.
Picasso. Peintures, Vauvenargues 1959–1961, preface by Maurice Jardot, Paris, Galerie Louise Leiris, 26 January–24 February 1962.
Picasso; incisioni su linoleum e tauromachia, introduction by Franco Russoli, Milan, Pinacoteca di Brera, 25 March–1 April 1962.
Picasso. Gravures, céramiques, preface by Daniel-Henry Kahnweiler, Lyons, Musée des Beaux-Arts, April–May 1962.
Picasso: An American Tribute, catalogue by John Richardson, New York, M. Knoedler and Co., Inc., Saidenberg Gallery, Paul Rosenberg and Co., Duveen Brothers, Inc., Perls Galleries, Staempfli Gallery, Inc., Cordier-Warren Gallery, The New Gallery, Otto Gerson Gallery, 25 April–12 May 1962.
Tableaux de Picasso. Œuvres offertes par des artistes français et de divers pays, Paris, Maison de la Pensée française, 27 April–4 May 1962.
Picasso, 80th Birthday Exhibition. The Museum Collection, Present and Future, New York, Museum of Modern Art, 14 May–18 September 1962.
Picasso. Le déjeuner sur l'herbe 1960–1961, introduction by Douglas Cooper, Paris, Galerie Louise Leiris, 6 June–13 July 1962.
Picasso: Graphik im Besitz des Kaiser-Wilhelm-Museums Krefeld, Krefeld, Kaiser-Wilhelm-Museum, July–September 1962.
Picasso. Les Déjeuners. Dessins originaux, poem by Jean Cocteau, text by Douglas Cooper, Cannes, Galerie Madoura, August 1962.
Picasso, New York, Kootz Gallery, 2–20 October 1962.

Pablo Picasso, introduction by Daniel-Henry Kahnweiler, Zagreb, Galerija Suvremene Umjetnosti, 4–28 October 1962.
Trois livres illustrés par Picasso, Barcelona, Syra, 3–15 November 1962.
Picasso; Guernica, Tokyo, Kokuritsu Kindai Bijutsukan, 3 November–23 December 1962.
Picasso: 44 linoleums originales, Barcelona, Sala Gaspar, 24 November–14 December 1962.
Picasso, Athens, Galerie Zygos, December 1962.

1962–1963
Picasso. Art graphique, céramiques, Orléans, Musée des Beaux-Arts, 24 November 1962–28 January 1963.

1963
Pablo Picasso: Lithographieën, aquatintes, bronzen, Amsterdam, Stedelijk Museum, 1963.
Picasso Sculpture . . . and Three Important Acquisitions, London, Felix Gallery, 1963.
Picasso: 42 incisioni su linoleum, Rome, Galleria II Segno, March–April 1963.
Picasso, linographies originales, Vallauris, Galerie Madoura, 4 April–5 May 1963.
Picasso: 54 Recent Colour Linocuts, London, Hanover Gallery, 30 April–31 May 1963.
Picasso, gravures, 1924–1962, Lunéville, Musée Municipal, 23 May–30 June 1963.
Pablo Picasso, 50 gravures sur linoléum, 1958–1963, Geneva, Galerie Gérald Cramer, 31 May–5 July 1963.
Picasso, deux époques, peintures 1912–1927, 1952–1961, Lucerne, Galerie Rosengart, summer 1963.
Picasso: 204 assiettes récentes (mai et juin 1963), Cannes, Galerie Madoura, 6 July–1 August 1963.
Picasso, preface by André Verdet, Geneva, Musée de l'Athénée, 11 July–21 September 1963.

1963–1964
Picasso: 15 linoleums recientes, Barcelona, Sala Gaspar, 28 December 1963–24 January 1964.

1964
Pablo Picasso: One Hundred and Two Linocuts, introduction by Bernhard Geiser, Auckland, City Art Gallery, 1964.
Pablo Picasso Graphik, introduction by Paul Westheim, Berlin, Galerie Nierendorf, 1964.
Picasso: 60 ans de gravure, Paris, Galerie Berggruen, 1964.
L'itinéraire de Picasso et l'œuvre gravé 1924–1964, Saint-Etienne-du-Rouvray, 1964.
Picasso and Man, catalogue by Jean Sutherland Boggs, John Golding, Robert Rosenblum and Evan H. Turner, Toronto, The Art Gallery, 11 January–16 February 1964; Montreal, Museum of Fine Arts, 28 February–31 March 1964.
Picasso. Peintures 1962–1963, preface by Michel Leiris, Paris, Galerie Louise Leiris, 15 January–15 February 1964.
Pablo Picasso: Keramik 1947 bis 1961, Mosaiken 1956 bis 1958, Linolschnitte seit 1961, Lithographien 1956 bis 1961, Plakate 1948 bis 1962, Hamburg, Museum für Kunst und Gewerbe, 31 January–22 March 1964.
Picasso, eaux-fortes, pointes sèches, aquatintes, Paris, Galerie Cahiers d'Art, 28 April–23 May 1964.
Picasso Bilder der Jahre 1945–1961, Picasso Painting 1945–1961, Zurich, Gimpel &

Hanover Galerie, 16 May–20 June 1964; London, Gimpel Fils Gallery, 30 June–15 August 1964.
Pablo Picasso, Retrospective 1899–1963, introduction by Daniel-Henry Kahnweiler and Alfred H. Barr, Tokyo, National Museum of Modern Art, 23 May–5 July 1964; Kyoto, National Museum of Modern Art, 10 July–3 August 1964; Nagoya, Prefectoral Museum of Art, 7–18 August 1964.
Picasso. Linogravures en couleurs, Paris, Galerie Cahiers d'Art, 26 May–27 June 1964.
Picasso, Graphik and illustrierte Bücher, Sammlung Oscar Stern, Bern, Kornfeld und Klipstein, 30 May 1964.
Picasso. Lithographies, Paris, Galerie Cahiers d'Art, 30 June–31 July 1964.
Picasso Drawings, Ottawa, The National Gallery of Canada, 17 July–7 September 1964.

1965
Pablo Picasso, gouaches en tekeningen 1959–1964, Amsterdam, Galerie d'Eendt, 1965.
Picasso: eaux-fortes, lithographies, 1905–1947, Bern, Gutekunst und Klipstein, 1965.
Picasso. Peintures, dessins, gravures rares, introduction by Gilberte Duclaud, Cannes, Galerie 65, 1965.
Picasso, Prague, Galerie Vincenc Kramar, 1965.
Picasso, his Later Works, 1938–1961, Worcester, Mass., Art Museum, 25 January–25 February 1965.
Picasso, 150 Handzeichnungen aus sieben Jahrzehnten, Frankfurt, Frankfurter Kunstverein, 29 May–4 July 1965; Hamburg, Kunstverein, 24 July–5 September 1965.
Picasso et le théâtre, preface by Jean Cassou, texts by Robert Mesuret, Douglas Cooper, Denis Milhau, catalogue by Denis Milhau, Toulouse, Musée des Augustins, 22 June–15 September 1965.
Picasso. Exposición Pintura, Tapiz, Dibujo, Grabado,, Barcelona, Sala Gaspar, 15 July–15 August 1965.
Picasso graficus; een Keuze uit zijn grafisch œuvre uit de jaren 1906–1963, Haarlem, Frans Hals Museum, 18 July–5 September 1965.
Picasso i Kiruna, text by Carl Nordenfalk, Stockholm, National-Museum, 4–12 September 1965.
Picasso: Graphisches Werk, 1904–1965, St Gallen, Kunstmuseum, 2 October–14 November 1965.

1966
Pablo Picasso, 85ᵉ anniversaire. Dessins et céramiques, Moscow, Pushkin Museum, 1966.
Picasso chez Boler, Paris, Galerie Boler, 1966.
Picasso, Paris, Galerie de l'Elysée, 1966.
Picasso; dessins, Paris, Galerie Françoise Ledoux, 1966.
Picasso: 17 tableaux récents, 29 gravures, Paris, Galerie Louise Leiris, 1966.
Livres illustrés par Picasso, Paris, Galerie Alexandre Loewy, 1966.
Hommage à Picasso, Paris, Galerie Alex Maguy, 1966.
Picasso: Œuvres gravées, Céramiques originales et éditées, Vallauris, Galerie Madoura, 1966.
Picasso: obra grafica, Barcelona, Sala Gaspar, January 1966.
Picasso, Exposición Antologica, Las Palmas

de Gran Canaria, Casa de Colon, January–February 1966.
Picasso, introduction by Daniel-Henry Kahnweiler and Maurice Jardot, Tel Aviv, Museum, Helena Rubinstein Pavilion, January–May 1966.
Picasso, Turin, Galleria Galatea, 19 January–14 February 1966.
Picasso, Selection of Graphic Work, Collection Georges Bloch, 1959–1965, Jerusalem, Israel Museum, 24 March–2 May 1966.
Picasso, gravures rares de 1904 à nos jours, Cannes, Galerie 65, 9 April–12 May 1966.
Picasso, Graphik, introduction by Daniel-Henry Kahnweiler, Dresden, Kupferstich-Kabinett der Staatlichen Kunstsammlungen Dresden im Albertinum, 17 April–21 August 1966.
Picasso since 1945, Washington, Gallery of Modern Art, 30 June–4 September 1966.
Picasso: deux époques: peintures 1960–1965 et des années 1934, 1937, 1944, text by Douglas Cooper, Lucerne, Galerie Rosengart, summer 1966.
Picasso. 20 ans de céramiques chez Madoura, 1946–1966, introduction by Georges and Suzanne Ramié, Vallauris, Galerie Madoura, July 1966.
Sixième biennale de peinture dédiée à Pablo Picasso, Menton, 1 July–15 September 1966.
Pablo Picasso, Bremen, Galerie Michael Hertz, July–September 1966.
Picasso: Zeichnungen und Druckgraphik 1905–1965, preface by Daniel-Henry Kahnweiler, Stuttgart, Staatsgalerie, September–December 1966.
Picasso. 85 gravures présentées à l'occasion de son 85ᵉ anniversaire, Paris, Galerie Berggruen, October 1966.
Picasso. Cent dessins et aquarelles 1899–1965, preface by Daniel-Henry Kahnweiler, Paris, Galerie Knoedler, October–December 1966.
Picasso. Sixty Years of Graphic Works, Los Angeles, Los Angeles County Museum of Art, 25 October–24 December 1966.
Picasso: 100 affiches, Paris, Librairie Fischbacher, November 1966.
Picasso: 150 grabados, 1927–1965, Buenos Aires, Instituto Torcuato di Tella, Centro de Artes Visuales, 15 November–11 December 1966.
Picasso, Paris, Galerie Lucie Weill, 15 November–15 December 1966.
Picasso. Papiers collés, 1910–1914, Paris, Galerie Au Pont des Arts, 16 November–15 December 1966.

1966–1967
Pablo Picasso, Le Peintre et son modèle; 44 gravures originales 1963–1965, Geneva, Galerie Gérald Cramer, 24 November 1966–21 January 1967.
Picasso, œuvres de 1900–1932, catalogue by Roland Penrose, Basel, Galerie Beyeler, 26 November 1966–31 January 1967.
Hommage à Pablo Picasso, preface by Jean Leymarie, Paris, Grand Palais and Petit Palais, November 1966–February 1967.
Pablo Picasso. Gravures, preface by Etienne Dennery, introduction by Jean Adhémar, Paris, Bibliothèque Nationale, November 1966–February 1967.
Picasso, gravures, Basel, Galerie Beyeler, November 1966–March 1967.
Picasso et le béton, texts by Pierre Gascar, Daniel Gervis, Georges Patrix, Michel Ragon,

Paris, Galerie Jeanne Bucher, November 1966; London, Institute of Contemporary Arts Gallery, 11 January–11 February 1967; St Gallen, Kunstmuseum, 9 April–12 May 1967.
Pablo Picasso: Druckgraphik aus dem Besitz der Kunsthalle Bremen, Bremen, Kunsthalle, 11 December 1966–22 January 1967.

1967
Hommage à Picasso, Helsinki, Atheneum Taidemuseo, 1967.
Picasso, gravuras, Lisbon, Sociedade Nacional de Belas Artes, 1967.
Picasso, Basel, Galerie Beyeler, February–March 1967.
Picasso, Two Concurrent Retrospective Exhibitions, introduction and text by Douglas Cooper, Fort Worth, Art Center Museum (drawings, gouaches, etc.); Dallas, Museum of Fine Arts (paintings), 8 February–26 March 1967.
Picasso, Amsterdam, Stedelijk Museum, 4 March–30 April 1967.
Picasso-Meistergraphik, Cologne, Wallraf-Richartz-Museum, 11 March–20 April 1967.
Picasso: Sculpture, Ceramics, Graphic Work, text by Roland Penrose, London, Tate Gallery, 9 June–13 August 1967.
Izlozba grafike Pabla Pikasa, Belgrade, Muzej Savremene Umetnosti, 10 June–1 August 1967.
Picasso gravures, preface by Mandy Epstein, Geneva, Musée d'Art et d'Histoire, Cabinet des Estampes, 24 June–10 September 1967.
Picasso, introduction by Bernard Dorival, Château de Culon, 1 July–10 September 1967.
Picasso. Œuvres récentes, preface by Hélène Parmelin, Colmar, Musée d'Unterlinden, July–September 1967.
Pablo Picasso, texts by Vladimir Gojovie and Georges Boudaille, Zagreb, Galerija Suvremene Umjetnosti, 17 November–31 December 1967.

1967–1968
Prints by Picasso: A Selection from 60 Years, catalogue by William S. Lieberman, New York, Museum of Modern Art, 11 October 1967–1 January 1968.
The Sculpture of Picasso, by Roland Penrose, New York, Museum of Modern Art, 11 October 1967–1 January 1968.
Picasso. 70 gravures, 1905–1965, preface by Patrice Hugues, Le Havre, Musée des Beaux-Arts, 18 November 1967–8 January 1968.
Picasso 1966–1967, New York, Saidenberg Gallery, 11 December 1967–31 January 1968.

1968
I Picasso atelé, Malmö, Museum, 1968.
347 Picasso. Graphische Blätter aus dem Jahr 1968, Stuttgart, Württembergischer Kunstverein, 1968.
Picasso in Chicago: Paintings, Drawings and Prints from Chicago Collections, Chicago, Art Institute, 3 February–31 March 1968.
Picasso. Dessins 1966–1967, preface by Michel Leiris, Paris, Galerie Louise Leiris, 28 February–23 March 1968.
Picasso los Minotauros, San Juan, Galeria Colibri, March 1968.
Picasso: pinturas, dibujos, grabados, colección Sala Gaspar, introduction by Jaime Sabartés, Barcelona, Libreria Tecnica Extranjera, March 1968.
Pablo Picasso, catalogue by Heribert Hutter, Vienna, Oesterreichisches Museum für angewandte Kunst, 24 April–30 June 1968.

Pablo Picasso: Das graphische Werk, Zurich, Kunsthaus, 25 May–28 July 1968.
25 Picasso-Blätter, Bremen, Galerie Michael Hertz, July–August 1968.
Pablo Picasso: das Spätwerk: Malerei und Zeichnung seit 1944, Baden-Baden, Staatliche Kunsthalle, 15 July–6 October 1968.
Pablo Picasso, Humlebaek, Louisiana Museum, 21 September–10 November 1968.
Picasso Drawings: 1961–1968, preface by R.S. Johnson, Chicago, R.S. Johnson Gallery, autumn 1968.
Picasso: litografii si gravuri, Bucharest, Muzeului de arta al R.S. Romania, October 1968.

1968–1969
Picasso. Graphik, Augsburg, Holbeinhaus, 1968–1969.
Picasso. 347 gravures, preface by Aldo and Piero Crommelynck, Paris, Galerie Louise Leiris; Chicago, Art Institute, 18 December 1968–1 February 1969.

1969
Pablo Picasso, Kupfergravuren aus dem Jahre 1968, Bremen, Galerie Michael Hertz, 1969.
La sculpture. Picasso: thèmes et variations, Saint-Denis de la Réunion, Musée des Beaux-Arts, 1969.
Picasso d'aujourd'hui. Dessins, gravures, linoléums, livres illustrés, céramiques, introduction by Jean-Marie Magnan, Arles, Musée Réattu, 4 April–1 June 1969.
Pablo Picasso: 347 graphische Blätter vom 16.3.1968 bis 5.10.1968, Zurich, Kunsthaus, 12 April–20 May 1969.
Pablo Picasso. Gemälde, Handzeichnungen, Druckgrafik, Keramik aus der Sammlung Kahnweiler, Paris, Düren, Leopold-Hoesch-Museum, 9 May–8 June 1969.
Picasso: Paintings, Sculpture, Ceramics, Drawings, Graphics, Dublin, University, Trinity College, 17 May–30 August 1969.
Pablo Picasso; 347 graphische Blätter aus dem Jahr 1968, Berlin, Akademie der Künste, 1–29 June 1969; Hamburg, Kunsthalle, 11 July–10 August 1969; Cologne, Kunstverein, 7 September–12 October 1969.
Grafik von Pablo Picasso, Bern, Kornfeld und Klipstein, 13 June 1969.
Picasso. Figures peintes entre le 30 janvier et le 7 mai 1969, Paris, Galerie Cahiers d'Art, 17 June–19 July 1969.
Picasso aujourd'hui: Œuvres récentes, text by Hélène Parmelin, Lucerne, Galerie Rosengart, summer 1969.
Picasso, gravures, Vallauris, Galerie Madoura, 20 August–25 September 1969.
Picasso. One Hundred Graphics, New York, Parke-Bernet Galleries, 11 December 1969.

1969–1970
Picasso, introduction by Daniel-Henry Kahnweiler, Toronto, Dunkelman Gallery, 26 November 1969–10 January 1970.

1970
Pablo Picasso: Bemalte Linos 1956 bis 1965, Bern, Kornfeld und Klipstein, 1970.
Picasso-Grafik, Bielefeld, Kunsthalle, 1970.
Picasso-Grafik, Bremen, Kunsthalle, 1970.
Picasso, 347 Engravings, 16.3.1968–5.10.1968, London, Institute of Contemporary Arts, 1970.
Picasso Drawings, London, Waddington Galleries, 10 February–7 March 1970.
Painted Linos by Picasso, Basel, Galerie Beyeler, 1 March–9 May 1970.

Pablo Picasso 1969–1970, introduction by Christian Zervos, Avignon, Palais des Papes, 1 May–30 September 1970.
Picasso, gravures récentes, Vallauris, Galerie Madoura, 6 May–30 June 1970.
Pablo Picasso, Florence, Galleria Michelucci, 4–30 June 1970.
Grafik von Pablo Picasso, Bern, Galerie Kornfeld und Klipstein, 9–16 June 1970.
Picasso: Graphik von 1904 bis 1968, Munich, Haus der Kunst, 20 June–27 September 1970.
Picasso: l'Idée pour une sculpture, thèmes et variations, preface by Roland Penrose, Lucerne, Galerie Rosengart, July–September 1970.
Picasso for Portland, Portland, Art Museum, 20 September–25 October 1970.
Pablo Picasso, Rome, Marlborough Galleria d'Arte, October 1970.
Picasso 1967–1970, New York, Saidenberg Gallery, 6 October–14 November 1970.
347× Picasso, Graphische Blätter aus dem Jahr 1968, Stuttgart, Württembergischer Kunstverein, 8 October–22 November 1970.
Picasso: Master Printmaker, catalogue by Riva Castleman, New York, The Museum of Modern Art, 15 October–29 November 1970.
Picasso: Women in the Graphic Work 1904–1968, Tokyo, Art Gallery, 13–25 November 1970.
Pablo Picasso, Blätter zum Thema 'Frauenraub', Bremen, Galerie Michael Hertz, 22 November–31 December 1970.
Picasso, 347 grabados, Barcelona, Sala Gaspar, December 1970.

1970–1971
Picasso in Milwaukee, Milwaukee, Art Center, 25 October 1970–28 January 1971.
Stiftung D.-H. Kahnweiler: 20 graphische Werke Picassos, Mannheim, Kunsthalle, 12 December 1970–17 January 1971.

1971
Picasso Paintings, Drawings and Sculptures from Southern California Collections, Los Angeles, Californian Museum of Art, 1971.
Picasso: 25 œuvres, 25 années: 1947–1971, Lucerne, Galerie Rosengart, 1971.
Picasso: Histoire naturelle de Buffon, New York, Weintraub Gallery, 1971.
De Picasso à Picasso, preface by Alex Maguy, Paris, Galerie de l'Elysée, 1971.
Picasso: portraits imaginaires, Paris, Galerie du Passeur, 1971.
Plakate von Picasso, Cologne, Kölnischer Kunstverein, 9 January–7 March 1971.
Picasso: 150 grabados, Caracas, Museo de Bellas Artes, March 1971.
Picasso: Master of Graphic Art, a Retrospective of Graphic Works, 1904–1968, Chicago, R.S. Johnson International Gallery, spring 1971.
Pablo Picasso; 347 Radierungen des Sommers 1968, Munich, Stuck-Villa, April–June 1971.
Picasso. Dessins en noir et en couleurs, Paris, Galerie Louise Leiris, 23 April–5 June 1971.
Picasso and the Vollard Suite, Ottawa, National Gallery of Canada, 1 June–31 December 1971.
Picasso. Dessins inédits du 3-12-70 au 4-11-71, preface by Jean-Maurice Rouquette, Arles, Musée Réattu, July–September 1971.
Picasso, gravures, dessins, Geneva, Musée de l'Athénée, 13 July–16 October 1971.
Picasso Summer Exhibition, London, The Brook Street Gallery, summer 1971.

Graphik von Picasso: 1904–1968, Mülheim an der Ruhr, Städtisches Museum, 9 September–3 October 1971.
Picasso: 20 Drawings, 1967–1971, Chicago, R.S. Johnson International Gallery, autumn 1971.
Obras de Picasso de la collection Hugue, Barcelona, Museo Picasso, October 1971.
Picasso. Pintura, dibujo, Barcelona, Sala Gaspar, October 1971.
Picasso in London. A Tribute on his 90th Birthday, text by Roland Penrose, Institute of Contemporary Arts, October 1971.
Homage to Picasso for his 90th Birthday, Years 1924–1971, introduction by John Richardson, New York, Marlborough Gallery, October 1971.
Homage to Picasso for his 90th Birthday, Years 1901–1924, introduction by John Richardson, New York, Saidenberg Gallery, October 1971.
Hommage à Picasso. 90 gravures présentées à l'occasion de ses 90 ans, Paris, Galerie Berggruen, October 1971.
Hommage à Pablo Picasso: livres illustrés, gravures originales, Geneva, Galerie Gérald Cramer, 20 October–27 November 1971.
Hommage à Picasso, Paris, Musée de Louvre, 21–31 October 1971.
Picasso: 45 Selected Graphics from 1904 to 1968, Beverly Hills, Frank Perls Gallery, 25 October–26 November 1971.
Picasso, Paris, Galerie Knoedler, 26 October–30 November 1971.
Picasso. 90, Dibuixos, gravats, linoleums, Palma de Mallorca, Sala Pelaires, December 1971.

1971–1972
Picasso: 90 dessins et œuvres en couleurs, Winterthur, Kunstmuseum, 9 October–15 November 1971; Basel, Galerie Beyeler, 20 November 1971–15 January 1972; Cologne, Wallraf-Richartz Museum, 25 January–end of February 1972.
Picasso dans les musées soviétiques, preface by Jean Leymarie, Paris, Musée National d'Art Moderne, November 1971–January 1972.

1972
Pablo Picasso, Druckgraphik, Bern, Gottfried-Keller-Stiftung, 1972.
Pablo Picasso, Bern, Kunstmuseum, 1972.
Pablo Picasso, Blick und Bildnis, Dortmund, Museum am Ostwall, 1972.
Picasso: Gli Amori secreti di Raffaello e la Fornarina, Milan, Galleria d'Arte 32, 1972.
Pablo Picasso, New York, Knoedler Gallery, 1972.
Picasso in the Collection of the Museum of Modern Art, texts by William Rubin, Elaine L. Johnson, Riva Castleman, New York, Museum of Modern Art, 23 January–2 April 1972.
Picasso 90, introduction by Jean Marcenac, Brussels, Galerie Veranneman, 29 January–26 February 1972.
Graphisch Werk Pablo Picasso, Antwerp, International Cultureel Centrum Meir, 18 March–30 April 1972.
En hommage à Pablo Picasso pour son 90e anniversaire, Paris, Galerie Félix Vercel, April–June 1972.
Picasso/200 Prints, Tel Aviv, Museum, April–June 1972.
Picasso, Dakar, Musée Dynamique, 6 April–6 May 1972.
Picasso: 347 Engravings, London, Waddington Galleries, 13 September–7 October 1972.
Œuvres graphiques de Picasso, Port-au-Prince, Musée d'Art Haïtien, 5–22 October 1972.
Exposición de libros con grabados originales de Picasso, Barcelona, Museo Picasso, October–November 1972.
Picasso. Œuvre gravé 1904–1968, preface by Michel Melot, Montreuil, Galerie municipale, 4 November–16 December 1972.

1972–1973
Picasso. 172 dessins en noir et en couleurs, Paris, Galerie Louise Leiris, 1 December 1972–13 January 1973.

1973
Homage to Picasso, Chicago, R.S. Johnson International Gallery, 1973.
Pablo Picasso, Blick und Bildnis II, Dortmund, Museum am Ostwall, 1973.
Une collection Picasso. Huiles, gouaches, dessins, collages et découpages. Œuvres de 1937 à 1946, Geneva, Galerie Jean Krugier, 1973.
Picasso. Œuvre gravé 1904–1968, preface and catalogue by Gérard Collot, Metz, Musée des Beaux-Arts, 1973.
Les affiches de Picasso, preface by Jean-Paul Crespelle, Paris, Galerie Multiples, 1973.
Picasso, His Graphic Work in the Israel Museum Collection, Jerusalem, The Israel Museum, January–March 1973.
Picasso. 156 gravures récentes, Paris, Galerie Louise Leiris, 24 January–24 February 1973.
Picasso: the Vollard Suite of Etchings, 1930–1937, introduction by Werner Spies, London, Fischer Fine Art, Ltd, February–March 1973.
Picasso: olii, gouaches, pastelli, Chine, disegni, dal 1921 al 1971, Milan, Galleria Levi, March–April 1973.
In Memoriam Pablo Picasso, 1881–1973, Cleveland, Museum of Art, 10 April–6 May 1973.
Hommage à Picasso, Arles, Musée Réattu, 12–30 April 1973.
Hommage à Picasso, Saint-Denis. Musée municipal d'Art et d'Histoire, 11 May–16 July 1973.
Picasso, 51 Linocuts, 1959–1973, Tokyo, Fuji Television Gallery, 15 May–2 June 1973.
Pablo Picasso, 1881–1973; Gedächtnis-ausstellung, Bremen, Kunsthalle, Kupferstich-kabinett, 20 May–8 July 1973.
Pablo Picasso 1970–1972, preface by René Char, Avignon, Palais des Papes, 23 May–23 September 1973.
Hommage à Picasso, 50 Picasso des collections belges, 1902–1969, Brussels, Palais des Beaux-Arts, 29 May–1 July 1973.
Picasso: Master Printmaker, Auckland, City Art Gallery, June–July 1973.
Graphik, Bücher und Handzeichnungen von Pablo Picasso, Bern, Kornfeld und Klipstein, 14–19 June 1973.
Picasso: dessins 1970–1972, Nuremberg, Pilatushaus, 24 June–5 August 1973.
Picasso et la paix, Céret, Musée d'Art Moderne, summer 1973.
Pablo Picasso, Druckgraphik und illustrierte Bücher, Depositum der Gottfried-Keller-Stiftung und eigene Bestände, Basel, Kunstmuseum, Kupferstich-Kabinett, 8 July–2 September 1973.
Picasso, preface by Roland Leroy, La Courneuve, Fête de l'Humanité, 5–9 September 1973.
Picasso Graphics, London, Waddington Galleries, 18 September–13 October 1973.
Picasso: maestro del grabado, Montevideo, Museo nacional de artes plasticas, October 1973.
Picasso in Hannover: Gemälde, Zeichnungen, Keramik, Übersicht über das graphische Werk, catalogue by Helmut R. Leppien, Hanover, Kunstverein, 21 October–25 November 1973.
Pablo Picasso, San Juan, Puerto Rico, Museo del Grabada Latino-americano, 9–24 November 1973.
Picasso. 100 estampes originales 1900–1937, Paris, Galerie Guiot, 27 November–29 December 1973.
Les estampes céramiques de Picasso, introduction by Georges Ramié, Avignon, December 1973.

1973–1974
Hommage à Picasso, Berlin, Nationalgalerie; Hanover, Kestner-Gesellschaft, 23 November 1973–13 January 1974.
Repeindre Picasso, Paris, Institut Goethe, 29 November 1973–31 January 1974.

1974
Picasso: œuvre gravé, 1904–1968, Clermont-Ferrand, Musée Bargoin, 1974.
Picasso, Malerier, Tegninger, Grafik, Hovikodden, Henie-Onstad Kunstsenter, February–April 1974.
Conoscere Picasso, text by Lara-Vinca Masini, Vinci, Biblioteca Communale, March 1974.
Pablo Picasso: Le Visage de la Paix, 28 dessins inédits, Geneva, Musée de l'Athénée, 18 April–8 June 1974.
Picasso. Œuvre gravé 1904–1968, preface and catalogue by Gérald Collot, Caen, Musée des Beaux-Arts, 20 May–30 June 1974.
Dessins et gravures de Pablo Picasso, Collection Geneviève Laporte, Paris, Galerie Françoise Tournié, June–July 1974.
Pablo Picasso: El Entierro del Conde de Orgaz; la Célestine, Geneva, Galerie Gérald Cramer, June–September 1974.
Pablo Picasso: from the Blue Period to the Last Years, Tokyo, Fuji Television Gallery, 8–14 June 1974.
Gravures de Picasso. Fonds Sabatier d'Espeyran, Montpellier, Musée Fabre, August–September 1974.
Picasso, Seoul, National Museum of Modern Art, 10 August–9 September 1974.
Picasso und die Antike, preface by Jürgen Thimme, Karlsruhe, Badisches Landesmuseum, 9 September to 11 November 1974.
Picasso, 67 acuarelas, dibujos, gouaches de 1897 a 1971, Barcelona, Sala Gaspar, October 1974.
Pablo Picasso 'La Célestine', 66 Original-radierungen, Düsseldorf, Galerie Ursus-Presse, 4 October–15 November 1974.

1974–1975
Pablo Picasso: Das graphische Werk, Hamburg, 19 October–8 December 1974; Frankfurt, Kunstverein, 8 December 1974–2 February 1975; Stuttgart, Staatsgalerie, 13 February–30 March 1975.
Hommage à Pablo Picasso, preface by Dominique Viéville, Calais, Musée des Beaux-Arts, December 1974–January 1975.

1975
Salut à Picasso, text by Jacques Lassaigne, Brussels, Galerie Jacques Damase, 1975.
Picasso Radierungen aus der Vollard-Suite: 1930–1937, Stuttgart, Wolf Donndorf,

11 April–31 May 1975.
Picasso: a Loan Exhibition for the Benefit of Cancer Care, New York, Acquavella Galleries, 15 April–17 May 1975.
Picasso (nus, portraits, compositions), texts by Hélène Parmelin and Pierre Barousse, Montauban, Musée Ingres, 27 June–7 September 1975.
Picasso linographe, introduction by Georges Ramié, Vallauris, Galerie Madoura, July–August 1975.
Hommage à Pablo Picasso, introduction by Jean Leymarie, Paris, Institut Goethe, 3 November–19 December 1975.

1976
Picasso, catalogue by William Rubin and Franz Meyer, Basel, Kunstmuseum, 15 June–12 September 1976.

1976–1977
Pablo Picasso: Estampes originales, livres illustrés, 1905–1972, Geneva, Galerie Patrick Cramer, 24 November 1976–14 January 1977.

1977
Picasso, texts by Rafael Alberti, Vicente Aleixandre, Jose Camón Aznar, Madrid, Fundación Juan March, September–November 1977.
Picasso: 19 plats en argent, par François et Pierre Hugo, preface by Douglas Cooper, Paris, Galerie Matignon, November–December 1977.

1977–1978
Picasso Exhibition, Retrospective 1898–1970, Tokyo, Metropolitan Museum of Art, 15 October–4 December 1977; Nagoya, Aichi Museum, 13–26 December 1977; Fukuoka, Cultural Center, 5–22 January 1978; Kyoto, National Museum of Modern Art, 28 January–5 March 1978.
Exposición Picasso, Barcelona, Fundación Juan March, Museo Picasso, 5 December 1977–10 January 1978.

1978
Picasso: Els 156 darrers gravats originals 24/10/68 – 25/3/72, Barcelona, Sala Gaspar, March–April 1978.
Pablo Picasso, 150 graphische Blätter 1970–1972, Zurich, Kunsthaus, 31 March–16 May 1978.
Picasso-Graphik, Leipzig, Museum der bildenden Künste, 28 April–25 June 1978.
Picasso en los sellos, Barcelona, Museo Picasso, 29 September–8 October 1978.
Pablo Picasso's Prints, Tokyo, Bridgestone Museum of Art, 5 October–24 December 1978.

1978–1979
Picasso. 156 gravures et leurs 87 états préparatoires, 1970–1972, Paris, Centre Culturel du Marais, 15 November 1978–11 February 1979 (same contents as the 1973 exhibition organized by the Galerie Louise Leiris, together with its catalogue; also shown at Antibes, Musée Picasso, 6 April–6 May 1979).
Picasso, Madrid, Galería Theo, December 1978–January 1979.

1979
Picasso erótico, Barcelona, Museo Picasso, 27 February–18 March 1979.
Pablo Picasso, his Last Etchings: a Selection, Chicago, R.S. Johnson International, March 1979.
Pablo Picasso, Letzte graphische Blätter, 1970–1972, Hanover, Kestner-Gesellschaft, 4–27 May 1979.
Pablo Picasso: Suite Vollard: A Selection, Chicago, R.S. Johnson International, autumn 1979.

1979–1980
Picasso, Œuvres reçues en paiement des droits de succession, catalogue by Dominique Bozo, Michèle Richet, Philippe Thiébaut, Paris, Grand Palais, 11 October 1979–7 January 1980.

1980
Picasso, from the Musée Picasso, Paris, Minneapolis, Walker Art Center, 10 February–30 March 1980.
Darrers gravats de Picasso, Barcelona, Museo Picasso, 6 May–31 July 1980.
Picasso, Letzte graphische Blätter, 1970–1972, Picasso Graphik aus der Sammlung Ludwig, Aachen, Leipzig, Galerie der Hochschule für Grafik und Buchkunst, 9 May–20 June 1980; Halle, Staatliches Museum Moritzburg, 29 June–7 September 1980.
Pablo Picasso: A Retrospective, New York, The Museum of Modern Art, 22 May–16 September 1980.
Picasso, Peintures 1901–1971, Paris, Galerie Claude Bernard, June 1980.
Picasso, Tokyo, The Seibu Museum of Art, 9 July–6 August, 1980.
Picasso, gravats, litografies, Barcelona, Sala Gaspar, November–December 1980.
Pablo Picasso, Images of the 1930's, Fort Lauderdale, Museum of Art, 9–28 December 1980.

1980–1981
Picasso, The Saltimbanques, catalogue by E.A. Carmean, Jr., Washington, National Gallery of Art, 4 December 1980–15 March 1981.
Pablo Picasso. Ausgewählte Graphik, Hanover, Kunstmuseum, 14 December 1980–1 February 1981.

1981
Picasso, Estampes 1904–1972, Martigny, Fondation Pierre-Gianadda, 1981.
Picasso, Gouaches, Lavis et Dessins, 1966–1972, preface by Pierre Daix, Paris, Galerie Berggruen, 1981.
Picasso, The Avignon Paintings, New York, Pace Gallery, 30 January–14 March 1981.
Picasso, 1953–1973, Marcq-en-Barœul, Fondation Anne et Albert Prouvost-Septentrion, 14 February–17 May 1981.
Master Drawings by Picasso, catalogue by Gary Tinterow, Cambridge, Mass., Fogg Art Museum, 20 February–5 April 1981; Chicago, Art Institute, 24 April–14 June 1981; Philadelphia, Museum of Art, 11 July–23 August 1981.
Pablo Picasso in der Staatsgalerie Stuttgart, Stuttgart, Staatsgalerie, 1 March–17 May 1981.
Picasso 1881–1973, Tokyo, Isetan Museum of Arts, 5 March–7 April 1981; Fukuoka, Municipal Museum, 21 April–9 May 1981; Nagoya, Aichi Prefecture Museum, 12–26 May 1981; Hiroshima, Museum, 30 May–21 June 1981.
Picasso fra Musée Picasso, Paris, Humlebaek, Louisiana Museum, 6 March–22 June 1981.

Picasso, Tout l'œuvre linogravé, Aix-en-Provence, Musée Granet, 7 March–6 September 1981; Montbéliard, Centre d'Action Culturelle, 19 September–31 October 1981.
Picasso, A Centennial Selection, Basel, Galerie Beyeler, April–July 1981.
Picasso, Obra Gráfica original, 1904–1971, Madrid, Subdirección general de artes plasticas, May–July 1981.
Pablo Picasso, Ingelheim am Rhein, 2 May–8 June 1981.
Picasso, Opere dal 1895 al 1971, dalla collezione Marina Picasso, catalogue by Giovanni Carandente and Werner Spies, Venice, Palazzo Grassi, 3 May–26 July 1981.
Pablo Picasso, Die letzten graphischen Blätter. Aus der Sammlung Ludwig, Aachen, Dresden, Kupferstich-Kabinett der Staatlichen Kunstsammlungen, Albertinum, 8 May–15 July 1981.
Pablo Picasso, 65 livres illustrés, Geneva, Galerie Patrick Cramer, 15 May–31 July 1981.
Pablo Picasso, Ausgewählte Graphik 1905 bis 1970, Essen, Museum Folkwang, 17 May–12 July 1981.
Picasso–347, Hovikodden, Henie-Onstad Kunstsenter, 23 June–23 August 1981.
Hommage à Picasso pour le centenaire de sa naissance, Antibes, Musée Picasso, summer 1981.
Picasso, La Chaise-Dieu, Festival, summer 1981.
Picasso 'Les Elues', Lucerne, Galerie Rosengart, summer 1981.
Picasso intime, Collection Maya Ruiz-Picasso, Geneva, Musée de l'Athénée, 4 July–6 September 1981.
Picasso, London, Waddington Graphics, 14 July–29 August 1981.
Picasso's Picassos, London, Hayward Gallery, 17 July–11 October 1981.
Picasso, Grafik aus dem Kupferstichkabinett Dresden, Gera, Kunstgalerie, 18 July–6 September 1981.
Picasso, Valbonne, Association Sophia Antipolis, 1–29 August 1981.
Pablo Picasso. Das Spätwerk, Themen 1964–1972, Basel, Kunstmuseum, 6 September–8 November 1981.
Picasso Centenaire, preface by Roland Leroy, La Courneuve, Fête de l'Humanité, 10–12 September 1981.
Picasso y los toros, Málaga, Museo de Bellas Artes, October–December 1981.
Picasso intime, Collection Maya Ruiz-Picasso, Tokyo, Seibu Museum of Art, 3 October–3 November 1981.
Picasso, Druckgraphik, Münster, Westfälisches Landesmuseum für Kunst und Kulturgeschichte, 4 October–22 November 1981.
Picasso, dessins et gouaches 1899–1972, Paris, Galerie Louise Leiris, 22 October–28 November 1981.
Picasso: Célébration du Centenaire de sa naissance, Paris, UNESCO, 26–30 October 1981.
Voir Picasso, Gentilly, Mairie, 14–29 November 1981.
Pablo Picasso zum 100. Geburtstag, 41 keramische Unikate aus der Sammlung Madame Jacqueline Picasso, Balingen, Kulturzentrum, 20 November–20 December 1981.
Picasso, grabados 1920–1955, série Caisse à remords, Murcia, Galería Yerba, December 1981.

1981–1982

Pablo Picasso, Werke aus der Sammlung Marina Picasso, catalogue by Werner Spies, Munich, Haus der Kunst, 14 February–20 April 1981; Cologne, Josef-Haubrich-Kunsthalle, 11 August–11 October 1981; Frankfurt, Städtische Galerie, 22 October 1981–10 January 1982; Zurich, Kunsthaus, 29 January–28 March 1982.

The Morton G. Neumann Family Collection, Volume III, Picasso Prints and Drawings, catalogue by E.A. Carmean, Jr., Washington, National Gallery of Art, 25 October 1981–24 January 1982.

Picasso, Bilder, Zeichnungen, Plastiken, Vienna, Rathaus, November 1981–January 1982.

Picasso 1881–1973. Exposición Antológica, Madrid, Museo Español de Arte Contemporáneo, November–December 1981; Barcelona, Museo Picasso, January–February 1982.

Els Picassos del Mas Manolo a Caldes de Montbui, Caldes de Montbui, Patronat Mas Manolo, December 1981–January 1982.

1982

Picasso Prints, Edinburgh, Scottish Arts Council, 1982.

Pablo Picasso: Works on Paper 1915–1963, London, Thomas Gibson Fine Art, 1982.

Picasso: la pièce à musique de Mougins, Paris, Centre Culturel du Marais, 1982.

Picasso, l'atelier du sculpteur, text by Hélène Seckel, Paris, Palais de Tokyo, 1982.

Picasso, céramiques, Barcelona, Galerie Dau al Set, January–February 1982.

Picasso and the Theatre, Brighton, Burstow Gallery and Great Hall, Brighton College, 1–30 May 1982.

Picasso ceramista, Barcelona, Palau Meca, 2 June–10 July 1982.

Pablo Picasso, 25 gravures, Châteaudun, Hôtel de Ville, 3 July–4 September 1982.

Hommage à Picasso, Salon-de-Provence, Château de l'Empéri, 16 July–31 August 1982.

Picasso, œuvres de la Fondation Zervos, Vézelay, Musée Lapidaire, 17 July–30 September 1982.

Picasso: rétrospective de l'œuvre gravé, 1947–1968, Cannes, Galerie Herbage, summer 1982.

Picasso, 1881–1973, Kstoletiju so dlja vrodenija, Moscow, Pushkin Museum, summer 1982.

The Sculpture of Picasso, text by Robert Rosenblum, New York, Pace Gallery, 16 September–23 October 1982.

Picasso graveur, Montigny-lès-Cormeilles, Centre Culturel Picasso, October 1982.

Picasso, Barcelona, Sala Gaspar, 25 October 1982.

Pablo Picasso, graphische Werke, 1904–1972, Bern, Galerie Kornfeld, 25 October–22 December 1982.

Picasso, 347 immagini erotiche, Milan, Galleria Bergamini, Studio Marconi, Galleria Seno, November 1982.

1982–1983

Los Picassos de Picasso en Mexico, introduction by Octavio Paz, Mexico, Museo Tamayo, November 1982–January 1983.

Picasso e il Mediterraneo, catalogue by Marie-Laure Bernadac, Rome, Villa Medici, 27 November 1982–13 February 1983; Athens, National Picture Gallery, March 1983.

1983

Picasso, Toulouse, Réfectoire des Jacobins, February–April 1983.

Picasso, London, Mayor Gallery; Zurich, Thomas Ammann Fine Art; Munich, Galerie Thomas, 3 February–16 March 1983.

Picasso, Caisse à Remords, 45 estampes 1919–1955, London, Edward Totah Gallery, 17 February–19 March 1983; Milan, Galleria Seno, 1983; Paris, Galerie Gianna Sistu, 1983.

Picasso, Estampes diverses, épreuves rares, Paris, Bouquinerie de l'Institut, 17 March–27 April 1983.

Picasso/117 gravats, 1919–1968, Barcelona, Museo Picasso, 19 March–31 May 1983.

Picasso, Masterpieces from Marina Picasso Collection and from Museums in U.S.A. and U.S.S.R., Tokyo, National Museum of Modern Art, 2 April–29 May 1983; Kyoto, Municipal Museum, 10 June–24 July 1983.

Pablo Picasso, The Last Prints, New York, Aldis Browne Fine Arts, 18 April–29 June 1983.

Picasso, Linocuts, London, Waddington Graphics, 27 April–4 June 1983.

Picasso, China Art Gallery, Peking, 2–22 May 1983; Shanghai, Museum of Fine Art, 30 May–30 June 1983.

Picasso, linogravures originales, 1958–1963, Bordeaux, Mécénart, 6–27 May 1983.

Picasso, Nîmes, Musée des Beaux-Arts, summer 1983.

Pablo Picasso, Paris, Grand Palais, FIAC, Galerie Gmurzynska, 23 September–2 October 1983; Cologne, Galerie Gmurzynska, 10 October–19 November 1983.

The Primacy of Design, Major Drawings in Black and Colored Media, from the Marina Picasso Collection, New York, Galerie Paul Rosenberg & Co., 26 October–3 December 1983.

1983–1984

Picasso the Printmaker: Graphics from the Marina Picasso Collection, catalogue by Brigitte Baer, Dallas, Museum of Art, 11 September–30 October 1983; New York, Brooklyn Museum, 23 November 1983–8 January 1984; Detroit, Institute of Arts, 31 January–25 March 1984; Denver, Art Museum, 7 April–20 May 1984.

Picasso Plastiken, catalogue by Werner Spies and Christine Piot, Berlin, Nationalgalerie, 7 October–27 November 1983; Düsseldorf, Kunsthalle, 11 December 1983–29 January 1984.

1984

Picasso. Todesthemen, catalogue by Ulrich Weisner, Bielefeld, Kunsthalle, 15 January–1 April 1984.

Picasso, The Last Years, 1963–1973, New York, Guggenheim Museum, 2 March–6 May 1984.

Picasso, Drawings from the Marina Picasso Collection, London, Fischer Fine Art Ltd, May–June 1984.

Picasso, 51 peintures 1904–1972, Paris, Galerie Louise Leiris, 17 May–9 June 1984.

Picasso, su ultima decada, 1963–1973, Mexico, Museo Tamayo, June–July 1984.

Hommage de Pablo Picasso à 'Monsieur Cézanne', Aix-en-Provence, Musée Granet, summer 1984.

Picasso, Tête à tête, la parabole du sculpteur, Antibes, Musée Picasso, 6 July–30 September 1984.

Picasso, Nice, Galerie des Ponchettes, Direction des musées de Nice, 15 July–16 September 1984.

Picasso, Melbourne, National Gallery of Victoria, 25 July–23 September 1984; Sidney, Art Gallery of New South Wales, 10 October–2 December 1984.

1984–1985

Picasso, l'œuvre gravé, 1899–1972, Paris, Musée des Arts Décoratifs, 26 September–29 October 1984; Nantes, Musée des Beaux-Arts, November–December 1984; Villeneuve-d'Ascq, Musée d'Art, January–February 1985.

Picasso, œuvres de jeunesse, Bern, Kunstmuseum, 6 December 1984–17 February 1985.

Select Bibliography

Bibliographies

Gaya Nuño, Juan Antonio, *Bibliografía crítica y antológica de Picasso*, San Juan, Puerto Rico, 1966.
Kibbey, Ray Anne, *Picasso, A Comprehensive Bibliography*, New York, London, 1977.
Matarasso, Henri, *Bibliographie des livres illustrés par Pablo Picasso/Œuvres graphiques 1905–1945*, Nice, 1956.

Picasso the Man

Brassaï, *Picasso & Co.*, New York, 1966, London, 1967.
Champris, Pierre de, *Picasso, ombre et soleil*, Paris, 1960.
Cocteau, Jean, *Le rappel à l'ordre*, Paris, 1926.
Connaître Picasso, Paris, 1974.
Crespelle, Jean-Paul, *Picasso and his Women*, London, 1969.
Duncan, David Douglas, *The Private World of Pablo Picasso*, New York, 1958.
Duncan, David Douglas, *Goodbye Picasso*, Paris, 1975.
Duncan, David Douglas, *The Silent Studio*, New York, London, 1976.
Duncan, David Douglas, *Viva Picasso, a Centennial Celebration 1881–1981*, New York, 1980.
Eluard, Paul, *A Pablo Picasso*, Geneva, 1944.
Gilot, Françoise and Lake, Carlton, *Life with Picasso*, New York, 1964, London, 1965.
Jacob, Max, 'Souvenirs sur Picasso', Paris, *Cahiers d'Art*, 1927, Vol. VI, pp. 199–203.
Kahnweiler, Daniel-Henry, *Mes galeries et mes peintres, Entretiens avec Francis Crémieux*, Paris, 1961.
Kahnweiler, Daniel-Henry, *Confessions esthétiques*, Paris, 1963.
Laporte, Geneviève, *Sunshine at Midnight*, London, 1975.
Malraux, André, *La tête d'obsidienne*, Paris, 1974.
Mili, Gjon, *Picasso et la troisième dimension*, Paris, 1970.
Mourlot, Fernand, *Gravés dans ma mémoire*, Paris, 1979.
Olivier, Fernande, *Picasso and his Friends*, London, 1964.
Otero, Roberto, *Forever Picasso*, New York, 1974.
Parmelin, Hélène, *Picasso Plain: an Intimate Portrait*, London, 1963.
Parmelin, Hélène, *Picasso Says . . .*, London, 1968.
Parmelin, Hélène, *Voyage en Picasso*, Paris, 1980.
Penrose, Roland, *Portrait of Picasso*, London, 1956, New York, 1957.
Ponge, Francis and Descargues, Pierre, *Picasso*, photographs by Edward Quinn, Paris, 1974.
Prévert, Jacques, *Portraits de Picasso*, photographs by André Villers, Paris, 1981.
Quinn, Edward, *Picasso at Work, an Intimate Photographic Study*, introduction and text by Roland Penrose, London, New York, 1965.
Sabartés, Jaime, *Picasso: an Intimate Portrait*, London, 1949.
Sabartés, Jaime, *Picasso. Documents iconographiques*, Geneva, 1954.
Salmon, André, *Souvenirs sans fin*, 2 vols., Paris, 1955–1956.
Stein, Gertrude, *The Autobiography of Alice B. Toklas*, New York, London, 1933.
Tzara, Tristan, *Picasso et les chemins de la connaissance*, Paris, 1948.
Verdet, André, *Pablo Picasso*, photographs by Roger Hauert, Geneva, 1956.
Weill, Berthe, *Pan! Dans l'œil! ou trente ans dans les coulisses de la peinture contemporaine 1900–1930*, Paris, 1933.

Reference Works

Bloch, Georges, *Pablo Picasso, Catalogue of the Graphic Work 1904–67*, Bern, 1968.
Cachin, Françoise and Minervino, Fiorella, *Tout l'œuvre peint de Picasso, 1907–1916*, Paris, 1977.
Czwiklitzer, Christophe, *Les affiches de Pablo Picasso*, Basel, Paris, 1970.
Daix, Pierre and Boudaille, Georges, *Picasso 1900–1906, catalogue raisonné de l'œuvre peint*, Neuchâtel, 1966.
Daix, Pierre and Rosselet, Joan, *Picasso: The Cubist Years 1907–1916*, London, 1979.
Duncan, David Douglas, *Picasso's Picassos*, London, New York, 1961.
Fairweather, Sally, *Picasso's Concrete Sculptures*, New York, 1982.
Geiser, Bernhard, *Picasso peintre-graveur*, 2 vols., Bern, 1933 and 1968.
Goeppert, Sebastian, Goeppert-Frank, Herma and Cramer, Patrick, *Pablo Picasso, catalogue raisonné des livres illustrés*, Geneva, 1983.
Moravia, Alberto, Lecaldano, Paolo and Daix, Pierre, *Tout l'œuvre peint de Picasso, périodes bleue et rose*, Paris, 1980.
Mourlot, Fernand, *Picasso lithographe*, 4 vols., Monte Carlo, 1949–1964.
Palau i Fabre, Josep, *Picasso, 1881–1907: Life and Work of the Early Years*, Oxford, 1981.
Ramié, Georges, *Céramique de Picasso*, Paris, 1974.
Spies, Werner, *Picasso Sculpture*, London, 1972.
Spies, Werner, *Picasso, Das plastische Werk* (sculpture catalogue in collaboration with Christine Piot), Stuttgart, 1983.
Zervos, Christian, *Pablo Picasso*, Paris, Vol. I, 1932, to Vol. XXXIII, 1978.

Monographs

Ashton, Dore, *Picasso on Art: A Selection of Views*, London, 1972.
Barr, Alfred Hamilton, *Picasso, Fifty Years of his Art*, New York, 1946, London, 1967.
Berger, John, *The Success and Failure of Picasso*, Harmondsworth, Baltimore, 1965.
Boeck, Wilhelm and Sabartés, Jaime, *Picasso*, London, New York, 1955.
Boudaille, Georges and Moulin, Raoul-Jean, *Picasso*, Paris, 1971.
Buchheim, Lothar Gunther, *Picasso. A Pictorial Biography*, New York, London, 1959.
Cabanne, Pierre, *Le siècle de Picasso*, 2 vols., Paris, 1975.
Cabanne, Pierre, *Picasso*, Neuchâtel, 1981.
Cassou, Jean, *Picasso*, New York, 1940, London, 1959.
Cassou, Jean, *Pablo Picasso*, Paris, 1975.
Chiari, Joseph, *Picasso. L'homme et son œuvre*, Paris, 1981.
Cocteau, Jean, *Picasso*, 1923.
Cocteau, Jean, *Picasso de 1916 à 1961*, Paris, 1962.
Daix, Pierre, *Picasso. The Man and his Work*, New York, 1964, London, 1965.
Daix, Pierre, *La vie de peintre de Pablo Picasso*, Paris, 1977.
Dale, Maud, *Picasso*, New York, 1930.
Damase, Jacques, *Pablo Picasso*, London, 1965.
Descargues, Pierre, *Picasso*, Paris, 1956.
Diehl, Gaston, *Picasso*, New York, 1960.
Dmitrieva, Nina Alexandrovna, *Pikasso*, Moscow, 1971.
Elgar, Frank and Maillard, Robert, *Picasso*, London, New York, 1956.
Elgar, Frank, *Picasso*, London, 1972.
Falkman, Kaj, *Picasso och hjärnan*, Stockholm, 1976.
Fermigier, André, *Picasso*, Paris, 1969.
Gaya Nuño, Juan Antonio, *Picasso*, Barcelona, 1957.
George, Waldemar, *Picasso*, Rome, 1924.
Gieure, Maurice, *Initiation à l'œuvre de Picasso*, Paris, 1951.
Guillén, Mercedes, *Picasso*, Madrid, 1973.
Hilton, Timothy, *Picasso*, New York, 1975, London, 1976.
'Hommage à Pablo Picasso', *XXe siècle*, special issue, 1971.
Jaffé, Hans Ludwig C., *Pablo Picasso*, New York, London, 1964.
Krestev, Kiril, *Picasso*, Sofia, 1982.
Lassaigne, Jacques, *Picasso*, London, 1955.
Level, André, *Picasso*, Paris, 1928.
Leymarie, Jean, *Picasso. Métamorphoses et Unité*, Geneva, 1985.
Lipton, Eunice, *Picasso Criticism, 1901–1939: the Making of an Artist-Hero*, New York, London, 1976.
Mahaut, Pierre, *Picasso*, Paris, 1930.
Martini, Alberto, *Picasso*, Milan, 1965.
McCully, Marilyn, *A Picasso Anthology: Documents, Criticism, Reminiscences*, London, 1981.
Merli, Juan, *Picasso, el artista y la obra de nuestro tiempo*, Buenos Aires, 1948.
Micheli, Mario de, *Picasso*, London, New York, 1967.
O'Brian, Patrick, *Pablo Ruiz Picasso*, London, 1976.
Ors, Eugenio d', *Pablo Picasso*, Paris, 1930.
Palau i Fabre, Josep, *Picasso*, Barcelona, 1965.
Penrose, Roland, *Picasso: His Life and Work*, London, 1958, New York, 1962.
Penrose, Roland, *Portrait of Picasso*, London, 1981.
Perry, Jacques, *Yo Picasso*, Paris, 1982.
Picasso, coll. Génies et Réalités, Paris, 1967.
Picasso 1881–1973, London, 1973 (new ed. *Picasso in Retrospect*, New York, 1980).
Raboff, Ernest, *Pablo Picasso. Art for Children*, New York, 1968.
Raynal, Maurice, *Picasso*, Munich, 1921, Paris, 1922.
Raynal, Maurice, *Picasso*, Geneva, 1959.
Reverdy, Pierre, *Pablo Picasso*, Paris, 1924.

Ripley, Elizabeth, *Picasso: a Biography*, Philadelphia, London, 1959.
Schiff, Gert (editor), *Picasso in Perspective*, Englewood Cliffs, London, 1976.
Schürer, Oscar, *Pablo Picasso*, Leipzig, 1927.
Stein, Gertrude, *Picasso*, London, 1939, New York, 1946.
Sutton, Keith, *Pablo Picasso*, New York, 1962, London, 1963.
Sweetman, D., *Picasso*, London, 1973.
Thomas, Denis, *Picasso and his Art*, New York, London, 1975.
Uhde, Wilhelm, *Picasso et la tradition française*, Paris, 1928.
Vallentin, Antonina, *Pablo Picasso*, Paris, 1957.
Walter, Gerhard, *Picasso*, Stuttgart, 1949.
Wiegand, Wilfried, *Picasso*, Hamburg, 1973.
Zennström, Per-Olov, *Pablo Picasso*, Stockholm, 1948.
Zervos, Christian, *Pablo Picasso*, Milan, 1937.

The Early Years; the Blue and Rose Periods

Apollinaire, Guillaume, 'Les jeunes: Picasso peintre', *La Plume*, 15 May 1905, pp. 478–483.
Blunt, Anthony and Pool, Phoebe, *Picasso. The Formative Years. A Study of his Sources*, London, Greenwich, 1962.
Boudaille, Georges, *Picasso. Première époque 1881–1906*, Paris, 1964.
Chevalier, Denys, *Picasso, époques bleue et rose*, Paris, 1969.
Cirici-Pellicer, Alexandre, *Picasso avant Picasso*, Geneva, 1950.
Cirlot, Juan Eduardo, *Pablo Picasso, naissance d'un génie*, Paris, 1972.
Elgar, Frank, *Picasso: Blue and Rose Periods*, London, 1956.
Francin, Francisco, *Picasso y Horta de Ebro*, Tarragona, 1981.
Guichard-Meili, Jean, *Picasso. De Barcelone à l'époque rose*, Paris, 1967.
Lieberman, William S., *Picasso. Blue and Rose Periods*, New York, 1952, London, 1955.
Marussi, Garibaldo, *Pablo Picasso. Il periodo blu e il periodo rosa*, Milan, 1955.
Pad'rta, Jiri, *Picasso: the Early Years*, New York, London, 1960.
Palau i Fabre, Josep, *Picasso en Cataluña*, Barcelona, 1979.
Pool, Phoebe, 'Sources and Background for Picasso's Art. 1900–1906', *The Burlington Magazine*, No. 101, 1959, pp. 176–182.
Pool, Phoebe, 'Picasso's Neo-classicism. First Period, 1905–1906', *Apollo*, February 1965, pp. 122–127.
Sabartés, Jaime, *Les Bleus de Barcelone*, Paris, 1963.

Les Demoiselles d'Avignon

Bandmann, Gunter, *Picasso. Les Demoiselles d'Avignon*, Stuttgart, 1965.
Daix, Pierre, 'Il n'y a pas d'art nègre dans *Les Demoiselles d'Avignon*', *Gazette des Beaux-Arts*, October 1970, pp. 247–270.
Golding, John, 'The Demoiselles d'Avignon', *The Burlington Magazine*, March 1958, pp. 155–163.
Hoog, Michel, '*Les Demoiselles d'Avignon* et la peinture à Paris en 1907–1908', *Gazette des Beaux-Arts*, October 1973, pp. 212–215.

Rosenblum, Robert, 'The Demoiselles d'Avignon revisited', *Art News*, April 1973, pp. 45–48.
Rubin, William, 'From Narrative to "Iconic" in Picasso: The Buried Allegory in "Bread and Fruitdish on a Table" and the Role of "Les Demoiselles d'Avignon"', *The Art Bulletin*, December 1983, pp. 615–649.
Steinberg, Leo, 'The Philosophical Brothel', *Art News*, September 1972, pp. 20–29, October 1972, pp. 38–47.

Cubism

Apollinaire, Guillaume, *Les peintres cubistes*, Paris, 1913.
Basler, Adolphe, 'Pablo Picasso und der Kubismus', *Der Cicerone*, April 1921, pp. 237–244.
Camón Aznar, José, *Picasso y el cubismo*, Madrid, 1956.
Cooper, Douglas, *The Cubist Epoch*, London, New York, 1971.
Cooper, Douglas and Tinterow, Gary, *The Essential Cubism*, London, 27 April–10 July 1983.
Le Cubisme, Université de Saint-Etienne, C.I.E.R.E.L., Travaux IV, 1973.
Elgar, Frank, *Picasso: Cubist Period*, London, 1957.
Fry, Edward, *Cubism*, London, New York, 1966.
Golding, John, *Cubism, A History and an Analysis, 1907–1914*, London, 1959.
Gomez de la Serna, Ramón, *Picasso y el cubismo*, Turin, 1945.
Kahnweiler, Daniel-Henry, *The Rise of Cubism*, New York, 1949.
Kramar, Vincenc, *Kubismus*, Brno, 1921.
Martini, Alberto, *Picasso e il cubismo*, Milan, 1967.
Paulhan, Jean, *La peinture cubiste*, Paris, 1971.
Phillips, Virginia, 'Concerning Picasso's Cubism', *Avenue*, February 1934, pp. 17–22, and March 1934, pp. 36–40.
Raynal, Maurice, *Les maîtres du cubisme: Pablo Picasso*, Paris, 1921.
Rosenblum, Robert, *Cubism and Twentieth Century Art*, rev. ed., New York, 1976, London, 1977.
Russoli, Franco, introduction, *L'opera completa di Picasso cubista*, Milan, 1972.
Schwartz, Paul, *The Cubists*, New York, London, 1971.

1917–1925

Blunt, Anthony, 'Picasso's Classical Period (1917–1925)', *The Burlington Magazine*, April 1968, pp. 187–191.
Carandente, Giovanni, 'Il viaggio in Italia: 17 febbraio 1917', in *Picasso: opere dal 1895 al 1971 dalla Collezione Marina Picasso*, Venice, 1981.
Cooper, Douglas, *Picasso and the Theatre*, London, 1968.
Galassi, Susan, G., 'Picasso's "The Lovers" of 1919', *Arts Magazine*, February 1982, pp. 76–82.
Meyer, Susan, *Ancient Mediterranean Sources in the Works of Picasso*, thesis, New York, 1980.
Pool, Phoebe, 'Picasso's Neo-Classicism: Second Period, 1917–1925', *Apollo*, March

1967, pp. 198–207.
Le retour à l'ordre dans les arts plastiques et l'architecture, Université de Saint-Etienne, C.I.E.R.E.L., Travaux VIII, 1975.
Schürer, Oskar, 'Picasso's Klassizismus', *Kunst für Alle*, April 1926, pp. 202–207.
Zervos, Christian, *Picasso, œuvres 1920–1926*, Paris, 1926.

1925–1936

Breton, André, *Surrealism and Painting*, New York, 1945.
Gassman, Lydia, *Mystery, Magic and Love in Picasso 1925–1937*, thesis, Ann Arbor, 1981.
Glozer, Laszlo, *Picasso und der Surrealismus*, Cologne, 1974.
Golding, John, 'Picasso and Surrealism', *Picasso 1881–1973*, London, 1973, pp. 77–121.
'Hommage à Picasso', *Documents*, No. 3, 1930.
Kaufmann, Ruth, 'Picasso's Crucifixion of 1930', *The Burlington Magazine*, September 1969, pp. 553–561.
Mujica Gallo, Manuel, *La Minotauromaquia de Picasso*, Madrid, 1971.
Picasso 1930–1935, pull-out from *Cahiers d'Art*, Vol. X, Nos. 7–10 of 1935, published in 1936.
Penrose, Roland, 'Beauty and the Monster', *Picasso 1881–1973*, London, 1973, pp. 156–195.
Ries, Martin, 'Picasso and the Myth of the Minotaur', *Art Journal*, Winter 1972–1973, pp. 142–145.
Rubin, William, *Dada and Surrealist Art*, New York, London, 1970.
Runnqvist, Jan, *Minotauros; en studie i for*, Stockholm, 1959.
Seckel, Curt, 'Picasso, Wege zur Symbolik der Minotauromachie', *Die Kunst und das schöne Heim*, May 1973, pp. 289–296.

1936–1945

Arnheim, Rudolf, *Picasso's Guernica. The Genesis of a Painting*, Berkeley, 1962.
Blunt, Anthony, *Picasso's Guernica*, London, 1969.
Cahiers d'Art, Nos. IV–V, 1937, special issue on *Guernica*.
Chipp, Herschel B., 'Guernica: Love, War and the Bullfight', *Art Journal*, Winter 1973–1974, pp. 100–115.
Desnos, Robert, *Picasso. Seize peintures, 1939–1943*, Paris, 1943.
Ferrier, Jean-Louis, 'Eléments pour Guernica', *XXe siècle*, special issue, 1971, pp. 48–51.
Guernica – Legado Picasso, Madrid, 1981.
Janis, Harriet and Sidney, *Picasso. The Recent Years, 1939–1946*, New York, 1946.
Larrea, Juan, *Guernica. Pablo Picasso*, New York, 1947.
Palau i Fabre, Josep, *El Guernica de Picasso*, Barcelona, 1979.
Russell, John, *Picasso: Paintings 1939–1946*, London, 1946.

1945–1973

Alberti, Rafael, *Picasso en Avignon*, Paris, 1971.
Alberti, Rafael, *Picasso. Le rayon ininterrompu*, Paris, 1974.
Cooper, Douglas, *Picasso: Variations on Manet's 'Déjeuners sur l'Herbe'*, London, 1963.
Dor de la Souchère, Romuald, *Picasso*,

Antibes, London, 1962.
Dufour, Pierre, *Picasso, 1950–1968*, Geneva, 1969.
Eluard, Paul and Sabartés, Jaime, *Picasso à Antibes*, photographs by Michel Sima, Paris, 1948.
Gallwitz, Klaus, *Picasso 1954–1973*, Paris, 1985.
Geelhaar, Christian, 'Themen 1964–1972', *Pablo Picasso. Das Spätwerk*, Basel, 1981.
Giraudy, Danièle, *L'œuvre de Picasso à Antibes*, Antibes, 1981.
Marchiori, Giuseppe, *L'ultimo Picasso*, Venice, 1949.
Parmelin, Hélène, *Picasso: Women, Cannes and Mougins 1954–63*, London, 1965.
Parmelin, Hélène, *The Artist and his Model and Other Recent Works*, New York, 1965.
Parmelin, Hélène, *At Notre-Dame de Vie*, New York, 1966.
'Picasso à Vallauris', *Verve*, Nos. 25–26, October 1951.
Roy, Claude, *La Guerre et la Paix*, Paris, 1952.
Sabartés, Jaime, *Les Ménines et la vie*, Paris, 1958.
Sabartés, Jaime, *Faune et flore d'Antibes*, Greenwich, Conn. 1960.
Schiff, Gert, 'The Musketeer and his *Theatrum Mundi*', *Picasso, The Last Years, 1963–1973*, New York, 1984.

Papiers collés

Apollinaire, Guillaume, 'Picasso', *Montjoie!*, 14 March 1913.
Daix, Pierre, 'Des bouleversements chronologiques dans la révolution des papiers collés (1912–1914)', *Gazette des Beaux-Arts*, October 1973, pp. 217–227.
Exhibition *Georges Braque, les papiers collés*, Paris, Centre Pompidou, 17 June–27 September 1982.
Greenberg, Clement, 'The pasted-paper revolution', *Art News*, September 1958.
Paulhan, Jean, 'L'espace cubiste ou le papier-collé', *L'Arc*, Spring 1960, No. 10.
Rosenblum, Robert, 'Picasso and the Coronation of Alexander III: A note on the dating of some "Papiers Collés"', *The Burlington Magazine*, October 1971.
Tzara, Tristan, 'Le papier collé ou le proverbe en peinture', *Cahiers d'Art*, 1931, No. 2.
Tzara, Tristan, introduction to the catalogue of the exhibition *Papiers collés, 1912–1914 de Picasso*, Paris, 20 February–20 March 1935.
Wescher, Herta, *Picasso. Papiers collés par Picasso*, Paris, 1960.

Sculpture

Argan, Giulio Carlo, *Scultura di Picasso*, Venice, 1953.
Ashton, Dore, 'Sculptures de Picasso', *XXe siècle*, June 1968, pp. 25–40.
Bowness, Alan, 'Picasso's Sculptures', *Picasso, 1881–1973*, London, 1973, pp. 122–155.
Breton, André, 'Picasso dans son élément', photographs by Brassaï, *Minotaure*, No. 1, May 1933, pp. 8–29.
Elsen, Albert, 'The Many Faces of Picasso's Sculpture', *Art International*, XIII/6, Summer 1969, pp. 24–34.
Elsen, Albert, 'Picasso's Man with a Sheep', *Art International*, XXI/2, March–April 1977, pp. 8–15, 29–31.

Gaffé, René, 'Sculpteur, Picasso?', *Artes*, Series 2, Nos. 3/4, 1947–1948, pp. 36–37.
Gonzalez, Julio, 'Picasso sculpteur', *Cahiers d'Art*, 1936, Nos. 6–7, pp. 189–191.
Henze, Anton, 'Neue Plastiken von Picasso', *Das Kunstwerk*, 9/XIII, March 1960, pp. 17–24.
Johnson, Ronald William, *The Early Sculpture of Picasso 1901–1914*, New York, 1976.
Kahnweiler, Daniel-Henry, *The Sculptures of Picasso*, photographs by Brassaï, London, 1949.
Laporte, Paul M., 'The Man with the Lamb', *Art Journal*, Spring 1962, pp. 144–150.
Lichtenstern, Christa, *Picasso 'Tête de Femme'*, Frankfurt, 1980.
Penrose, Roland, *Picasso*, London, 1961.
Penrose, Roland, *Picasso: Sculptures*, New York, 1965.
Penrose, Roland, *The Sculpture of Picasso*, New York, 1967.
Piot, Christine, *Décrire Picasso*, thesis, Paris, October 1981.
Prampolini, Enrico, *Picasso scultore*, Rome, 1943.
Prejger, Lionel, 'Picasso découpe le fer', *L'Œil*, No. 82, October 1961, pp. 28–33.
Rosenblum, Robert, 'Notes on Picasso's Sculpture', *Art News*, January 1983, pp. 60–66.
Russoli, Franco, *Picasso*, Milan, 1966.
Salles, Georges, 'Les baigneurs de Picasso', *Quadrum*, No. 5, 1958, pp. 4–10.
Smith, Laura, E., 'Iconographic issues in Picasso's "Woman in the garden"', *Arts Magazine*, No. 5, January, 1982, pp. 142–147.
Tucker, William, 'Picasso Cubist Constructions', *Studio International*, No. 179, May 1970, pp. 201–205.
Verdet, André, *L'homme au mouton de Pablo Picasso. Poème*, Paris, 1950.
Verdet, André, *La Chèvre*, Paris, 1952.
Veronesi, Giulia, 'Sculture di Picasso', *Emporium*, April 1951, pp. 146–153.
Zervos, Christian, 'Projets de Picasso pour un monument', *Cahiers d'Art*, 1929, Nos. 8–9, pp. 342–344.
Zervos, Christian, 'L'homme à l'agneau de Picasso', *Cahiers d'Art*, 1945–1946, pp. 84–112.

Ceramics

Bloch, Georges, *Pablo Picasso, catalogue de l'œuvre gravé céramique, III, 1949–1971*, Bern, 1972.
Cahiers d'Art, special issue, Vol. 23, No. 1, 1948.
Kahnweiler, Daniel-Henry, *Picasso-Keramik*, Hanover, 1957.
Ramié, Suzanne and Georges, *Céramiques de Picasso*, New York, 1955.
Ramié Georges, 'Céramiques', *Verve*, Vol. VII, Nos. 25–26, 1951.
Sabartés, Jaime, *Picasso ceramista*, Milan, 1953.
Verdet, André, *Faunes et nymphes de Pablo Picasso*, Geneva, 1952.

Drawings

Boeck, Wilhelm, *Picasso: Zeichnungen*, Cologne, 1973.
Boudaille, Georges, introduction, *Pablo Picasso. Carnet de la Californie*, Paris, 1959.

Boudaille, Georges and Dominguin, Luis Miguel, *Pablo Picasso, Toros y Toreros*, London, 1961.
Bouret, Jean, *Picasso/Dessins*, Paris, 1950.
Carlson, Victor I., *Drawings and Watercolors, 1899–1907, in the Collection of the Baltimore Museum of Art*, Baltimore, 1976.
Carnet Royan, 30.5.40, Paris, 1948.
Char, René and Feld, Charles, *Picasso. Dessins du 27-3-66 au 15-3-68*, Paris, 1969.
Cooper, Douglas, *Pablo Picasso. Carnet catalan*, Paris, 1958.
Cooper, Douglas, *Pablo Picasso, Pour Eugenia*, Paris, 1976.
Dessins de Picasso, époques bleue et rose, Lausanne, 1960.
Eluard, Paul, *Picasso. Dessins*, Paris, 1952.
George, Waldemar, *Picasso. Dessins*, Paris, 1926.
Jardot, Maurice, *Picasso. Dessins d'un demi-siècle*, Paris, 1956.
Jardot, Maurice, *Pablo Picasso: Drawings*, New York, 1959.
Keller, Horst, introduction, *Picasso, 90 dessins et œuvres en couleurs*, Basel, no date.
Lambert, Jean-Clarence, *Picasso. Dessins de Tauromachie, 1917–1960*, Paris, 1960.
Lasarte, Juan Aynaud de, *Carnet Picasso. La Coruña, 1894–1895*, Barcelona, 1971.
Leiris, Michel, *Picasso and the Human Comedy, A Suite of 180 Drawings by Picasso*, New York, 1954.
Leymarie, Jean, *Picasso, dessins*, Geneva, 1967.
Longstreet, Stephen, introduction, *The Drawings of Picasso*, Alhambra, 1974.
Marcenac, Jean, *Picasso. Le goût du bonheur. A Suite of Happy, Playful and Erotic Drawings*, New York, 1970.
Migel, Parmenia, *Pablo Picasso. Designs for The Three Cornered Hat*, New York, 1978.
Millier, Arthur, *The Drawings of Picasso*, Los Angeles, 1961.
Ocaña, Maria Teresa, introduction, *Picasso, Viatge a Paris*, Barcelona, 1979.
Palau i Fabre, Josep, *Picasso. Dessins pour ses enfants*, Paris, 1979.
Parmelin, Hélène, *Picasso, La flûte double*, Saint-Paul-de-Vence, 1967.
Picasso. Fifteen Drawings, New York, 1946.
Picasso, 145 dessins pour la presse et les organisations démocratiques, Paris, 1973.
Picasso, Line Drawings and Prints, New York, 1981.
Picasso, Der Zeichner, 1893–1972, Zurich, 1982, 3 vols.
Picon, Gaëtan, *Pablo Picasso, 'La chute d'Icare'*, Geneva, 1971.
40 dessins en marge du Buffon, Paris, 1957.
Richardson, John, *Pablo Picasso Watercolours and Gouaches*, London, 1964.
Sabartés, Jaime, *A los toros avec Picasso*, Monte Carlo, 1961.
Salas, Xavier de, introduction, *Carnet Picasso. Madrid, 1898*, Barcelona, 1976.
Salles, Georges, *Picasso. Mes dessins d'Antibes*, Paris, 1958.
Serullaz, Maurice, introduction, *Picasso's Private Drawings*, New York, 1969.
Solmi, Sergio, *Disegni di Picasso*, Milan, Hoepli, 1945.
'Une anatomie – dessins de Picasso', *Minotaure*, No. 1, 15 February 1933, pp. 33–37.
Verve, special issue, Nos. 29–30, 1954.
Zervos, Christian, *Dessins de Picasso, 1892–1948*, Paris, 1949.

Picasso in Montmartre about 1904 (Picasso Archives)

Chronology

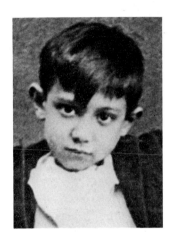

Picasso, aged seven
(Picasso Archives)

First number of *La Coruña*,
16 September 1894 (M.P. 402)

1880
8 December: marriage in Málaga of Don José Ruiz Blasco (1838–1913) and Doña Maria Picasso y López (1855–1939). José Ruiz Blasco studied at the Provincial Fine Arts School of Málaga, has taught drawing there since 1879 and becomes curator of the Municipal Museum in June 1880.

1881
25 October: birth of Pablo, the eldest child.

1884
20 December: birth of Pablo's first sister, Dolorès, known as Lola (1884–1958).

1887
30 October: birth of the second sister, Concepción or Conchita (1887–1895).

1888–1889
Picasso begins to paint under his father's tuition.

1891
Don José takes up a teaching post at the Instituto da Guarda in Corunna.
October: the family goes there by sea and sets up home at 14, Calle Payo Gómez. Pablo enters secondary school.

1892
September: enters the Corunna School of Fine Arts where he is listed under No. 88 and attends the decorative drawing classes conducted by his father.

1893
October: transfers to the figure drawing class under No. 11. Writes and designs a magazine – *Azul y Blanco* – the first issue of which is dated 8 October.

1894
First accurately dated sketchbooks.
16 September: first issue of the manuscript periodical *La Coruña*, illustrated with portraits and caricatures signed 'P. Ruiz'.
Attends three courses: copying plaster casts; figure drawing from plaster casts; and painting and copying from nature.
Paints the first oil portraits of his family and friends.

1895
March: Don José, appointed to teach at the Barcelona School of Fine Arts, in the La Lonja building, immediately takes up his post and leaves his family in Corunna to finish the school year.
July: Picasso's discovery of Madrid and the Prado on the way to Málaga where he is to spend the holidays. A sea voyage to Barcelona follows, resulting in some small seascapes.

September: the family moves into 3, Calle Cristina, at the corner of the Calle Llauder, near La Lonja.

15 and 30 September: entrance examinations for the Senior Course, Classical Art and Still-life Section. From the very start at La Lonja Picasso makes friends with Manuel Pallarés, six years his senior. Produces several portraits of his new friend.

1896

The First Communion (Barcelona, Museo Picasso) is shown at the Barcelona Fine Arts and Industry Exhibition, 23 April–26 July.

Reaches Málaga in June, where he paints landscapes and the *Portrait of Aunt Pepa* (Barcelona, Museo Picasso).

Family moves during the summer to 3, Calle de la Merced. Picasso has his first studio at 4, Calle de la Plata, which he shares with Pallarés. His attendance at the La Lonja classes becomes irregular.

1897

At the beginning of the year, paints *Science and Charity* (Barcelona, Museo Picasso), which is sent to Madrid in May to the General Fine Arts Exhibition, where it earns a distinction on 8 June, then to the Fine Arts Exhibition at Málaga, where it wins a gold medal.

12 June: opening of Els Quatre Gats, a cabaret modelled on the Chat Noir in Paris.

Summer: holidays in Málaga.

September–October: leaves for Madrid, where he stays at 5, Calle San Pedro Martir. Passes entrance examination for the San Fernando Academy. Joins the landscape course and the course for drawing from classical models and drapes. Spends time at the Prado. Gives up the Academy during the winter.

1898

Spring: Picasso weakened by scarlet fever. Returns to Barcelona in May.

June: leaves for Horta de Ebro – now Horta de San Juan – with Pallarés, a native of this village. Spends a short time with the Pallarés family, then visits Mount Santa Barbara and camps out in the hills. Landscape studies.

Returns to Horta about mid-August.

1899

Mid-February: returns to Barcelona. Sets himself up in a studio at 2, Carrer de Escudillers Blancs. Frequents the Círculo Artístico, where he produces drawings of an academic kind. The first issue of the *Quatre Gats* magazine, edited by Pere Romeu, is published in February. Picasso makes himself at home in Els Quatre Gats circles, where he meets the painters Junyer-Vidal, Nonell, Sunyer and Casagemas, the art collector Carlos Junyer-Vidal, the sculptor Manolo Hugué (known as Manolo), the Fernandez de Soto brothers, the writer Ramón Reventos and the poet Sabartés, who is later to become his secretary and his closest friend. An older generation includes Eugenio d'Ors, the painter and writer Santiago Rusiñol, the art historian Miguel Utrillo and the painter Ramón Casas. First Art Nouveau drawings. Discovers the art of Steinlen and Toulouse-Lautrec through Casas.

3 June: publication of first number of *Pél y Ploma* review produced by Utrillo and Casas. First etching: *The Picador*, known as *El Zurdo* (*The Left-hander*) because of the reversed print. At the end of the year, No. 30 of *Pél y Ploma* carries the announcement of a poster competition for the 1900 carnival. Picasso enters a *Pierrot* (M.P. 427).

1900

Beginning of the year: Picasso moves, together with Casagemas, to a studio at 17, Riera de San Juan.

1 February: opening of an exhibition of some 150 drawings by Picasso at Els Quatre Gats, mostly portraits of his friends; reviewed in *Vanguardia* on 3 February and *Diario de Barcelona* on 7 February.

Paints bullfight scenes.

Les derniers moments (*The Last Moments*), a picture later overpainted with *La vie* (*Life*) of

Design for a menu for
Els Quatre Gats,
1899–1900 (M.P. 416R)

1903, is chosen for display at the Paris International Exhibition which opens on 14 April. The review *Joventut* publishes drawings by Picasso in No. 22 of 12 July and No. 27 of 16 August as illustrations of two poems by Bridgman.

In September, the *Catalunya Artística* review publishes two more drawings.

October: departure for Paris with Casagemas; they stay in Montmartre, at 49, rue Gabrielle, in the studio vacated by Nonell.

Visit to the International Exhibition's Painting Section and contacts with the local Spanish colony, especially Paco Durio and Manolo.

The Catalan dealer Pedro Mañach offers Picasso 150 francs per month in return for some works and introduces him to Berthe Weill, who buys three pastels of bullfights from him on the spot. The collector Olivier Sainsère begins to buy drawings from him.

Paints *Le Moulin de la Galette* (New York, The Solomon R. Guggenheim Museum).

Casagemas has fallen in love with the model Laure Gargallo, known as Germaine, and is reluctant to return to Spain with Picasso.

20 December: departure for Barcelona.

End of year spent at Málaga. Casagemas goes back to Paris and Picasso decides to settle in Madrid.

1901

Mid-January: departure for Madrid and short visit to Toledo.

17 February: Casagemas's suicide in Paris.

28 February: obituary of Casagemas in *Catalunya Artística* with a portrait drawn by Picasso. Meets the Catalan writer Francisco de Asis Soler with whom he founds the *Arte Joven* review. The first of the four numbers published appears on 31 March and announces the birth of another review, *Madrid, Notas d'Arte* which never sees the light of day.

Towards the end of his stay in Madrid he sometimes signs his works 'P. Ruiz Picasso', 'P.R. Picasso' or, on other occasions, simply 'Picasso'.

End of April: departure for Barcelona. Increasing use of Pointillist technique featuring large dabs of paint. Paintings and pastels of society ladies. *The Woman in Blue* (Madrid, Museo Nacional de Arte Moderno) is sent to the National Exhibition of Fine Arts which opens in Madrid on 29 April.

May: departure for Paris with Jaime Andreu and move to 130 ter, boulevard de Clichy, where Casagemas's studio had been.

June: Miguel Utrillo shows pastels by Picasso at the Sala Parés in Barcelona. The catalogue is published in *Pèl y Ploma* with a text by Utrillo.

17 June: article by Gustave Coquiot in *Le Journal* announcing an exhibition of works by Picasso and Iturrino at the Galerie Vollard.

24 June: opening of the exhibition organized by Mañach. Picasso shows sixty-four works, including the *Yo Picasso* self-portrait (New York, private collection) the *Portrait of Mañach* (Washington, National Gallery of Art), cabaret scenes, women drinking, landscapes and still-life pictures, as well as drawings. Picasso first meets Max Jacob, his senior by five years, on this occasion.

July: favourable review by Félicien Fagus in *La Revue blanche*.

August: Casagemas's death used as a theme in *L'enterrement de Casagemas* (*Burial of Casagemas*) or *Evocation* (Musée d'Art Moderne de la Ville de Paris).

September–October: influence of Toulouse-Lautrec, who dies on 9 September.

Adoption of purely blue colouring. Series of mother-and-child pictures, the *Portrait of Sabartés* or *The Glass of Beer* (Moscow, Pushkin Museum) and *Self-portrait* (cat. 4).

Picasso in the studio at 130 ter, boulevard de Clichy with Mañach, Fuentes-Torres and his wife, 1901 (Picasso Archives)

1902

January: Picasso's contract with Mañach broken. Return to Barcelona.

Rents a studio at 6, Calle Nueva (now Calle Conde del Asalto). Blue monochrome style further developed in mother-and-child scenes and pictures of grieving women, culminating in *The Meeting* or *The Two Sisters* (Leningrad, The Hermitage Museum).

Meets Julio Gonzalez.

1–15 April: exhibition of pictures and pastels by Louis Bernard-Lemaire and Picasso, Galerie Berthe Weill.

October: Picasso leaves for Paris, probably with Sebastian Junyer. Stays first at the Hôtel des Ecoles, rue Champollion, then rue de Seine, at the Hôtel du Maroc, in the attic of the sculptor Agero, and finally shares the room rented by Max Jacob at 87, boulevard Voltaire.

He is too poor to buy canvases and does much drawing.

15 November: joint exhibition with Pichot, Girieud and Launay in the Galerie Berthe Weill. The Blue pictures revealed.

Favourable article in the December issue of the *Mercure de France* by Charles Morice, a friend of Gauguin, who gives Picasso a copy of *Noa-Noa* when they meet.

Study for *La vie* (*Life*), 1903
(M.P. 473)

1903

January: return to Barcelona. He goes back to the studio in the Riera de San Juan and sets out on a highly productive period.

Beginning of the 'Embraces' series.

May: culmination of the 'Embraces' in the great allegorical *Life* composition (The Cleveland Museum of Art). The male figure, which has often been endowed with Picasso's own features in the sketches, takes on those of Casagemas in the completed painting.

Summer and autumn: series of Soler family portraits. *The Blind Man's Meal* (New York, The Metropolitan Museum of Art), *The Old Guitarist* (The Art Institute of Chicago) and *The Old Jew* (Moscow, Pushkin Museum) recall El Greco's distortions by their elongated Mannerist treatment. The strong blues express the physical discomfort of old age, deprivation and ill-health.

End of the year: move to 28, Calle del Commercio, a studio made available by Gargallo.

Picasso's arrival in Paris with Sebastian Junyer-Vidal in April 1904. Drawing in a sketchbook in the Museo Picasso, Barcelona

1904

Paints *La Célestine* (Paris, private collection) and a *Portrait of Sabartés* (Oslo, Kunsternes Museum).

April: departure for Paris and move to the Bateau-Lavoir, place Ravignan (now place Emile-Goudeau), to a studio handed over to him by Paco Durio. He renews contact with the Spanish colony, especially Ricardo Canals and his wife, Manolo and Totote, as well as Ramón Pichot and Germaine.

Max Jacob introduces him to André Salmon. He frequents the Lapin Agile and the Cirque Médrano.

Blue works continue. A series of erotic drawings.

Summer: liaison with Madeleine, probably the model for the *Woman with a Helmet of Hair* (The Art Institute of Chicago). Meets Fernande, whom he portrays at the end of the year in *Meditation* (*Contemplation*) (New York, private collection), a watercolour.

Autumn: meets Guillaume Apollinaire.

Prompted by Ricardo Canals, Picasso again tries his hand at etching in *Le repas frugal* (*The Frugal Meal*).

24 October: opening of group exhibition at the Galerie Berthe Weill, including a dozen pictures by Picasso produced during the previous three years.

Gradual abandonment of the monochrome blue treatment.

The Actor (New York, The Metropolitan Museum of Art) represents the transition to the Rose period.

The Bateau-Lavoir about 1904. Picasso has indicated the location of his studio windows (Musée Picasso Document)

1905

25 February–6 March: exhibition, jointly with Albert Trachsel and Auguste Gérardin, at the Galerie Serrurier on the theme of the circus. Introduction to the catalogue by Charles Morice and illustrated review by Apollinaire in *La Plume* of 15 May.

Frequents the Closerie des Lilas in Montparnasse, to which he is taken by Salmon and Apollinaire; this is a meeting place for painters and writers belonging to the circle of Paul Fort and Jean Moréas.

Van Gogh and Seurat retrospective exhibition at the Salon des Indépendants.

Produces *Le fou* (*The Jester*, cat. 272) which Vollard arranges to have cast in bronze.

Works on *The Family of Saltimbanques* (Washington, National Gallery of Art).

Summer: a stay at Schoorl, in Holland, where he has been invited by a young writer, Tom Schilperoort. He paints *Les trois hollandaises* (*The Three Dutchwomen*, Paris, Musée National d'Art Moderne, on loan to the Musée Picasso) there.

October: Salon d'Automne, with the 'Cages aux Fauves' and an Ingres retrospective exhibition. *The Turkish Bath* is shown on this occasion.

Autumn: he meets Gertrude and Leo Stein through the dealer Clovis Sagot and enjoys their hospitality.

Winter: *La mort d'Arlequin* (*The Death of Harlequin*, private collection), the first work bought by Wilhelm Uhde several months later.

A start on the *Portrait of Gertrude Stein* (New York, The Metropolitan Museum of Art).

Winter 1905–1906: display at the Louvre of recently excavated Iberian sculptures from Osuna and Cerro de los Santos.

1906

Drawings, watercolours and paintings on the theme of *L'abreuvoir* (*The Watering Place*).

Early March: Manet exhibition at Durand-Ruel.

Vollard buys the bulk of the Rose period canvases for 2,000 gold francs, thereby providing Picasso with the necessary measure of financial security to enable him to travel.

Gertrude Stein introduces him to Matisse who is showing *La Joie de Vivre* at the Salon des Indépendants. He meets Derain a little later.

Picasso and Ramón Reventos in Barcelona in 1906 (Picasso Archives)

Studies for self-portraits, 1906 (cf. cat. 8)
(M.P. 524R)

Work on Gertrude Stein's portrait continues, but he has difficulties with the rendering of the face.

Beginnings of the 'Coiffure' theme.

Beginning of May: departure for Barcelona with Fernande. Spends a short time there with his family and meets his friends again.

Mid-May: departure with Fernande for Gosol, an isolated village in Upper Catalonia.

Picasso absorbs the atmosphere and environment there. This leads to a monochrome treatment dominated by ochre tonalities on themes such as *Les deux frères* (*The Two Brothers*, Basel, Kunstmuseum, and cat. 6). *The Toilette* (New York, Albright-Knox Gallery) and *The Harem* (The Cleveland Museum of Art), a parody of *The Turkish Bath*, revert to the theme of *La Coiffure* (New York, The Metropolitan Museum of Art). He sketches studies of peasants. Fernande's face also appears in some works.

Hasty departure from Gosol, scared away by a typhoid epidemic.

Autumn: completion of Gertrude Stein's portrait. The face displays a stylized archaizing treatment derived from the stay in Gosol and from Iberian sculptures.

A series of self-portraits (cat. 8 and Philadelphia Museum of Art among them) in which this trend becomes more marked.

22 October: death of Cézanne, ten of whose works are shown at the Salon d'Automne.

The Two Nudes (New York, The Museum of Modern Art) represent the culmination of a series combining all these elements.

Winter 1906–1907: a start with the studies leading up to *Les Demoiselles d'Avignon*.

Fernande Olivier about 1906
(Musée Picasso Document)

1907

Early March: Picasso buys two Iberian heads from Géry-Piéret, Apollinaire's secretary, without realizing that he has stolen them from the Louvre.

The theme of *Les Demoiselles d'Avignon* is developing into a brothel scene, with five nude women, accompanied by a sailor seated in the middle and a student carrying a death's head in the earlier studies and a book in the later ones.

20 March: Salon des Indépendants, at which Matisse shows the *Nu bleu, souvenir de Biskra* (*Blue Nude, Souvenir of Biskra*) and Derain exhibits *Les baigneuses* (*The Bathers*).

End of April–early May: a start made with the large canvas of *Les Demoiselles d'Avignon*. In the final watercolour, the sailor has been eliminated and the student replaced by a nude woman holding a curtain aside.

Study for *Les Demoiselles d'Avignon*, spring 1907 (M.P. 533)

Salmon in front of *Les trois femmes* (*The Three Women*) at the Bateau-Lavoir, summer 1908 (Picasso Archives)

Interior of the studio at Horta de San Juan, 1909 (Musée Picasso Document)

Mid-May: several female head-and-shoulders studies in oils stressing angular shapes which recur in the *Self-portrait* (Prague, National Gallery).

End of May: first version of *Les Demoiselles d'Avignon*.

June: the month in which Picasso is said to have discovered the Musée du Trocadéro and the impact of African sculpture.

17–29 June: exhibition of seventy-nine watercolours by Cézanne at the Galerie Bernheim-Jeune.

End of June–beginning of July: final version of *Les Demoiselles d'Avignon* (New York, The Museum of Modern Art).

Summer: first visit to the Bateau-Lavoir by Kahnweiler, who has just opened his gallery at 28, rue Vignon. He is bowled over by the recently completed painting. Some friends of Picasso who also now see it for the first time give it a title, a joking reference to the brothels in the Calle d'Avignon in Barcelona. This work is only publicly displayed in 1916, at the exhibition 'L'art moderne en France' at the Salon d'Antin.

September: completion of the *Nu à la draperie* (*Nude with Drapery*, Leningrad, The Hermitage Museum) which was started this summer and is bought on the spot by the Steins, together with all its preliminary studies.

October: Cézanne retrospective exhibition at the Salon d'Automne, comprising fifty-six works.

Apollinaire brings Braque to the Bateau-Lavoir, where the sight of the *Nude with Drapery* contributes to his *Grand nu* (*Large Nude*), which is also indebted to the earlier influences of Cézanne and of Matisse's *Blue Nude*.

Winter 1907–1908: *L'amitié* (*Friendship*, Leningrad, The Hermitage Museum).

1908

Spring: Picasso paints the rhythmic version of *Les trois femmes* (*The Three Women*, Hanover, Kunstmuseum).

June: suicide at the Bateau-Lavoir of the German painter Wiegels.

Composition à la tête de mort (*Composition with Death's Head*, Leningrad, The Hermitage Museum).

Still-life pictures.

August: stays with Fernande at La Rue-des-Bois, some forty miles north of Paris, and brings back figure studies and a series of landscapes with reverse perspective in the manner of Cézanne.

End of September: meeting with Braque; the six landscapes he has brought back from L'Estaque have been rejected by the Salon d'Automne.

October: definitive version of *The Three Women* (Leningrad, The Hermitage Museum).

9 November: Braque exhibition at the Galerie Kahnweiler. The introduction to the catalogue is by Apollinaire. In his review for *Gil Blas* on 14 November, Louis Vauxcelles refers to 'cubes', an expression which gains currency among the majority of artists from the end of this year. Picasso's links with Braque become closer.

November: banquet in honour of Douanier Rousseau organized at the Bateau-Lavoir by Picasso and Fernande. Apollinaire, Marie Laurencin, Salmon, Braque and Gertrude Stein are among those present.

1909

At the beginning of the year, the *Carnaval au bistrot* is turned into a still-life, *Pains et compotiers sur une table* (*Loaves and Fruit Bowls on a Table*, Basel, Kunstmuseum).

Spring: *Femme à l'éventail* (*Woman with a Fan*, Moscow, Pushkin Museum) and *Portrait of Clovis Sagot* (Hamburg, Kunsthalle).

May: departure for Barcelona with Fernande, where he meets his family and friends; *Portrait of Pallarés* (Detroit Institute of Arts).

A further stay at Horta after eleven years' absence. The series of landscapes, portraits of Fernande and still-life pictures carried out on this occasion marks the beginnings of Analytical Cubism, with works whose visual approach is closely related to that of Cézanne and runs counter to classical perspective.

September: return to Paris.

Move to 11, boulevard de Clichy, where Picasso and Fernande hold open house for friends on Sundays.

Still-life pictures in which the arbitrary impact of light stresses the facets of the subject and separate volumes increasingly acquire depth.

These discoveries are now applied to sculpture, first in a *Pomme* (*Apple*), modelled in plaster, with facets (cat. 285), then in *Tête de femme (Fernande)* (*Head of a Woman* [*Fernande*], cat. 286) cast in bronze.

End of the year: starts on the *Portrait of Vollard*.

Braque in the boulevard de Clichy studio, 1909–10 (Picasso Archives)

1910

The *Portrait of Vollard* (Moscow, Pushkin Museum) and *Portrait of Wilhelm Uhde* (private collection), a young art collector and critic, in which the fragmentation of the planes fails to conceal the likeness of the sitters.

May: exhibition at the Galerie Notre-Dame-des-Champs, mainly of 1908 and 1909 canvases.

End of June: departure for Barcelona with Fernande, then on to Cadaqués, where he rents a house.

July: Derain and his wife come to join them.

Works on etchings for *Saint-Matorel* by Max Jacob, four of which are included in the edition published the following year by Kahnweiler.

September: return to Paris. Paints the *Portrait of Kahnweiler* (The Art Institute of Chicago).

8 November–15 January 1911: takes part in the 'Manet and the Post-Impressionists' exhibition organized by Roger Fry at the Grafton Galleries in London.

1911

January–February: two works sent to a collective exhibition at the Paul Cassirer gallery in Berlin.

28 March–25 April: exhibition of eighty-three watercolours and drawings at the Photo Secession Gallery, New York, at which Stieglitz buys a drawing.

1 May: inauguration of the Berlin Secession, to which Picasso contributes four works, including *La Coiffure* of 1906 (New York, The Metropolitan Museum of Art).

Early July: departure of Picasso, on his own, at the invitation of Manolo, for Céret where he stays at the Maison Delcros.

Eva Gouel (Marcelle Humbert), 1911–12 (Musée Picasso Document)

Early August: Braque and Fernande join him, as well as Max Jacob. He is now collaborating very closely with Braque.

Paints *L'Indépendant* (private collection); the theme of a café table covered with a variety of objects is supplemented by the introduction of letters into the composition by means of newsprint.

Early September: rushes back to Paris because of the Iberian heads case.

6 September: Picasso and Apollinaire take the two Iberian heads bought in 1907 to the offices of *Paris-Journal*.

7–12 September: Apollinaire jailed.

21 September: reportage by André Salmon about Picasso in *Paris-Journal*.

1 October: Cubist room at the Salon d'Automne; Picasso and Braque stay away, as they did at the last Salon des Indépendants.

Autumn: start of his liaison with Eva Gouel (Marcelle Humbert), Louis Marcoussis's mistress, whom he has met at the Steins and calls '*Ma Jolie*' in his canvases, a name taken from the refrain of a popular song.

Paints *Homme à la mandoline* (*Man with a Mandolin*, cat. 33), one of the nine monumental compositions in this series.

Picasso at Sorgues, in front of *L'aficionado*, summer–autumn 1912 (Picasso Archives)

Le Grand Café at Céret, from an old postcard
(Musée Picasso Document)

1912

In January, takes part in the 'Knave of Diamonds' exhibition in Moscow, that of the 'Blaue Reiter' in Munich in February and the Berlin Secession later in the spring.

18 May–21 June: stays at Céret with Eva.

25 May–30 September: contributes to the 'Sonderbund' exhibition in Cologne.

21 June: leaves Céret for Avignon with Eva.

25 June: moves to the Villa Les Clochettes at Sorgues, north of Avignon.

July: joined by Braque and his wife.

Early September: Picasso goes to Paris to move from the studio he has kept at the Bateau-Lavoir to a new studio at 242, boulevard Raspail, found for him by Kahnweiler.

Braque produces the first *papier collé* while he is away.

Returns to Sorgues on 18 September.

Towards the end of his stay, paints a series of pictures with figures, culminating in *L'aficionado* (Basel, Kunstmuseum).

October: returns from Sorgues and moves to boulevard Raspail.

'La Section d'Or' exhibition at the Galerie de la Boétie brings together the Cubists who have taken part in the Salon des Indépendants and the Salon d'Automne since 1911. Picasso and Braque are not included.

18 December: contract letter between Picasso and Kahnweiler covering a three-year period; it becomes void when the latter has to leave France as a German citizen in August 1914.

In the course of the year, the first construction – the *Guitare en carton* (*Cardboard Guitar*) – has been followed by the *Guitare en tôle* (*Sheet-iron Guitar*, New York, The Museum of Modern Art) and the first collage – *Nature morte à la chaise cannée* (*Still-life with Chair-caning*, cat. 35) – with imitation caning on oilcloth, as well as the first *papiers collés*.

1913

Cubist portrait of Guillaume Apollinaire as a frontispiece for the first edition of *Alcools* (Paris, Mercure de France), completed for publication on 20 April.

17 February–15 March: 'International Exhibition of Modern Art, Armory Show', New York, which includes eight works by Picasso.

Mid-March: departure with Eva for Céret, where they are joined by Max Jacob.

17 March: publication of Apollinaire's *Les Peintres Cubistes: Méditations Esthétiques*, Paris, Eugène Figuière.

Second group of more abstract and colourful *papiers collés*.

Simplification to the limit in the *Guitar* (cat. 37) and the *Head* (London, Penrose collection).

3 May: Picasso goes to Barcelona for his father's funeral.

Man with a Guitar (New York, The Museum of Modern Art), with its toned-down colours and the inclusion of collage, introduces the new abstract and geometrical compositions dating from 1915–1916.

20 June: Eva and Picasso fall ill and return to Paris.

22 July: return to Céret.

19 August: return to Paris and move to 5 bis, rue Schoelcher.

Autumn: paints *Woman in an Armchair* (New York, private collection) for which he has done a large number of preliminary sketches. In this he returns, with much humour, to a theme very characteristic of the earlier years.

Devises a series of *Constructions* which Apollinaire reproduces in the first issue of the new *Soirées de Paris* series, published on 15 November.

Guitar Player construction, Paris, boulevard Raspail, 1913 (since destroyed) (Musée Picasso Document)

1914

Winter: third series of *papiers collés*.

14 January: Kahnweiler publishes *Le siège de Jérusalem* by Max Jacob, illustrated with three engravings by Picasso.

Spring: further constructions. Produces *Le verre d'absinthe* (*The Glass of Absinthe*); Kahnweiler orders six bronze copies of it, variously painted.

June: departure for Avignon with Eva. After some time in a hotel, he moves to 14, rue Saint-Bernard. The Braques are at Sorgues and the Derains at Montfavet this summer. Lively colours and rounded forms burst forth in still-life pictures and portraits replete with fun and lyrical feeling. *Portrait de jeune fille* (*Portrait of a Girl*, Paris, Musée National d'Art Moderne).

August: Apollinaire, Braque and Derain mobilized. Kahnweiler leaves for Italy and his gallery in the rue Vignon is sequestrated.

End of November: return to Paris. The colours in his paintings become more sombre, reflecting the dreary mood of the times.

1915

January: Max Jacob poses for a naturalistic portrait in pencil (Paris, private collection).

18 February: Max Jacob baptized; Picasso is his godfather.

Summer: Eva falls ill.

Portrait drawing of Vollard (New York, The Metropolitan Museum of Art).

Autumn: *Harlequin* (New York, The Museum of Modern Art), an austere composition of large geometrical monochrome areas on a black background.

In Kahnweiler's absence, Léonce Rosenberg sells some canvases.

Picasso, Henri-Pierre Roché and Max Jacob in front of La Rotonde in Montparnasse in 1915 (Musée Picasso Document)

L'arlequin (*Harlequin*), Paris,
end of 1915 (New York,
The Museum of Modern Art)

Edgar Varèse brings Cocteau to meet Picasso.
November: Eva to hospital.
14 December: Eva dies.

1916
Liaison with Gaby, Madame L . . .
17 March: Apollinaire wounded.
May: Cocteau introduces Diaghilev to Picasso at the rue Schoelcher. Planning with Erik Satie for a ballet which is to become *Parade*.
July: first showing of *Les Demoiselles d'Avignon* at the Salon d'Antin organized by André Salmon, in fact held at Paul Poiret's establishment.
24 August: Picasso agrees to work on the *Parade* project.
Move to 22, rue Victor-Hugo, Montrouge, during the summer.
19 November–5 December: exhibition at the Salle Huyghens, jointly with Matisse, Modigliani and Ortiz de Zarate, organized by Cocteau.
31 December: banquet in honour of Apollinaire and the publication of the *Poète assassiné*. The character of the artist in the book, 'the bird of Benin', is based on Picasso.

1917
January: brief visit to his family in Barcelona.
Works on the *Parade* set.
17 February: goes with Cocteau to Rome to join Diaghilev and the Ballets Russes. Spends eight weeks there. Produces sets and costumes for *Parade*. Draws caricatures and portraits of his close friends. Meets Stravinsky and Olga Kokhlova, one of the dancers in the company.
End of March: visit to Naples and Pompeii.
End of April: return to Paris.
18 May: première of *Parade*, badly received: the audience reacts violently and claims that it is a provocation.
Early June: departure for Madrid, then Barcelona with the Ballets Russes. The company then leaves for South America, while Olga remains with Picasso.

Picasso in Rome, 1917 (Picasso Archives)

Picasso and the stage hands sitting on the drop curtain for *Parade*, Rome, 1917
(Musée Picasso Document)

12 July: banquet held in honour of Picasso by his painter friends, Miguel Utrillo, Angel de Soto, Ricardo Canals and Iturrino.
Paints, in realist fashion, *Portrait d'Olga à la mantille* (*Portrait of Olga with a Mantilla*, private collection) and *La Salchichona* (Barcelona, Museo Picasso) using a Pointillist technique.
End of November: return to Paris and Montrouge, with Olga.
Le retour du baptême, d'après Le Nain (*The Return from the Christening, after Le Nain*, cat. 51) is an entirely Pointillist paraphrase.

1918

23 January–15 February: Matisse-Picasso exhibition at the Galerie Paul Guillaume with an introduction to the catalogue by Apollinaire.
Spring: moves with Olga to the Hôtel Lutetia.
Change in life style; frequents the circle around the Ballets Russes.
2 May: witness, together with Vollard, at Apollinaire's marriage to Jacqueline Kolb.
18 May: meets Proust and James Joyce at a supper in honour of the Ballets Russes.
12 July: marries Olga at the Russian Church, rue Daru, Paris. The witnesses are Cocteau, Max Jacob and Apollinaire. Leaves immediately afterwards for Biarritz, to stay with Eugenia Errazuriz at the Villa La Mimoseraie. He meets Paul Rosenberg and Georges Wildenstein there, and draws portraits of their wives. Paints *Les baigneuses* (*The Bathers*, cat. 55).
End of September: return to Paris. Paul Rosenberg becomes his agent.
9 November: death of Apollinaire.
End of November: move to two floors at 23 bis, rue La Boétie, with the studio above an apartment comfortably fitted out by Olga.

1919

Paints *La fillette au cerceau* (*The Little Girl with a Hoop*, Paris, Musée National d'Art Moderne) and still-life pictures in a Synthetic Cubist style.
Spring: visit by Joan Miró whom he welcomes and encourages on his arrival in Paris.
Early May: goes to London where Diaghilev has invited him to work on a new ballet, *The Three-Cornered Hat*, with music by Manuel de Falla and choreography by Massine. Stays three months in London. Personally paints the drop curtain, assisted by Vladimir Polunin. Draws portraits of the dancers, of Massine and of Diaghilev.
22 July: première of *The Three-Cornered Hat* at the Alhambra Theatre in London.
From August on, stays first at the Hôtel Continental, then at the Hôtel des Bains in Saint-Raphaël with Olga. Many Cubist still-life watercolours from windows opening on light and sea.

Trois danseuses
(*Three Dancers*), 1919,
with Olga on the left (M.P. 834)

Olga and Picasso in London in the workshop where the drop curtain for *The Three-Cornered Hat* was being made, 1919 (Picasso Archives)

Study for *Pulcinella* costume and mask (M.P. 1792)

Olga in the rue La Boétie apartment. On the wall, her portrait (cat. 50) and some drawings for *The Three-Cornered Hat*, 1920 (Picasso Archives)

20 October: these works are shown at the Galerie Paul Rosenberg, 21, rue La Boétie.
November: frontispiece for Aragon's *Feu de Joie*, ready for publication on 10 December.
3 December: death of Renoir.
Paints *Les amoureux* (*The Lovers*, cat. 57) as a tribute to Manet.
Begins work on *Pulcinella*, a ballet on a Commedia dell'Arte theme.

1920
22 February: Kahnweiler returns to France.
15 May: première of *Pulcinella* at the Opéra, choreographed by Massine, with music by Stravinsky on themes by Pergolesi and a libretto by Massine and Diaghilev based on old Neapolitan texts. The final version of the scenery inclines to Cubism, while the costumes are more in the Italian tradition.
Mid-June: departure with Olga, first to the Hôtel Continental at Saint-Raphaël, then (in July) to the Villa Les Sables at Juan-les-Pins. Works on the colourful gouaches started in Paris in May on Commedia dell'Arte themes.
Three Women Bathing (New York, private collection).
September: inauguration of Kahnweiler's new gallery, the Galerie Simon – his partner's name – at 29 bis, rue d'Astorg.
End of September: return to Paris.

1921
4 February: birth of Paulo.
April: first monograph devoted to Picasso, by Maurice Raynal, Munich, Delphin Verlag (published in France by Editions Crès in 1922).
Hurriedly redesigns the first *Pulcinella* set for a new ballet, *Cuadro Flamenco*.
22 May: première of *Cuadro Flamenco* at the Théâtre de la Gaité-Lyrique with traditional music adapted by Manuel de Falla.
30 May: sale at the Hôtel Drouot of the Uhde collection, sequestrated by the French government during the war, including thirteen works by Picasso, the art dealer's Cubist portrait among them.
13–14 June: first of four sales at the Hôtel Drouot of works from the Galerie Kahnweiler sequestrated in 1914. Thirty-six items by Picasso are included, Kahnweiler's Cubist portrait among them. The dealer is able to buy back some of the works involved.
June: Max Jacob goes into seclusion at Saint-Benoît-sur-Loire.
July: move to a rented house in Fontainebleau with Olga and Paulo.
Intensive work: he paints the two versions of *The Three Musicians* (New York, The Museum of Modern Art, and Philadelphia Museum of Art) and of *Trois femmes à la fontaine* (*Three Women at the Fountain*, New York, The Museum of Modern Art, and cat. 69) which mark the transition to monumental composition in both Cubist and classical styles.
Series of pastel figures carried out in a similar classical mood.
September: return to Paris.
17–18 November: second Kahnweiler sale, with forty-six items by Picasso, mainly still-life pictures. The third sale is held on 4 July 1922 and the fourth on 7–8 May 1923, comprising fifty canvases by Picasso in all.

1922
June–September: stay in Dinard, first at the Hôtel des Terrasses then at the Villa Beauregard.
Paints *Deux femmes courant sur la plage (La course)* (*Two Women Running on the Beach [The Race]*, cat. 74), at once an idealization of the previous year's monumental figures and – as a new element – the treatment of movement; this picture will be used as a model for the drop curtain of *Le Train bleu* in 1924.
Portrait of Olga and Paulo (The Baltimore Museum of Art), in which psychology returns to his portraiture.
December: stage set for *Antigone*, freely adapted by Cocteau and produced at the Atelier, with costumes by Chanel.

Façade of Picasso's house at Fontainebleau (M.P. 961)

1923

Return to the Harlequin theme in four portraits of the painter Salvado posing in a costume given to Picasso by Cocteau (Paris, Musée National d'Art Moderne, and Basel, Kunstmuseum, in particular).

Olga's portraits now show her in a more pensive mood.

19 May: interview with Picasso by Marius de Zaya in *The Arts*, New York, published in French by Florent Fels in 1925.

Summer at Cap d'Antibes with Olga and Paulo. He paints *La flûte de Pan* (*The Pipes of Pan*, cat. 76) there and produces large numbers of pencil studies of women bathing, a series started in Paris.

Spends much time with the American painter Gerald Murphy and Etienne de Beaumont.

Picasso on the beach of La Garoupe at Antibes, summer 1923 (Picasso Archives)

1924

André Breton and Aragon persuade Jacques Doucet to purchase *Les Demoiselles d'Avignon* for 25,000 francs.

Works on the *Mercure* ballet for which he uses the soft shapes derived from Fluid Cubism and characteristic of his large contemporary still-life pictures.

18 June: première of *Mercure*, with music by Satie and choreography by Massine, at the Théâtre de la Cigale, as part of the Soirées de Paris organized by Etienne de Beaumont. The ballet is badly received by the audience and the critics, but Picasso is supported by the Surrealist group, which publishes a tribute to him in *Paris-Journal* on 20 June.

20 June: première of *Le Train bleu*, with a drop curtain by Picasso (an enlargement of the gouache painted in Dinard in 1922, cat. 74), text by Cocteau, music by Darius Milhaud.

Summer: at the Villa La Vigie, Juan-les-Pins.

October: publication of the *Manifeste du Surréalisme* by André Breton.

1925

15 January: two pages of abstract drawings done at Juan-les-Pins are reproduced in the second issue of *La Révolution Surréaliste*.

March–April: visit to Monte Carlo with Olga and Paulo during the Ballets Russes season there. Realistic sketches of the dancers.

June: completion of *The Dance* (London, Tate Gallery), reproduced in *La Révolution Surréaliste*, No. 4 of 15 July.

End of June: move to the Villa Belle-Rose at Juan-les-Pins, where he paints *The Studio with Plaster Head* (New York, The Museum of Modern Art) and *Le baiser* (*The Kiss*, cat. 81).

14 November: opening in the Galerie Pierre of 'La Peinture Surréaliste', the first Surrealist exhibition. Picasso contributes to this exhibition.

The Dance, 1925, London, Tate Gallery

1926

January: first issue of *Cahiers d'Art*, founded by Christian Zervos.

Le peintre et son modèle (*The Painter and his Model*, cat. 82) and *L'atelier de la modiste* (*The Milliner's Workshop*, Paris, Musée National d'Art Moderne) use a geometrical layout derived from Cubism, in monochrome greys with curved shapes.

Spring: a series of *Guitars* made up of aggressive combinations of textiles, taut pieces of string and long nails or tacks offer a Surrealist solution for a Cubist theme. One of these (cat. 249) is reproduced in *La Révolution Surréaliste*, No. 7.

June–July: the exhibition at the Galerie Paul Rosenberg recapitulates the output of the last few years.

Summer: stay in Juan-les-Pins and Antibes.

October: visit to Barcelona with Olga.

Picasso photographed by Man Ray at Juan-les-Pins, summer 1926 (Musée Picasso Document)

Marie-Thérèse photographed by
Picasso at Dinard, summer 1929
(Musée Picasso Document)

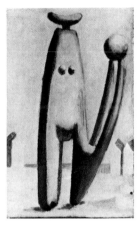

Baigneuse au ballon (*Bather
with a Beach Ball*, cat. 104),
Dinard, 1 September 1929
(M.P. 118)

1927

January: meets Marie-Thérèse Walter, then aged seventeen.

May: death of Juan Gris.

Summer: spent at the Chalet Madrid in Cannes with Olga and Paulo.

Carnet des Métamorphoses, with Indian ink drawings of monstrous bathing women and sexually aggressive themes.

Autumn: return to Paris.

End of year: engravings on the theme of 'The Studio': these plates are the first in the series for Balzac's *Le Chef-d'œuvre inconnu*, which Vollard asked him to illustrate in 1926 and which is published in 1931.

1928

1 January: large collage of the *Minotaur* (Paris, Musée National d'Art Moderne), the first appearance of this theme.

Models the *Metamorphoses I* and *II* (cat. 302, bronze; cat. 303, plaster) after the drawings of the previous year reproduced in *Cahiers d'Art*.

The Painter and his Model (New York, private collection) in the series of *The Studio* (New York, The Museum of Modern Art).

March: renews contact with Gonzalez.

April–May: drawings foreshadowing wire sculpture.

Summer: holidays with Olga and Paulo at the Hôtel des Terrasses and the Villa Les Roches in Dinard, and, secretly, with Marie-Thérèse, who inspires some lithographs.

Autumn: production of iron sculptures with Gonzalez: the *Tête* (*Head*, cat. 304) and *Figures* (cat. 306, 307), suggested as designs for a monument to Apollinaire.

1929

Spring: starts on *La femme au jardin* (*The Woman in the Garden*, cat. 310), still in conjunction with Gonzalez. The format has increased and the style is in line with the paintings of this period.

A series of harsh paintings – among them, in May, the *Grand nu au fauteuil rouge* (*Large Nude in a Red Armchair*, cat. 99) – which reflect his deteriorating relations with Olga.

Summer: holidays spent at the Hôtel Gallic, Dinard.

1930

7 February: finishes *The Crucifixion* (cat. 108), 'the application of Hallucinatory Expressionism to the field of historical painting' (Daix).

Aragon pays tribute to Picasso in *La Peinture au défi*.

April: special number of *Documents* devoted to Picasso.

June: purchase of the Château de Boisgeloup, near Gisors.

Summer at Juan-les-Pins, where he produces a number of sand-coated reliefs.

Agrees to illustrate Ovid's *Metamorphoses* for Albert Skira, a young publisher; produces thirty etchings between 13 September and 25 October inspired by Marie-Thérèse's face.

Marie-Thérèse moves to 44, rue La Boétie during the autumn.

October: Picasso is awarded the Carnegie Prize for his *Portrait of Olga in Profile* (Switzerland, private collection).

Picasso in his sculpture studio at Boisgeloup, 1931
(Picasso Archives, photo Bernès-Marouteau)

1931

2 March: finishes *Grand nature morte au guéridon* (*Large Still-life with a Pedestal Table*, cat. 112), a concealed portrait of Marie-Thérèse.

May: at Boisgeloup, where he fits out a studio.

Carries out the series of large sculptured heads which represent variations on Marie-Thérèse's face.

Summer at Juan-les-Pins. Works on a series of engravings which will later form part of the *Vollard Suite*.

Autumn: continues to work as a sculptor. In his canvas of *Le sculpteur* (*The Sculptor*, cat. 113), dated 7 December 1931, the artist is looking at a bust of Marie-Thérèse.

Two books are published in the course of the year: *Les Métamorphoses d'Ovide* (Lausanne, Albert Skira, 30 etchings) and Balzac's *Le Chef-d'œuvre inconnu* (Paris, Vollard, 13 etchings).

The Château de Boisgeloup, near Gisors
(Musée Picasso Document)

1932

January–March: paints a series of representations of sleeping women featuring Marie-Thérèse and culminating in the *Girl before a Mirror* (New York, The Museum of Modern Art) of 14 March.

16 June–30 July: first retrospective exhibition, Galeries Georges Petit, with 236 items selected by the artist and ranging from 1901 to the latest works.

June: special issue of *Cahiers d'Art* devoted to Picasso.

15 June: interview with Tériade published in *L'Intransigeant*.

Summer at Boisgeloup: Olga and Paulo probably go on their own to Juan-les-Pins.

11 September–30 October: augmented repeat of the Galeries Georges Petit exhibition at the Kunsthaus in Zurich. An article by Carl C. Jung published in the *Neue Zürcher Zeitung*, No. 13.

October: publication of the first volume of the *catalogue raisonné* by Christian Zervos covering the period 1895–1906.

Series of drawings after Grünewald's *Crucifixion*.

1933

March: in Paris, a set of engravings in the 'Sculptor's Studio' series, including forty-one plates, mostly etchings, produced before the beginning of May. Marie-Thérèse appears in most of them.

17 May: the image of the Minotaur has replaced that of the sculptor.

1 June: first issue of Albert Skira's review *Minotaure*, published by Tériade, for which Picasso designs the cover (layout: New York, The Museum of Modern Art).

Summer: holidays at the Hôtel Majestic in Cannes, with Olga and Paulo.

Second half of August: visit to Barcelona with Olga and Paulo; they stay at the Ritz and he meets his Catalan friends and his family again.

Beginning of September: return to Paris.

September: paints two *Corridas* (*Bullfights*, cat. 122, 123).

Layout for cover of the *Minotaure* review, Paris, 1933 (New York, The Museum of Modern Art)

Autumn: publication of Fernande Olivier's memoirs, *Picasso et ses amis*, which he tries to suppress for fear of a fit of jealousy on Olga's part.

In the course of the year, publication in Bern of the first volume of Bernhard Geiser's *Picasso, peintre-graveur, catalogue raisonné des gravures et des lithographies, 1899–1931*.

1934

The 'Sculptor's Studio' theme is continued in engravings.

In the field of sculpture, *La femme au feuillage* (*The Woman with Leaves*, cat. 360) and *La femme à l'orange* (*The Woman with an Orange*, cat. 361) produced at Boisgeloup.

June–September: fresh series of paintings, drawings and engravings dealing with bullfights.

Second half of August: journey with Olga and Paulo to Madrid, including visits to the Escorial, Toledo and Saragossa.

Early September: stays in Barcelona and visits the Museum of Catalan Art, where he admires the paintings recently transferred there from Romanesque churches.

Mid-September: return to Paris with Olga and Paulo.

September–November: four engravings on the theme of the *Blind Minotaur Guided by a Little Girl*.

In the course of the year, publication of Aristophanes' *Lysistrata*, translated by Gilbert Seldes (New York, Limited Editions Club, 6 etchings and 34 lithographs).

Picasso, Olga and Paulo at Toledo during their visit to Spain, summer 1934 (Picasso Archives)

1935

Beginning of the year: Marie-Thérèse is expecting a child.

20 February–20 March: exhibition of *papiers collés*, 1912–1914, at the Galerie Pierre, with a catalogue by Tristan Tzara.

March–April: 'Les Créateurs du Cubisme' exhibition at the Galerie des Beaux-Arts, with a catalogue by Raymond Cogniat and introduction by Maurice Raynal.

Spring: *Minotauromachie* engraved.

May: no more paintings produced until February 1936. Begins to write Surrealist poetry and continues to do so until the outbreak of war.

June: separation from Olga, who moves to the Hôtel California, rue de Berri, Paris.

July: invites Sabartés, then resident in South America, to come back and become his business manager.

Spends the summer in Paris and at Boisgeloup.

5 September: birth of María de la Concepción, so christened in memory of Picasso's sister who died in Corunna, but known as Maya.

13 November: Sabartés arrives in Paris.

1936

Off-printed special edition of *Cahiers d'Art*, Vol. X, Nos. 7–10, *Picasso 1930–1935*, containing his writings and Surrealist poems, with illustrations.

8 January: portrait drawing of Paul Eluard: the two men have known each other since the mid-1920s, but a faithful and lasting friendship develops between them from the end of 1935 on.

13 January: Eluard opens the Picasso exhibition organized in Barcelona by the ADLAN – Friends of the New Arts – group and gives a lecture on 17 January.

25 March: Picasso leaves for Juan-les-Pins with Marie-Thérèse and Maya.

April: begins a series of drawings, watercolours and gouaches on the 'Minotaur' theme, which he carries on after his return to Paris on 14 May.

Works with Lacourière on illustrations for Buffon's *Histoire Naturelle*, not published until 1942.

14 July: performance of *14 juillet* by Romain Rolland at the Alhambra with a drop curtain by Picasso (Toulouse, Musée des Augustins, donated by the artist in 1965), after a gouache in the *Minotaur* series (M.P. 1166).

18 July: Civil War breaks out in Spain.

Picasso appointed Director of the Museo del Prado.

Early August: departure for Mougins, in the hills inland from Cannes.

Meets Paul and Nusch Eluard there. They are joined by the Zervoses, Man Ray and René Char. Dora Maar, whom he had met in Paris through Eluard and the Surrealists, stays at Saint-Tropez, then at Mougins. Beginning of their liaison.

Discovery of Vallauris, a potter's village since classical times.

Autumn: forced to give up Boisgeloup as part of the division of property with Olga. Moves with Marie-Thérèse and Maya to a studio at Le Tremblay-sur-Mauldre, lent to him by Vollard.

Two books by Paul Eluard illustrated by Picasso are published during the year: *La Barre d'appui* (Editions des Cahiers d'Art, with 3 etchings and aquatints) and *Les Yeux fertiles* (Editions G.L.M., with a drawing of the author, the 3 engravings from *La Barre d'appui* and the etching from *Grand Air*).

1937

8–9 January: engravings of *Sueño y mentira de Franco* and the accompanying poem.

Move to a new studio at 7, rue des Grands-Augustins.

February–early March: works at Le Tremblay-sur-Mauldre on a series of portraits of Marie-Thérèse.

The Spanish Republican government invites Picasso to carry out a mural for the Spanish Pavilion at the Paris International Exhibition.

26 April: bombing of Guernica. *Ce Soir* and *L'Humanité* publish photographs of the destruction on the following days.

La dépouille du Minotaure en costume d'Arlequin (The Remains of the Minotaur in Harlequin Costume), 28 May 1936 (M.P. 1166)

The house at Le Tremblay-sur-Mauldre, with Maya at her window, 1936–37 (Musée Picasso Document)

Picasso and Dora Maar at Golfe-Juan, 1937 (Musée Picasso Document, photo Roland Penrose)

Picasso at Golfe-Juan, summer 1937 (Picasso Archives, photo Dora Maar)

1 May: Picasso sets to work in his new studio and turns out fifty or more studies for *Guernica* (Madrid, Museo del Prado).

11 May: beginning of the composition of *Guernica* on canvas. Dora Maar photographs the work as it progresses.

Mid-June: *Guernica* set up in the Spanish Pavilion.

June: opening of the exhibition 'Les Maîtres de l'Art indépendant' at the Petit Palais, including thirty-two works by Picasso.

12 July: opening of the Spanish Pavilion at the International Exhibition with, in addition to *Guernica*, two Picasso sculptures: a *Tête de femme* (*Head of a Woman*, cf. cat. 340) of 1931 and *La femme au vase* (*The Woman with a Vase*, Madrid, Museo del Prado) of 1933.

July: leaves for the Hôtel Vaste Horizon at Mougins with Dora Maar, where they meet Paul and Nusch Eluard. Portraits of Dora and Nusch.

End of September: return to Paris.

Mid-October: visit to Switzerland, where he meets Paul Klee in Bern.

October–December: paints *La femme qui pleure* (*The Weeping Woman*, cat. 143) and *La suppliante* (*The suppliant*, cat. 146), thereby rounding off the works that followed *Guernica*.

The house at 7, rue des Grands-Augustins where Picasso's studio was situated (Musée Picasso Document)

Picasso painting *Guernica* in the Grands-Augustins studio, 1937 (Picasso Archives, photo Dora Maar)

Picasso in the Grands-Augustins studio, 1938 (Picasso Archives, photo Peter Rose Pulham)

1938

January: two portraits of *Maya à la poupée* (*Maya with a Doll*, one of them cat. 148).

15 February: *The Woman with a Cock* (The Baltimore Museum of Art).

March: 'The Cock' comes to the fore as a theme in drawings and pastels.

Spring: large collage of *Femmes à leur toilette* (*Women at their Toilette*, cat. 219).

Increasingly systematic use in paintings and drawings of stripes and chevrons built into tight grids occasionally mimicking basketwork.

July: leaves with Dora Maar for the Hôtel Vaste Horizon at Mougins, where he meets Paul and Nusch Eluard again. Paints sailors and *Homme au chapeau de paille et au cornet de glace* (*Man with a Straw Hat and an Ice Cream Cone*, cat. 152).

End of September: return to Paris.

October: stay with the Zervoses at Vézelay.

1939

13 January: death of Picasso's mother in Barcelona.

21 January: paints Dora Maar and Marie-Thérèse on the same day in an identical pose (private collection and cat. 154).

26 January: fall of Barcelona.

5–29 May: *Guernica* and the preliminary studies for it shown at the Valentine Gallery, New York. These works then go to the Stendahl Gallery in Los Angeles, the Arts Club in Chicago and the Museum of Fine Arts in San Francisco.

Royan, 1940. Picasso's studio was in the second house from the right (Musée Picasso Document)

Picasso and Sabartés in the Royan studio with *La femme nue se coiffant* (*Woman Dressing her Hair*), 1940 (Musée Picasso Document)

Sequence of 'Women with a Hat' started in Paris (cat. 156, 157) in May–June, then in Royan during the autumn (cat. 158).

Beginning of July: departure with Dora Maar for Antibes, where they stay with Man Ray.

22 July: death of Ambroise Vollard. Brief visit to Paris for the funeral.

28 July: Sabartés accompanies Picasso to the South of France.

August: *Night Fishing at Antibes* (New York, The Museum of Modern Art).

25 August: return of Picasso, Sabartés and Dora Maar to Paris.

1 September: they leave again for Royan to stay at the Hôtel du Tigre. Marie-Thérèse and Maya are already there, at the Villa Gerbiers-de-Joncs.

7 September: returns to Paris for one day to obtain a residence permit for Royan.

Mid-October: spends two weeks in Paris. Brassaï photographs him for *Life* magazine in cafés and in his studio.

22 October: return to Royan.

15 November–7 January 1940: 'Picasso: Forty Years of his Art' exhibition organized by Alfred H. Barr, Jr., in New York, at The Museum of Modern Art, with 344 works, including *Guernica* and its attendant studies.

5 December: return to Paris.

21 December: back again to Royan.

1940

Works at Royan, in a studio on the fourth floor of the Villa Les Voiliers.

5–29 February: visit to Paris.

4–14 March: a sketchbook (M.P. 1878) devoted at Royan to *La femme nue se coiffant* (*Woman Dressing her Hair*).

Mid-March: return to Paris.

16 May: arrives in Royan with Dora Maar.

June: further study drawings for *Woman Dressing her Hair* and completion of the canvas (New York, Mrs Bertram Smith collection).

25 August: return to Paris.

Autumn: leaves his apartment in the rue La Boétie for the duration of the war and moves into the studio in the rue des Grands-Augustins, the vast proportions of which enable him to resume sculpture.

Paul Rosenberg is in the United States. Kahnweiler leaves Paris for the Unoccupied Zone. Publication during the year of the first of nine works by Iliazd, illustrated by Picasso: *Afat* (Paris, Le Degré Quarante et Un, with 2 aquatints and 4 engravings).

1941

14–17 January: writes *Le désir attrapé par la queue* (*Desire Caught by the Tail*), illustrated with three drawings and a frontispiece. This six-act play written as automatic poetry will be published by Gallimard in 1945 and 1973.

Spring: Marie-Thérèse and Maya return to Paris and go to live in the boulevard Henri-IV. Picasso sees them every weekend.

Paints *Woman with an Artichoke* (Cologne, Museum Ludwig) during the summer.

Bronze *Head of Dora Maar*, a copy of which is set up in Paris as a tribute to Apollinaire in the square of Saint-Germain-des-Prés in 1959.

1942

27 March: death of Julio Gonzalez.

Spring: *Tête de taureau* (*Head of a Bull*, cat. 370), an assemblage.

5 April: paints *Still-life with Steer's Skull* (Düsseldorf, Kunstsammlung Nordrhein-Westfalen).

4 May: completion of *L'Aubade* (Paris, Musée National d'Art Moderne, donated by Picasso in 1947).

6 June: Picasso denounced by Vlaminck in *Comoedia*, thus prompting young painters and intellectuals in the Resistance Movement to rally round him.
July: first drawings on the theme of 'Man with a Sheep'.
Summer: Eluard requests to be reinstated as a member of the Communist Party and goes underground.
9 October: *Portrait of Dora Maar in a Striped Blouse* (New York, Stephen Hahn collection).
Publication during the year of two illustrated books: Georges Hugnet's *Non Vouloir* (Paris, Editions Jeanne Bucher, 1 etched and engraved plate and 4 zincographs) and Buffon's *Histoire Naturelle* (Paris, Martin Fabiani, 31 aquatints, etchings and drypoints).

Studies for *L'homme au mouton* (*Man with a Sheep*, cf. cat. 375), 18 August 1942 (M.P. 1290)

1943

January: gives Dora Maar a copy of Buffon's *Histoire Naturelle* embellished with forty drawings.
Drawings on the 'Man with a Sheep' theme.
February or March: *L'homme au mouton* (*Man with a Sheep*, modelled in clay on an iron armature, and later cast in bronze, cat. 375).
Sculpture: *Tête de mort* (*Death's Head*, bronze, cat. 373).
May: meets Françoise Gilot. Goes back to painting.
End of June: set of Vert-Galant landscapes.
August: *Femme assise dans un rocking-chair* (*Woman in a Rocking Chair*, Paris, Musée National d'Art Moderne, donated by Picasso in 1947).

1944

28 February: Max Jacob arrested at Saint-Benoît-sur-Loire; sent to Drancy concentration camp and dies there on 5 March.
19 March: play-reading at the Leirises of *Le désir attrapé par la queue* (*Desire Caught by the Tail*), in which Albert Camus, Zanie and Jean Aubier, Louise and Michel Leiris, Simone de Beauvoir, Jean-Paul Sartre, Dora Maar, Germaine Hugnet, Raymond Queneau and Jacques-Laurent Bost take part. Georges Hugnet composes a musical accompaniment for it. Spectators include Brassaï, Braque and his wife, Valentine Hugo, Jacques Lacan, Cécile Eluard – Paul's daughter – and Sabartés. Françoise Gilot begins to appear in drawings.
Mid-August: Picasso lodges with Marie-Thérèse during the Paris rising.
25 August: liberation of Paris and return to the rue des Grands-Augustins.
Autumn: many visitors call at his studio, including a number of Americans and English.
September: visit by Geneviève Laporte, a young student and president of the National Student Front who will look back to her liaison with Picasso in her reminiscences – *Si tard le soir, le soleil brille, Pablo Picasso* (Editions Plon, 1973; English translation, *Sunshine at Midnight*, 1975).
5 October: announcement in *L'Humanité* that Picasso has joined the French Communist Party.
6 October: opening of the Salon d'Automne, incorporating a Picasso retrospective exhibition comprising seventy-four paintings and five sculptures, the artist's very first contribution to an annual Salon in France. Violent demonstrations, against both his output and his political commitment. The National Committee of Writers drafts a petition in his support.
Return to painting with a series of still-life works.
Publication during the year of *Contrée* by Robert Desnos (Paris, Robert J. Godet, 1 etching) and *Au Rendez-vous allemand* by Eluard (Paris, Editions de Minuit, 1 engraving – a *Portrait of Paul Eluard*).

1945

February: work starts on *The Charnel House* (New York, The Museum of Modern Art); Zervos photographs the picture at the various stages of its production.
16 February: *La casserole émaillée* (*The Enamel Saucepan*, Paris, Musée National d'Art Moderne, donated by the artist in 1947).

Meeting, at Picasso's house, of the 'actors' in *Le désir attrapé par la queue* (*Desire Caught by the Tail*), 16 June 1944 (Picasso Archives, photo Brassaï)

April–May: final version of *The Charnel House*, a vast black-and-white picture aimed at conveying 'the intrusion of death into everyday life, in fact a continuation of the subject emerging in the final state of *Guernica*' (Daix).

23 May: three realistic portraits of Maurice Thorez, a political assertion of commitment to the Party.

June: Tenth Congress of the French Communist Party; a tribute is paid to Picasso, but he is also criticized in Roger Garaudy's report on the intellectuals as part of an attempt to reassure the Party's official painters.

July: leaves for Cap d'Antibes with Dora Maar to stay with his friends, the Cuttolis. He has rented a room for Françoise at Golfe-Juan with the engraver Louis Fort, but she remains in Brittany, where she has been spending her holidays.

Buys a house at Ménerbes, in the Vaucluse, and gives it to Dora Maar.

August: returns to Paris.

2 November: goes back to lithographic work in the studio of Fernand Mourlot, whom he has met through Braque. His first proofs are those of the *Head of Françoise*, who rejoins him on 26 November.

December: exhibition of paintings by Picasso and Matisse at the Victoria and Albert Museum in London, comprising twenty-six works by Picasso, including *Night Fishing at Antibes*.

Publication during the year of Paul Eluard's *A Pablo Picasso* (Geneva and Paris, Editions des Trois Collines, 1 etching). This book appeared in a standard edition in Geneva in 1944.

Picasso at work in the Antibes studio, 1946 (Picasso Archives, photo Michel Sima)

1946

Completes the *Hommage aux Espagnols morts pour la France* (Mougins, Jacqueline Picasso collection) which is shown, together with the *Charnel House*, at the 'Art et Résistance' exhibition, 15 February–15 March at the Musée National d'Art Moderne.

The theme of 'Owl on a Chair' with a skull or flowers and a mirror now appears in his paintings.

Mid-March: joins Françoise Gilot at Golfe-Juan, with Louis Fort, then calls with her on Matisse in Nice.

End of April: return to Paris. Françoise goes to live with him.

Set of canvases involving Françoise, the best known being the *Femme-fleur* (*Woman Flower*) of 5 May (Françoise Gilot collection).

14–15 June: eleven lithograph portraits of Françoise printed by Mourlot.

Beginning of July: leaves for Ménerbes with Françoise to stay in the house that he has given Dora Maar. He paints landscapes and a pastoral scene as part of a return to Mediterranean subjects.

End of July: they go to stay with the Cuttolis at Cap d'Antibes, then with Louis Fort at Golfe-Juan early in August.

Françoise pregnant.

Works in oils on paper, producing fauns' heads and still-life pictures.

August: publication of *Picasso: Fifty Years of his Art* by Alfred H. Barr, Jr., New York, The Museum of Modern Art, which revises and supplements the book published in connection with the 'Picasso: Forty Years of his Art' exhibition in 1939.

September: Romuald Dor de la Souchère, the curator of the Antibes museum, whom Picasso has met through the photographer Michel Sima, gives him the run of the rooms at his disposal. Picasso sets up a makeshift studio there and collects some asbestos sheeting and plywood on which he uses marine paints, traditional materials being now in short supply.

Early October–late November: produces some twenty works there on Mediterranean subjects: still-lifes with fish, sea-urchins, squids and water-melons; local characters, such as fishermen and *Le gobeur d'oursins* (*The Sea-urchin Eater*); mythological compositions, such as

La joie de vivre; and female figures – all of which remain *in situ* in the museum.
Spends time with Nusch and Paul Eluard, now in Cannes, and Breton, back from exile in the United States.
End of November: return to Paris.
28 November: sudden death of Nusch while Paul Eluard is away in Switzerland.
Publication of *Picasso: Portraits et souvenirs* by Jaime Sabartés (Paris, Louis Carré and Maximilien Vox).

1947
Still-life works with an owl on a chair, both painted and lithographed.
Fauns, centaurs and bacchantes recall the Antibes sequence. Doves appear, as forerunners of the 'Dove of Peace'. Return in lithographs to the theme of a seated woman watching a sleeping person.

Picasso at work on pottery, about 1947 (Picasso Archives, photo P. Manciet)

30 March: beginning of lithographic variations on Lucas Cranach's *David and Bathsheba*.

Spring: publication of *Dos Contes* by Ramón Reventos (Paris and Barcelona, Editions Albor, 4 engravings). The engravings dated 4, 5 and 6 February return to the Mediterranean themes of Antibes, while those used to illustrate the French version – *Deux Contes* – are not produced until February 1948.

May: in response to a suggestion by Georges Salles and Jean Cassou, gift to the Musée National d'Art Moderne of ten major canvases, including *L'atelier de la modiste* (*The Milliner's Workshop*) of 1926, *L'Aubade* of 1942, a series of still-life pictures including *La casserole émaillée* (*The Enamel Saucepan*) of 1945, the *Femme assise dans un rocking-chair* (*Woman Sitting in a Rocking-chair*) of 1943 and portraits of Dora Maar. Until now, the only paintings by Picasso in French museums have been the *Portrait of Gustave Coquiot* in the foreign galleries of the Jeu de Paume in Paris (now on deposit in the Musée Picasso) and two works in the museum at Grenoble.

15 May: birth of Claude.

June: departure for Golfe-Juan with Françoise and the baby.

August: further visit to the Ramié pottery works at Vallauris, where Picasso has tried his hand at a few ceramic items the previous year.

Start of his intense activity as a potter: some two thousand pieces are turned out in a few months, embodying innovations in form, technique and the use of colours.

Except for a short stay in Paris, spends the winter months in the South of France.

December: *Oedipus Rex* by Sophocles at the Théâtre des Champs-Elysées, with sets by Picasso and costumes by Françoise Ganeau.

Publication, during the course of the year, of a work by Juan Larrea, with an introduction by Alfred H. Barr, Jr., *Guernica: Pablo Picasso*, including photographs by Dora Maar (New York, Curt Valentin).

Picasso in Cracow in 1948, with Paul Eluard on his right, and Aimé Césaire and Pierre Daix in the second row on the right (Picasso Archives)

Picasso at Madoura, 'drawing' with light, 1949 (Picasso Archives, photo Gjon Mili)

1948

Visite à Picasso, filmed by a Belgian director, Paul Haesaerts, at Vallauris and at the museum in Antibes, provides a valuable document about the artist's working methods.

March: Mourlot brings the plates which allow Picasso to complete the illustration of Pierre Reverdy's *Chant des Morts* (Paris, Tériade, 125 red-tinted lithographs). Each page of Reverdy's text is decorated with abstract signs reminiscent of fine oriental calligraphy. This work is carried out between January 1946 and March 1948.

Summer: Françoise and Picasso move to a villa – La Galloise – in the hills around Vallauris.

25 August: goes to Wroclaw with Eluard to attend the Congress of Intellectuals for Peace. He speaks out on this occasion for the release of Pablo Neruda, a victim of persecution in Chile; also visits Cracow and Auschwitz.

Early September: return to Vallauris.

October: return to Paris. Françoise is again pregnant.

November: exhibition of 149 ceramic items at the Maison de la Pensée Française in Paris. Stylized painted and lithographed portraits of Françoise.

Paints the two versions of *La cuisine* (*The Kitchen*, cat. 174 and New York, The Museum of Modern Art, the latter dated 9 November), constructed by means of rhythms and lines of force without any use of colour.

During the course of the year, publication of *Vingt Poèmes* by Gongora (Paris, Les Grands Peintres modernes et le Livre, 41 etchings and sugar aquatints).

1949

January: publication of *Les Sculptures de Picasso*, with a text by Daniel-Henry Kahnweiler and photographs by Brassaï (Paris, Editions du Chêne).

8 January: lithograph of *La colombe* (*The Dove*).

February: *The Dove* chosen by Aragon for the poster of the Peace Congress due to be held in April.

February–March: publication of *Carmen* by Prosper Mérimée (Paris, La Bibliothèque Française, 38 engravings and 4 sugar aquatints). The engravings date from May–November 1948.

19 April: birth of Paloma, meaning 'Dove' in Spanish.

20 April: opening of the Peace Congress, at the Salle Pleyel in Paris.

Spring: return to Vallauris and purchase of workshops in the rue du Fournas, former warehouses in which he fits out one studio for painting, another for sculpture and sets aside rooms for storing ceramics.

Begins to collect made objects and rejects in order to put them to further use.

Intensifies work on sculpture, which he has resumed during the previous year. *Femme enceinte* (*Pregnant Woman*, on a long iron rod, cat. 378) and some naturalistic works.

July: shows sixty-four of his recent works at the Maison de la Pensée Française in Paris.

Autumn: concentrates on sculpture.

1950

La femme enceinte (*The Pregnant Woman*, second state, cat. 385), cast in bronze in 1959.

February: two painted paraphrases: *Les demoiselles des bords de Seine* (*Young Women on the Banks of the Seine*, Basel, Kunstmuseum) after Courbet, and *Portrait d'un peintre* (*Portrait of a Painter*, Lucerne, Angela Rosengart collection) after El Greco.

Carries out a series of large sculptures: *Petite fille sautant à la corde* (*Little Girl Skipping*, cat. 381), *La femme à la poussette* (*Woman with a Push Chair*, cat. 382), *La chèvre* (*The Goat*, cat. 383, 384), in which he uses miscellaneous items and rejects with great humour and imagination.

Goes on producing pottery, especially owls.

25 June: beginning of the Korean War.

6 August: Laurent Casanova unveils *L'homme au mouton* (*Man with a Sheep*) in the market-place of Vallauris.

October: Françoise remains at Vallauris, while Picasso attends the Second World Peace Conference in Sheffield, England. The poster again takes up the theme of the Dove, but this time in flight, after a lithograph dated 9 July.

Picasso modelling the plaster version of *La femme à la poussette* (*Woman with a Push Chair*, cat. 382), Vallauris, 1950 (Picasso Archives)

November: awarded the Lenin Peace Prize.
November 1950–January 1951: exhibition of sculptures and drawings at the Maison de la Pensée Française in Paris; the introduction to the catalogue is signed by Aragon.
Publication of *Corps perdu* by Aimé Césaire (Paris, Editions Fragrance, 1 etching, 1 drypoint, 10 aquatints and 20 engravings).

1951

12 January: *Fumées à Vallauris* (*Smoke Clouds at Vallauris*, cat. 176).
Set of satirical lithographs with knights and pages.
18 January: *Massacre en Corée* (*Massacre in Korea*, cat. 177), a deliberate effort, in its subject-matter and realistic treatment, to meet the demands made on him by the Communist Party.
End of February: return to Paris.
May: *Massacre in Korea* is shown at the Salon de Mai and given a mixed reception.
14 June: Paul Eluard's second marriage, to Dominique Lemor, which Picasso and Françoise attend in Saint-Tropez.
25 June: inauguration of chapel decorated by Matisse in Vence. Picasso, accompanied by Françoise, calls on the artist.
Summer: eviction from the rue La Boétie and purchase of two other apartments in the rue Gay-Lussac.
Return to Vallauris.
October: *La guenon et son petit* (*Baboon with Young*, cat. 390), *L'arrosoir fleuri* (*The Flowering Watering Can*, 1951–53, cat. 391), *Crâne de chèvre, bouteille et bougie* (*Goat's Skull, Bottle and Candle*, 1951–53, cat. 392).
Early winter: return to Paris.
Publication of Paul Eluard's *Le Visage de la Paix* (Paris, Editions Cercle d'Art, 1 lithograph), the last of Eluard's works completed before his death. The lithograph, dated 29 September 1951, represents a dove framing a woman's face.

Le visage de la Paix (*The Face of Peace*), lithograph, 1951

1952

31 March: execution of Beloyannis, a Greek resistance fighter, commemorated in a drawing, *L'homme à l'œillet* (*The Man with the Carnation*, private collection).
April: Picasso decides to decorate a deconsecrated fifteenth-century chapel near the Vallauris market-place; the suggestion for this 'Temple of Peace' was probably not unconnected with the work on Matisse's chapel at Vence.
End of April: preparatory drawings for the two panels of *War* and *Peace*.
Summer: at Vallauris, where he paints the *Portrait of Hélène Parmelin* (Paris, H. Parmelin collection), the wife of his friend, the painter Edouard Pignon.
End of October: goes to Paris alone. His relations with Françoise are deteriorating.
18 November: death of Paul Eluard, whose funeral Picasso attends in Paris.
25 November: series of lithograph portraits of *Balzac*, one of which he picks out for an edition of *Le Père Goriot* (Monte Carlo, André Suaret, lithograph frontispiece). In 1957, Michel Leiris uses the seven lithographs dated 25.11.52 and one dated 7.12.52 for *Balzacs en bas de casse et picassos sans majuscule* (Paris, Galerie Louise Leiris, 1957).
Beginning of December: return to Vallauris. Finishes the two large panels of *War* and *Peace*.
Completes, at La Galloise, *Les Quatre Petites Filles*, a six-act play, the first version of which was written at Golfe-Juan and Vallauris in November 1947–August 1948. It is published by Gallimard in 1968.
Set of lithographs: Claude, Paloma and Françoise all treated with great tenderness.

1953

Mid-January: return to Paris.
30 January–9 April: 'Le Cubisme, 1907–1914' exhibition at the Musée National d'Art Moderne, in which *Les Demoiselles d'Avignon* is shown.
Mid-February: return to Vallauris.
5 March: death of Stalin. Aragon asks Picasso to provide a portrait of Stalin for *Les Lettres françaises*. He draws on an old lithograph dating from 1903 for this likeness, which is published in the 12–19 March issue. This picture of the subject as a young man shocks the

Portrait of Stalin, published in *Les Lettres françaises* of 12–19 March 1953

Picasso, Françoise Gilot, Claude and Paloma at Vallauris, 1952–53
(Picasso Archives, photo E. Quinn)

Party leaders, who would have preferred the portrait of an older man. Their disapproval spills over into politics and bursts into the open in a communiqué published a week later. From then on, Picasso distances himself from the Communist Party.

End of March: Françoise leaves for Paris with her children.

May–5 July: important retrospective exhibition at the Galleria Nazionale d'Arte Moderna in Rome, with a catalogue by Lionello Venturi, at which the *War* and *Peace* panels are shown.

June: retrospective exhibition at the Lyons museum, comprising 179 works.

Summer: series of heads and busts inspired by Françoise, who has returned to Vallauris with the children.

Mid-August: goes to Perpignan with Maya at the invitation of the Lazermes, who are friends of Manolo. After a short stay in Paris, Picasso returns to Perpignan with Maya, Paulo and Javier Vilato.

5 September: the Communists at Céret arrange a celebration in his honour, which he attends, accompanied by Paulo, Edouard Pignon and Hélène Parmelin.

19 September: return to Vallauris.

Françoise and the children leave for Paris and go to live in the rue Gay-Lussac.
23 September–31 December: an enlarged version of the Rome retrospective exhibition opens in Milan, with a catalogue by Franco Russoli.
End of November: start of the series of drawings of *Le peintre et son modèle* (*The Painter and his Model*).
13 December–20 February 1954: retrospective exhibition at the Museum of Modern Art in São Paulo, which includes *Guernica*. Catalogue by Maurice Jardot.

1954

Work on the series of *The Painter and his Model* drawings continues until 3 February, supplemented by traditional themes, such as the circus, harlequins and mythological subjects.
10 February: produces a lithograph to illustrate *La Guerre et la Paix* by Claude Roy (Paris, Editions Cercle d'Art, 1 lithograph), a comprehensive set of documents bearing on the genesis of the paintings and on conversations with Picasso, whom the author has known since the early 1950s.
April: meets Sylvette David, a twenty-year-old girl who poses for him. Some forty drawings and paintings result within the space of a month, followed by a few painted sheet-iron works.
2–3 June: three portraits of Madame Z . . ., Jacqueline Roque, a young woman whom he had met at Madoura.
July: 'Picasso: Deux périodes, 1900–1914, 1950–1954' exhibition at the Maison de la Pensée Française in Paris. The paintings belonging to the Shchukin collection, which have emerged for the first time from Soviet museums, are withdrawn and sent home a week after the exhibition opens. Picasso makes works available as replacements, including a *Portrait of Madame Z.*
5–8 July: stays at Perpignan with the Lazermes, together with Paulo and Maya.
6 August–September: further stay in Perpignan with Paulo, his future wife Christine, and Maya. Draws portraits of Madame de Lazerme. Françoise and her children also come to stay, as well as Jacqueline Roque and her daughter Catherine. Many of Picasso's friends call at the house in the rue de l'Ange, including Kahnweiler, the Leirises, the Ramiés, Roland Penrose, the Vilatos, the Pignons, the Manolos and Douglas Cooper.
19 September: Françoise and her children leave for Paris. Picasso goes to Vallauris with Jacqueline Roque on 25 September, then settles at the Grands-Augustins in Paris with her.
11 October: paints *Jacqueline à l'écharpe noire* (*Jacqueline with a Black Scarf*, Mougins, Jacqueline Picasso collection).
3 November: death of Matisse.
13 December: start of the set of variations on Delacroix's *Les femmes d'Alger* (*The Women of Algiers*). Up to 14 February 1955, fifteen paintings and two lithographs are produced in connection with this theme. There is a striking likeness between Jacqueline and the woman on the right of Delacroix's painting.

1955

11 February: death of Olga in Cannes.
May: stay at Perpignan with the Lazermes, together with Jacqueline, Paulo and Maya, where they meet the Leirises and Jean Cocteau. They go to Céret for the Whitsun bullfight.
June–October: major retrospective exhibition at the Musée des Arts Décoratifs in Paris, 'Picasso: Paintings, 1900–1955', which includes *Guernica*. After Paris, this exhibition goes on to Munich, Cologne and Hamburg until April 1956.
June: purchase of a new house in the South of France, a turn-of-the-century (Belle Epoque) villa, La Californie, on the high ground at Cannes, overlooking Golfe-Juan and Antibes and surrounded by a large garden with palms and eucalyptus trees, soon also to be studded with statues.
Summer: filming of Henri-Georges Clouzot's *Le Mystère Picasso* in the studio of La Victorine in Nice. The film director uses the camera to capture the way in which a picture comes into being, by following the ink as it soaks through paper, thus making it possible to trace the evolution of a painting, *La plage de la Garoupe* (*The Beach of La Garoupe*, Marina Picasso collection).

Portrait de Jacqueline aux mains croisées (*Portrait of Jacqueline with Clasped Hands*), 1954 (Private collection)

La Californie: steps into the garden, with sculptures, about 1955 (Picasso Archives)

Picasso during the filming of *Le Mystère Picasso* by Henri-Georges Clouzot, 1955 (Picasso Archives)

The huge rooms of La Californie are transformed into studios and prompt a series of 'Interior Landscapes'.

Many friends visit Picasso and he frequently attends bullfights at Arles and Nîmes. He strikes up a friendship with Luis-Miguel Dominguín. Claude and Paloma come to see him.

20 November: paints *Jacqueline au costume turc* (*Jacqueline in Turkish Dress*, Mougins, Jacqueline Picasso collection).

During the course of the year, publication of *A Haute Flamme* by Tristan Tzara (Paris, published by the author, 6 engravings).

1956

4 January: paints *Femmes à la toilette* (*Women at their Toilette*, cat. 184).

16 February: paints *Deux femmes sur la plage* (*Two Women on the Beach*, Paris, Musée National d'Art Moderne, Cuttoli donation), a return to the theme of bathers.

Summer: this theme also spreads to sculpture with *Les baigneurs* (*The Bathers*), first constructed in wood (Stuttgart, Staatsgalerie) and later cast in bronze (cat. 394–399).

Seventy-fifth birthday celebrated at Madoura with the potters of Vallauris.

22 November: signs a letter to the Central Committee of the French Communist Party, together with Edouard Pignon, Hélène Parmelin and seven other activists, expressing concern about the situation in Hungary.

During the course of the year, publication of Roch Grey's *Chevaux de Minuit* (Cannes and Paris, Le Degré Quarante et Un, text by Iliazd, 1 drypoint, 12 engravings) and *Nuit* by René Crevel (Alès, Pierre-André Benoit, 1 engraving). In spring 1956, Pierre-André Benoit sends Picasso a sheet of celluloid for an illustration by him of Crevel's poem. This is to be the start of a collaboration between them which is to last ten years.

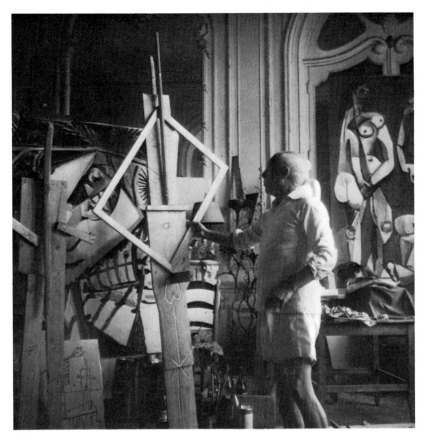

Picasso and one of *Les baigneurs* (*The Bathers: The Fountain Man*, cat. 396), La Californie, 1956 (Picasso Archives)

1957

4 May–8 September: 'Picasso: 75th Anniversary Exhibition', New York, The Museum of Modern Art, then The Art Institute of Chicago, 29 October–8 December, and Philadelphia Museum of Art, 6 January–23 February 1958.

17 August: start of the variations on *Las Meninas* by Velázquez, on which work is to continue until 30 December.

Autumn: commission for a mural at the new UNESCO building in Paris.

6 December: a gouache featuring a studio with a nude and a canvas on a theme closely related to *The Bathers* provides the initial conception for this work.

From 15 December on: two sketchbooks devoted to the UNESCO project display the nude and the bathers competing for the space available, while the painter first appears, then vanishes from the vicinity of the model.

During the year, production of the first carved concrete works by Carl Nesjar, after designs by Picasso, for three walls in a government building in Oslo: *Scene on a Beach*, *Fishermen* and *Faun and Satyr*. Also first models of heads in painted wood or cut-out sheet-iron (cat. 401, 402), for eventual enlargement to a monumental scale.

1958

18 January: further progress on the UNESCO mural: the diver watched by bathers now replaces the studio scene. Picasso pins the separate component elements to a model of the whole. The work is completed on 29 January.

Series of sculptures constructed from scrap pieces of wood in the spirit of *The Bathers*.

19 April–9 June: paints *La baie de Cannes* (*The Bay of Cannes*, cat. 186) seen from the top of La Californie.

In painting, there are renewed allusions to the studio at La Californie and to the baroque rhythm of its windows.

Unveiling of *La chute d'Icare* (*The Fall of Icarus*) at Vallauris, March 1958. Picasso, Jean Cocteau and Maurice Thorez (Picasso Archives, photo E. Quinn)

The Château de Vauvenargues, from a postcard (Musée Picasso Document)

September: the UNESCO mural placed in position. Georges Salles, who accepts the work on UNESCO's behalf, suggests *La chute d'Icare* (*The Fall of Icarus*) as a title for it.

The town of Cannes is growing and new buildings begin to surround the villa. Picasso now looks for a quieter working place and buys the Château de Vauvenargues, a fourteenth-century building standing at the foot of the Montagne-Sainte-Victoire near Aix-en-Provence and surrounded by landscapes associated with Cézanne.

1959

January: writes a long poem in Spanish, *Trozo de Piel*, published in 1961 in Spain by the poet Camilo José Cela.

The linocut technique, which Arnera, a young printer from Vallauris demonstrated to him some years earlier, has been used by Picasso to produce several posters for pottery exhibitions and one for a bullfight in 1956. He goes on to employ it on a par with other engraving techniques, and the *Buste de femme* (*Head and Shoulders of a Woman*) after Cranach the Younger, which involves six separately coloured plates, is a triumph in terms of technique.

Paints several large sculptural nudes.

February: first stay at Vauvenargues.

Back at La Californie, on 23 March, starts *Le buffet de Vauvenargues* (*The Dresser at Vauvenargues*, cat. 188).

Still-life work: a parody of *El Bobo*, after Murillo (private collection).

Several portraits of Jacqueline, including *Jacqueline of Vauvenargues* (private collection) on 20 April.

5 June: unveiling of the *Monument to Apollinaire* (the bronze *Head* of Dora Maar, 1941) in Paris, square Saint-Germain-des-Prés.

August: at Vauvenargues, a start on the Manet *Déjeuner sur l'Herbe* variations; the work is done in the course of some ten periods of activity between August 1959 and December 1961 in three studios: at Vauvenargues, La Californie and Mougins.

19 September: official opening of the chapel at Vallauris containing the *War* and *Peace* panels. The building becomes a national museum.

Linocuts on Mediterranean themes: bacchanals, centaurs and fauns.

Publication during the year of *La Tauromaquia o arte de torear* by José Delgado, otherwise known as Pepe Illo (Barcelona, Gustavo Gili, 1 drypoint, 26 aquatints, supplemented by 2 sugar aquatints).

1960

Drawings and paintings of women in the bath or washing their feet.

February: further period of work on the *Déjeuners*.

6 July–18 September: 1895–1959 retrospective exhibition at the Tate Gallery, London, including 270 works catalogued by Roland Penrose.

20 August: version of *Le Déjeuner sur l'Herbe* (cat. 189), begun on 3 March, completed at Vauvenargues.

15 October: makes a start on the maquettes for the wall decorations at the Colegio Oficial de los Arquitectos in Barcelona. These are carved in concrete, after enlargement, by Carl Nesjar in 1960 and 1961. They consist of two external friezes and two interior walls, one of the latter portraying a sardana, a popular Catalan dance.

Jacqueline at La Californie, 1961 (Musée
Picasso Document, photo A. Gomes)

Picasso, Jacqueline, Michel Leiris and Paulo at a bullfight, about 1960
(Picasso Archives, photo E. Quinn)

1961

2 March: marries Jacqueline Roque at Vallauris.

Works in Cannes on cut-out and painted sheet-iron *La chaise* (*The Chair*, cat. 405), *Femme aux bras écartés* (*Woman with Outstretched Arms*, cat. 407), *Femme au chapeau* (*Woman with a Hat*, cat. 408), *Femme à l'enfant* (*Woman and Child*, cat. 410), *Pierrot assis* (*Seated Pierrot*, cat. 411) and *Footballers* (cat. 412, 413).

June: moves to the Mas Notre-Dame-de-Vie at Mougins, above Cannes.

25 October: celebration of Picasso's eightieth birthday at Vallauris.

1961–1962

Jacqueline in an Armchair (New York, The Museum of Modern Art).

1962

2 January: paints *Femme assise au chapeau jaune et vert* (*Seated Woman with a Yellow and Green Hat*, Mougins, Jacqueline Picasso collection).

1 May: is awarded the Lenin Peace Prize for the second time. Further work on the sheet-iron heads.

Produces seventy *Jacquelines* during the year – paintings, drawings, ceramic tiles and engravings – twenty-two of which during November–December.

August: Serge Lifar suggests to Picasso that he should design a set for *Icare* (*Icarus*), a ballet due to be produced at the Paris Opéra. He does a gouache on 28 August.

November: *L'enlèvement des Sabines* (*The Rape of the Sabines*, one version in Paris, at the Musée National d'Art Moderne, donated by D.-H. Kahnweiler).

Carl Nesjar's six-metre-high enlargement in concrete of the *Femme aux bras écartés* (*Woman with Outstretched Arms*) is produced in the course of the year for Kahnweiler's garden at Chalo-Saint-Mars.

1963

Thirteen variations on the theme of 'Jacqueline' during the first days of the year.
February: starts on the 'Painter and his Model' sequence in painting.
9 March: opening of the Museo Picasso in Barcelona, at the Palacio Aguilar, a fifteenth-century building in the Calle Montcada.
26 May: a painting, *Femme assise* (*Seated Woman*, cat. 192).
31 August: death of Braque.
11 October: death of Cocteau.
October: close collaboration with the Crommelynck brothers, Aldo and Piero, who set up their line-engraving studio at Mougins. Picasso met Aldo, who was then working in Lacourière's studio, during the 1940s. The brothers print the extensive series of engravings produced during the artist's final years. Picasso's daring experiments and fusion of techniques are represented in two series: the *Etreintes* (*Embraces*, 14–20 October) and *Le peintre et son modèle* (*The Painter and his Model*, 31 October–7 December).
In the course of this year, Nesjar creates a set of wall carvings at the Château de Castille in Remoulins, the residence of Douglas Cooper, a collector, art historian and friend of Picasso.

1964

January–May: a sequence of some twenty canvases on the theme of 'The Woman with a Cat', most of which recall Jacqueline.
A whole volume – Tome XXIV – of Christian Zervos's catalogue is devoted to 1964. It includes female faces and nudes, men's heads in coloured crayons and four self-portrait drawings. During the last months of the year, about a hundred canvases pick up the 'Painter and his Model' theme and that of the 'Man's Head' and 'Seated Nude'.
Work on engraving is broken off on 8 February, but resumes in August with the use of soft colour varnishes.
Preparation of a model for a monumental sculpture, based on *Head of a Woman* (The Art Institute of Chicago) of 1962, designed for the new Chicago business quarter. The final stainless-steel version, twenty metres high, was erected in the Chicago Civic Center in 1965 and officially unveiled in 1967.
During the year, publication of Brassaï's *Conversations avec Picasso* (Paris, Gallimard), illustrated by the author's photographs. (English translation, *Picasso & Co.*, 1966.)

Le déjeuner sur l'herbe, carved concrete, Stockholm, Moderna Museet (Musée Picasso Document, photo E. Rudling)

1965

February: a sequence of tortured landscapes.
The 'Painter and his Model' theme continues, with some thirty canvases during March.
New themes emerge in painting: the man carrying a child, the family, the water-melon eater.
By the spring, painting and engraving are back in step.
May: new series of landscapes.
October: goes from a series of men's heads to another of mother and child. Then ill-health intervenes. The attempt to stop the French-language edition of Françoise Gilot's *Vivre avec Picasso* (English title, *Life with Picasso*) merely boosts its sales.
November: hospitalization and operation at the American Hospital in Neuilly.

1965–1966

Le Déjeuner sur l'Herbe figures enlarged in carved concrete by Carl Nesjar and set up in the park of the Moderna Museet in Stockholm.

1966

Spring: resumption of drawing, then of painting, with the emergence of the 'Musketeers', a breed of Spanish Golden Age noblemen.
Flute players, water-melon eaters and painting musketeers radiate fantasy, humour and gaiety.

Picasso at the Mas Notre-Dame-de-Vie, about 1965 (Musée Picasso Document, photo A. Gomes)

August: resumption of engraving, with some sixty plates of great virtuosity by spring 1967, although none are printed until 1970.

19 November: 'Hommage à Picasso' exhibition opened at the Grand Palais and Petit Palais in Paris by André Malraux, the Minister of Culture since 1959. The exhibition, organized by Jean Leymarie, is highly successful and allows the public to become acquainted with the artist's sculptural output as a whole, since many of the works retained by Picasso have never been exhibited before.

Publication during the year of *Sable Mouvant* by Pierre Reverdy (Paris, Louis Broder, 10 aquatints), his last poem before he died at Solesmes on 17 June 1960. Picasso has agreed to illustrate this posthumous edition as a tribute to him. The ten aquatints are picked from the large graphic series of *Le peintre et son modèle* (*The Painter and his Model*) dating from the winter of 1963–64 and February–March 1965.

1967

Picasso refuses the award of the Legion of Honour.

Spring: he is evicted from his studio in the rue des Grands-Augustins.

Goes back to painting.

21 May: first appearance of a foreshortened frontal nude as part of a sequence which continues to grow until October.

Determined self-portraiture.

Picasso at the Mas Notre-Dame-de-Vie with the *Femme à l'enfant (Woman and Child,* cat. 410) of 1961 (M.P. 361) (Musée Picasso Document, photo A. Gomes)

1968

13 February: death of Jaime Sabartés, born in 1881. As a tribute to his memory, Picasso donates the fifty-eight canvases of the *Las Meninas* series and a Blue period portrait of Sabartés to the Museo Picasso, Barcelona. Sabartés had given his library to the Museo Provincial de Bellas Artes in Málaga in 1953. He later donated his collection of works to the Museo Picasso, Barcelona, as a contribution to its initial holding.

16 March–5 October: a *tour de force* – 347 engravings are produced during this period and put on show in December at the Galerie Leiris: complex constructions on varied and interrelated subjects, such as circuses, bullfights, the theatre and the Commedia dell'Arte, culminating in erotic scenes with a touch of humour. The Crommelynck brothers print these engravings in their Mougins studio.

Publication of *Le Cocu magnifique* (Paris, Editions de l'Atelier Crommelynck, 7 etchings, 4 aquatints and etchings, 1 aquatint, drypoint and etching) by Fernand Crommelynck, the engravers' father. This book is published two years before the playwright's death. Its illustrations are taken from the series of sixty-five engravings produced between 6 November and 19 December 1966.

A monumental concrete bust of *Sylvette* is set up at New York University.

1969

A major contribution to the painted output in the course of this year: faces imbued with a searching gaze; couples, with a marked preference for the theme of *Le baiser* (*The Kiss*, as in cat. 194 of 26 October); nudes; swordsmen; smokers; and still-life works.

April: publication of *El Entierro del Conde de Orgaz*, with a prologue by Rafael Alberti (Barcelona, Editorial Gustavo Gili, Ediciones de la Cometa, 1 engraving, 12 etchings, 3 aquatints). This 'literary flight of fantasy' was written by Picasso between 6 January 1957 and 20 August 1959, while the engravings were picked from his 1966–67 output.

October: after visiting Mougins, Yvonne and Christian Zervos decide to organize an exhibition of recent works to be held the following year in the Palace of the Popes at Avignon.

1970

January: gift to the Museo Picasso, Barcelona, of the works left with his family in Spain, comprising the artist's early output, first at Corunna and, later, Barcelona, as well as works produced in 1917 during his stay there with the Ballets Russes.

20 January: death of Yvonne Zervos. Christian Zervos writes the introduction for the catalogue of the Avignon exhibition, which opens on 1 May with 167 paintings and 45 drawings.

Christian Zervos dies on 12 September.

Painting continues, including *La famille* (*The Family*, cat. 195) on 30 September and *Le matador* (*The Matador*, cat. 197) on 4 October.

1971

Winter: Picasso gives The Museum of Modern Art, New York, the sheet-iron *Guitar* of 1912, his first metal construction.

25 May: gift of fifty-seven drawings carried out between 31 December 1970 and 4 February 1971 to the Musée Réattu in Arles, a city which he enjoyed for its bullfights.

30 August: *Maternité* (*Mother and Child*, cat. 200).

25 October: Picasso's ninetieth birthday; in connection with it, a selection of his works drawn from public collections in France is shown in the Great Gallery of the Louvre.

Publication of Fernando de Rojas, *La Célestine* (Paris, Editions de l'Atelier Crommelynck, 66 etchings and aquatints). This dramatized novel in twenty-one acts was first published in Burgos in 1499 and is one of the major works of Spanish literature. The engravings, dated 11 April–18 August 1968, are taken from the *Suite 347*.

1972

31 March: *Paysage* (*Landscape*, cat. 201).

June–July: series of self-portrait drawings in which the head sometimes turns into a death mask with protruding eyes.

1973

24 January–24 February: exhibition at the Galerie Leiris of 156 engravings produced between the end of 1970 and March 1972. Ever since 1953, this gallery has shown works as soon as they have appeared and has played a major part in disseminating them.

8 April: Picasso dies at the Mas Notre-Dame-de-Vie in Mougins.

10 April: buried in the garden of the Château de Vauvenargues. His widow arranges to have the bronze of *La femme au vase* (*Woman with a Vase*) of 1933 placed on his grave.

23 May–23 September: 'Pablo Picasso, 1970–1972' exhibition in the Palace of the Popes at Avignon. René Char writes the introduction for the catalogue. This is a display of the last works chosen for the occasion by the artist himself.

1979

As a result of the law authorizing a settlement in lieu of death duties, a significant part of the output which the artist has so passionately held on to passes into the French national collections, in the unusual form of a ready-made museum. It represents Picasso's personal selection and it was his wish that it should be put to such a purpose.

L.M.

View of the exhibition at the Palace of the Popes, Avignon, 1973 (Musée Picasso Document)

Concordances

M.P. inventory numbers	Catalogue numbers	M.P. inventory numbers	Catalogue numbers	M.P. inventory numbers	Catalogue numbers
1	1	59	54	117	103
2	2	60	56	118	104
3	3	61	55	119	105
4	4	62	57	120	106
5	5	63	58	121	107
6	6	64	59	122	108
7	7	65	60	123	264
8	8	66	65	124	261
9	9	67	61	125	259
10	10	68	62	126	260
11	11	69	63	127	262
12	see Cat. of Drawings	70	64	128	263
13	see Cat. of Drawings	71	66	129	265
14	12	72	67	130	266
15	13	73	71	131	109
16	14	74	69	132	110
17	15	75	70	133	111
18	16	76	72	134	112
19	17	77	73	135	113
20	18	78	74	136	114
21	19	79	76	137	115
22	20	80	75	138	116
23	21	81	77	139	117
24	22	82	78	140	118
25	24	83	79	141	119
26	25	84	80	142	120
27	23	85	81	143	121
28	26	86	249	144	122
29	28	87	250	145	123
30	29	88	251	146	124
31	30	89	252	147	125
32	31	90	253	148	126
33	32	91	254	149	127
34	34	92	255	150	128
35	33	93	256	151	129
36	35	94	258	152	130
37	36	95	257	153	131
38	37	96	82	154	132
39	39	97	83	155	133
40	40	98	84	156	134
41	41	99	85	157	135
42	42	100	88	158	136
43	243	101	86	159	137
44	43	102	87	160	138
45	245	103	89	161	139
46	246	104	90	162	140
47	247	105	91	163	141
48	248	106	92	164	142
49	44	107	93	165	143
50	45	108	94	166	144
51	46	109	95	167	145
52	47	110	96	168	146
53	48	111	97	169	147
54	49	112	98	170	148
55	50	113	99	171	149
56	51	114	100	172	150
57	52	115	101	173	151
58	53	116	102	174	152

M.P. inventory numbers	Catalogue numbers	M.P. inventory numbers	Catalogue numbers	M.P. inventory numbers	Catalogue numbers
175	153	241	284	307	350
176	219	242	285	308	351
177	154	243	286	309	358
178	155	244	287	310	359
179	156	245	288	311	352
180	157	246	241	312	354
181	158	247	289	313	356
182	159	248	242	314	360
183	160	249	290	315	362
184	268	250	291	316	363
185	269	251	244	317	365
186	270	252	292	318	364
187	161	253	293	319	368
188	162	254	294	320	369
189	163	255	295	321	366
190	164	256	296	322	367
191	165	257	297	323	343
192	166	258	298	324	372
193	167	259	300	325	371
194	168	260	301	326	373
195	169	261	302	327	361
196	170	262	303	328	374
197	171	263	304	329	391
198	172	264	306	330	370
199	173	265	307	331	375
200	174	266	305	332	376
201	175	267	310	333	377
202	176	268	327	334	378
203	177	269	312	335	472
204	178	270	311	336	381
205	179	271	328	337	382
206	180	272	314	338	385
207	181	273	315	339	383
208	182	274	316	340	384
209	183	275	317	341	392
210	184	276	318	342	390
211	185	277	319	343	386
212	186	278	320	344	387
213	187	279	321	345	484
214	188	280	322	346	485
215	189	281	323	347	388
216	190	282	324	348	389
217	191	283	313	349	393
218	192	284	325	350	401
219	193	285	326	351	402
220	194	286	308	352	394
221	196	287	309	353	395
222	195	288	329	354	396
223	197	289	330	355	397
224	198	290	331	356	398
225	199	291	332	357	399
226	200	292	333	358	404
227	201	293	334	359	405
228	202	294	335	360	407
229	203	295	347	361	410
230	271	296	342	362	412
231	272	297	336	363	413
232	276	298	337	364	411
233	275	299	338	365	408
234	273	300	339	366	432
235	278	301	340	367	204
236	279	302	341	368	205
237	280	303	344	369	206
238	281	304	345	370	207
239	282	305	346	371	208
240	283	306	349	372	209

M.P. inventory numbers	Catalogue numbers	M.P. inventory numbers	Catalogue numbers	M.P. inventory numbers	Catalogue numbers
373	210	3682	448	3748	514
374	211	3683	450	3749	515
375	212	3684	449	3750	516
376	213	3685	451	3751	518
377	214	3686	487	3752	517
378	38	3687	440	3753	519
379	215	3688	444	3754	520
380	216	3689	452	3755	445
381	217	3690	457	3756	446
382	218	3691	458	3757	521
383	223	3692	459	1980–1	27
384	224	3693	460	1980–111	348
385	225	3694	453	1980–112	353
386	226	3695	461	1980–113	355
387	227	3696	462	1981–3	277
388	228	3697	463	1982–162	220
389	229	3698	464	1982–163	221
390	230	3699	465	1982–164	222
391	231	3700	466	1982–169	267
392	232	3701	467	1983–2	357
393	233	3702	468	1983–6	240
394	234	3703	469		
395	235	3704	470		
396	236	3705	471		
397	237	3706	456		
398	238	3707	473		
399	see Cat. of Drawings	3708	474		
400	239	3709	475		
803	279	3710	476		
804	380	3711	478		
965	68	3712	479		
1136	125a	3713	480		
1790	299	3714	482		
1827	409	3715	483		
1828 (1–4)	400	3716	488		
1829 (1–3)	403	3717	490		
1830	406	3718	491		
1831	414	3719	492		
1832 (1 and 2)	418	3720	477		
1833	419	3721	493		
1834	415	3722	443		
1835	420	3723	486		
1836	421	3724	481		
1837	422	3725	494		
1838	423	3726	495		
1839	424	3727	454		
1840	425	3728	455		
1841	416	3729	496		
1842	426	3730	497		
1843	427	3731	498		
1844	428	3732	499		
1845	429	3733	500		
1846	430	3734	501		
1847	417	3735	502		
1848 (1–3)	431	3736	503		
1850	433	3737	504		
3541	274	3738	505		
3673	434	3739	506		
3674	435	3740	507		
3675	436	3741	508		
3676	437	3742	509		
3677	438	3743	510		
3678	439	3744	511		
3679	441	3745	512		
	442	3746	489		
	447	3747	513		

Zervos numbers	Catalogue numbers	Zervos numbers	Catalogue numbers	Zervos numbers	Catalogue numbers
1,3	2	II²,840	292	VIII,260	127
1,4	1	II²,846	247	VIII,324	137
1,91	4	II²,847	246	VIII,331	136
1,142	5	II²,848	291	VIII,351	138
1,322	272	II²,849	290	IX,78	151
1,323	273	II²,881	44	IX,99	148
1,329	277	II²,852	244	IX,103	219
II¹,1	8	II²,853	289	IX,136	144
II¹,38	17	II²,926	293	IX,205	152
II¹,79	26	II²,927	294	IX,217	141
II¹,135	27	III,83	50	IX,296	155
II¹,196	29	III,96	51	IX,301	156
II¹,290	33	III,139	53	IX,353	158
II¹,294	35	III,146	54	IX,357	159
II¹,343	211	III,237	55	IX,375	160
II¹,352	36	III,258	217	XI,88	161
II²,332	210	III,414	297	XI,155	162
II²,425	214	III,415	298	XI,200	163
II²,459	216	III,443	58	XIII,64	164
II²,468	40	IV,179	61	XIII,65	165
II²,470	39	IV,226	60	XIII,95	166
II²,510	47	IV,365	66	XIII,302	167
II²,573	286	IV,368	300	XIV,69	169
II²,574	278	IV,380	74	XIV,77	170
II²,575	241	V,141	76	XIV,78	168
II²,580	295	V,177	77	XIV,290	172
II²,607	281	V,178	79	XV,107	174
II²,617	16	V,188	78	XV,153	175
II²,651	10	V,217	301	XV,173	177
II²,662	14	V,374	80	XV,174	176
II²,667	279	V,460	81	XV,184	178
II²,668	280	VI,720	6	XV,201	180
II²,681	19	VII,9	250	XV,237	181
II²,688	22	VII,20	258	XVI,100	182
II²,720	30	VII,21	256	XVI,323	183
II²,721	32	VII,30	82	XVII,54	184
II²,729	31	VII,68	85	XVII,56	185
II²,757	213	VII,129	89	XVIII,83	186
II²,758	38	VII,137	86	XVIII,237	187
II²,770	287	VII,210	93	XVIII,395	188
II²,771	205	VII,216	94	XIX,204	189
II²,774	204	VII,223	95	XX,89	190
II²,779	288	VII,234	96	XX,90	191
II²,782	206	VII,262	101	XXI,178	3
II²,784	242	VII,263	99	XXVI,12	12
II²,791	236	VII,276	100	XXVI,18	15
II²,793	238d	VII,287	108	XXVI,262	18
II²,795	237b	VII,291	98	XXVI,361	23
II²,796	238b	VII,301	107	XXVI,364	20
II²,797	237c	VII,310	106	XXVI,365	21
II²,798	237a	VII,317	112	XXVI,392	25
II²,801	238c	VII,325	110	XXVI,394	24
II²,802	238a	VII,328	109	XXVI,412	28
II²,812	239	VII,329	111	XXVII,35	193
II²,806	235	VII,330	116	XXVIII,57	34
II²,815	230	VII,332	120	XXVIII,60	212
II²,816	234	VII,339	119	XXVIII,243	207
II²,817	233	VII,346	113	XXVIII,284	208
II²,818	240	VII,358	115	XXVIII,301	209
II²,819	232	VII,419	105	XXIX,35	42
II²,820	231	VII,423	91	XXIX,42	45
II²,822	227	VIII,138	122	XXIX,45	243
II²,825	228	VIII,167	124	XXIX,384	56
II²,828	46	VIII,210	125	XXIX,457	218
II²,830	248	VIII,214	123	XXIX,465	296
II²,838	245	VIII,215	125bis	XXX,236	65

Zervos numbers	Catalogue numbers
XXX,270	71
XXXI,484	194
XXXII,265	196
XXXII,271	195
XXXII,273	197
XXXII,293	198
XXXII,307	199
XXXIII,168	200
XXXIII,331	201
XXXIII,350	202
XXXIII,397	203

Spies numbers	Catalogue numbers
1(I)	271
4	272
6	273
6A	274
6B	276
6C	275
7	277
12	278
15	280
17	279
17A	283
19	281
20A	282
23	284
24	286
26	285
29	288
30	287
32	242
33(b)	241
42	245
45	248
46	292
49	247
50	246
51	244
52	291
53	290
53A	243
54	289
55	295
57	293
58	294
61A	296
61B	298
61D	297
61E	299
62	300
63	301
64	258
65	256
65A	251
65B	252
65C	253
65D	254
65E	255
65F	257
65G	249
65H	250
66A	304
67(II)	302
67A(I)	303
68	306
69	307
71	305
72(I)	310
75	264
76	259
77	260
78	265
79	327
80	312
81	311
84	328
86(I)	314
88(I)	315

Spies numbers	Catalogue numbers
89(I)	316
90(I)	317
91(I)	318
92(I)	322
93(I)	319
94(I)	320
95(I)	321
99(I)	323
100(I)	324
101(I)	313
102(I)	325
103(I)	326
104(II)	308
105(I)	329
106(II)	309
108	330
109(II)	331
110(I)	332
110(II)	333
111(I)	334
111(II)	335
113(I)	344
114(II)	345
115	346
116	267
117	266
118	261
118A	262
119	263
120(I)	347
120(II)	348
127(II)	342
130(II)	336
131(II)	337
131(III)	338
132(IIa)	339
133(Ia)	340
133(II)	341
138	349
141	350
144	351
148	358
149	359
151(I)	352
151(II)	353
152(I)	354
152(II)	355
153(II)	356
157(II)	360
162	362
165	363
171A	365
181(II)	264
182	268
183	269
185	270
194	368
208	369
219(II)	373
220	366
221	367
222	343
236(II)	361
238A(II)	371
239(I)	391
240(I)	370

nces

Spies numbers	Catalogue numbers	Daix Boudaille	Catalogue numbers	Daix Rosselet	Catalogue numbers
246	357	VI.5	3	2	9
277	374	VI.35	4	15	10
278(II)	372	VIII.1	5	18	11
280(II)	375	XV.8	6	22	12
334(II)	376	XVI.26	8	23	15
335(II)	377			24	16
347	378			26	14
350(II)	385			28	13
407(II)	382			52	17
408(I)	381			62	19
409(I)	383			71	18
409(II)	384			152	24
410(IIa)	392			153	25
461(I)	386			156	20
462(I)	387			157	21
463(I)	390			164	22
470	389			178	23
475(I)	388			187	26
493	401			227	27
495(2)	402			251	28
496	403			339	29
498(II)	393			379	30
503(II)	394			427	34
504(II)	395			428	33
505(II)	396			431	32
506(II)	397			433	31
507(II)	398			466	35
508(II)	399			485	36
539(II)	404			517	204
592(2)	405			518	205
594(1)	406			531	207
596	407			551	206
599(2)	410			555	287
604(2)	411			556	288
605	412			594	208
606(2)	413			597	37
612(1)	409			598	209
626(2b)	408			603	213
631(2)	432			606	38
640	400			611	210
642	416			612	211
652(a,1)	416			613	212
652(b,1)	414			617	214
652(c,1)	415			630	241
652(d,1)	417			632	289
C3	489			652	242
C4	513			673	215
C5	520			687	243
C6	519			693	216
				721	41
				731	42
				736	43
				748	292
				750	244
				751	290
				752	291
				759	40
				760	39
				788	248
				789	247
				790	246
				833	293
				834	294
				835	295